Acting Movie Scripts
or
Fulfilling Prophecies?

Daniel Ukadike Nwaelene, ThD

ACTING MOVIE SCRIPTS OR FULFILLING PROPHECIES?

ISBN (Paperback): 979-8-9922386-0-0
ISBN (Hardback): 979-8-9922386-1-7

Printed in the United States of America

Note:
Except where it is specifically mentioned, all Bible quotations in this book are from the Authorized King James Version (AKJV).

DEDICATION

This book is dedicated to the following:

Reverend Stephen Okeleke Eneanya (1953 – 2005).

Steve, as I called him, was my childhood Christian friend and brother. Our relationship dated back to our days in the children's church of the Pilgrim Baptist Church, Issele-Uku. He was eventually my "best man" at my wedding.

Shortly before he passed away, Steve always expressed dismay and displeasure that many Christians are no longer heaven conscious. When he died I felt it was too early. But since the Bible says, "*The righteous perisheth and no man layeth it to heart: and merciful men are taken away, none considering that the righteous is taken away from the evil to come*" (Isaiah 57:1), I am no longer too surprised that God took Steve as early as He did.

Ms. Rose Nwaka Halim (1950 – 2014).

Rose was a good friend of Patricia, my wife. At our wedding, Rose was my wife's chief bridesmaid.

To God be all glory for the lives of these two friends and the families they left behind.

TABLE OF CONTENTS

Preface

These days of Hollywood (America), Nollywood (Lagos, Nigeria), Pinewood (Buckinghamshire, England), and Bollywood (Bombay, India), this '–wood' and that '–wood' all over the world, professionals have made acting so popular and financially rewarding that many plays and novels are often acted out (dramatized) in theatres and halls. And they pull crowds! Many real-life events have been put into movies.

The works of many literary giants, especially playwrights, have thus been acted out over the centuries; and in recent times many more plays and movies have been produced and are in circulation. Some of the popular playwrights include William Shakespeare, George Bernard Shaw, John Webster (Great Britain), Zulu Sofola, Rotimi Ola, Wole Soyinka (Nigeria), Lorraine Hansberry, Arthur Miller, Suzanne-Lori Parks, Tennessee Williams, Tony Kushner, Langston Hughes, (United States of America)[1], etc. And with the advent of television and digital technology, many dramas and movies are now watched in people's living rooms and bedrooms.

It should be noted, however, that these plays and novels, unlike prophecies, are principally based on stories of past and/or contemporary societal events and issues. So, there is the tendency for some minds to sometimes wonder whether Jesus Christ was acting some manmade movie script like professional actors and movie stars do. However, sound Bible study, education and fulfillment of His prophecies reveal that the whole Bible, from Genesis to Revelation, points to Jesus Christ, notwithstanding that the Bible is a collection (literally a library) of sixty-six (66) books that were written by many inspired men at different locations in the then known world, and over many centuries.

The Bible comprises two parts: the Old Testament and New Testament. The Old Testament (OT), consisting of thirty-nine (39) books, in summary, presents the

---

[1] William Shakespeare (1564 - 1616), George Bernard Shaw (1856 - 1950), John Webster (1580 - 1634), Zulu Sofola (1935 – 1995), Rotimi Ola (1938 - 2000), Wole Soyinka (1934), Lorraine Hansberry (1930 – 1965), Arthur Miller (1915 – 2005), Suzanne-Lori Parks (1963), Tennessee Williams (1911 – 1983), Tony Kushner (1956), Langston Hughes (1902 – 1967).

stories about the beginnings including creation, the fall of man, and the plan of God for the redemption of man. Hence the 39 books comprise The Law and the Prophets, History, and Literature. The OT is also known as God's revelation of Himself. Hill and Walton say that one of the functions of the OT was to expose sin (disobedience and rebellion against God) as sin inherent in mankind.[2]

The other part of the Bible – the New Testament (NT) – consists of twenty-seven (27) books that were written in and around Palestine by eight or nine[3] men, within the first Century A.D. These books contain the Gospels (four in number) – Matthew, Mark, Luke, and John – which are historical narrations of the life and teachings of Jesus Christ. Note the opening two verses of *The Acts Of The Apostles* (the fifth book of the NT) authored by the author of the Gospel According to Luke:

Acts 1:1-2 "The former treatise have I made, O Theophilus, of all that Jesus began both to do and teach, [2] Until the day in which he was taken up, after that he through the Holy Ghost had given commandments unto the apostles whom he had chosen . . .."

These books (the Gospels) present the fulfillment of the prophecies of God's plan for the salvation of mankind as stated severally in the books of the OT.

The next book of the NT mentioned above (The Acts of the Apostles) is a historical account of the spread of the gospel of Christ from Jerusalem to the other parts of the world encompassing the old Roman Empire. The next twenty-one (21) books are letters (epistles) written to believers in Christ by apostles of Christ. And the last book (Revelation to John) is also known as the apocalypse of the end times - mainly the future return to earth of Jesus Christ to reign over the whole earth as King of kings, as well as the eternal state.

---

[2] Andrew E. Hill and John H Walton. A Survey of The Old Testament. (Grand Rapids: Zondervan, 2009), 71.

[3] The author of the Epistle to the Hebrews is not certain. If it was Apostle Paul, then 8 men wrote the 27 books; but 9 men if someone else yet to be properly identified wrote the epistle.

The supernatural events in the ministry of Jesus Christ, the virgin birth, death, resurrection, and ascension stories all help to prove that Jesus Christ was not just acting some man-made-up scripts, but was fulfilling prophecies of old.

In this book, most of the Bible references are fully quoted from the King James Version (KJV) so that you may compel yourself to read the actual words in the Bible as stated, except where such references are within excerpts. Nevertheless, I encourage you to own a copy of the Bible and read it through, as there is a lot more therein than the few passages quoted in this book.

Bible students and teachers, young people and the old, and all persons who are sincerely searching for where (i.e. in what or whom) to place their faith, and who may perhaps, be wondering why it must be Jesus Christ rather than anyone or anything else, will find this book invaluable. You will find in this book the miracles and parables of Jesus Christ, all of which will help to strengthen the faith of those that believe.

This book is aimed at helping people that are in doubt or at crossroads in their faith, to understand that Jesus Christ had a divine mission on earth and was not an actor, Rather He was the real and only SAVIOR of mankind. It is my prayer that the Lord will reveal great things including Himself to you as you read the book. May God bless you richly.

Daniel U. Nwaelene, ThD
Yonkers, New York. USA
August 2017.

ACKNOWLEDGMENTS

The Lord is good. He gave me the grace, and enabled me, to start and complete writing this book, which appeared too dry at inception. But because "[It is] *Not by might, nor by power, but by my spirit, saith the Lord of hosts*" (Zechariah 4:6), the work came through. So, I hereby express my sincere gratitude to the almighty God and ascribe all the glory to Him.

Some other writings were consulted while this book was being constructed and all such works consulted, cited, or quoted have been duly acknowledged as footnotes and/or in the Bibliography as the case may be, in this one. Notwithstanding I feel constrained to, and do hereby say, 'thank you' to all the authors of these works for permitting me to reference them and for the availability of their works.

I cannot fail to appreciate friends and family members that contributed in one way or another to make this work a success. Amongst these is a Christian brother, work colleague, and friend, Mr. Roland J. Bishop, Jr. for his invaluable counsel and suggestions that should not pass without mention. Thank you, sir. Also, I appreciate my wife, Mrs. Patricia Ifeanyi Nwaelene (nee Ojei). She assisted in no small measure with her usual cooperation and helpful suggestions. Thank you, Pat.

My appreciation also goes to our son, Chiedu Nwaelene (representing *CreativeMoveWorks*) for designing the cover of this book, as he did for the earlier one, "JESUS CHRIST: SAVIOR, JUDGE, AND KING OF THE WORLD." I also appreciate our daughter, Ebelechukwu. She helped me to produce the index for the book. Chiedu and Ebele, thanks. May God bless you.

Finally, I appreciate you, the reader of this book. You have made the efforts of putting into writing the book worthwhile. I pray that God will bless you with wisdom, to make you a blessing to your generation. Thank you very much.

Daniel U. Nwaelene, ThD.

PART 1

CHAPTER 1

INTRODUCTION.

1.1 Background

Professional actors and artists had in the past acted in some plays and movies so well that it would look like they were in the mind of the authors of such plays, no matter the length of the play, such as Shakespearean plays. Going to *'YouTube'* on the Internet, you can watch many plays/movies, which depict the issues of the day in various societies. Many plays and movies have been written and acted on based on the Scriptures' records of the life and teachings of Jesus Christ. On the list of such movies/plays are the following: -

1. Jesus Christ Superstar (Released 1973).

2. Jesus in the Stars: Tracing the Christ Story in the Constellations (Released 2000).

3. The Life and Passion of Christ from the Manger to the Cross (Released 1905).

4. Visual Bible, The Acts (Released 1996).

5. Frontline – From Jesus to Christ the First Christians (Released 1998).

6. Christ: The Spiritual Message for the New.

7. Jesus Christ Vampire Hunter (Released 2001).

8. The Passion of Jesus Christ (Released 2007).

9. The Life of Jesus Christ Volume 5.

10. History of Jesus Christ.

11. Resurrection of Jesus Christ.

12. Crucifixion of Jesus Christ.

13. Crucify Jesus Christ.

14. Miracles of Jesus Christ.

15. Official Nativity Story Birth of Jesus Christ.

Over the years too – even from ancient times – many critics, anti-Christian novelists, playwrights, and actors have written, produced, or nearly produced films aimed at disproving the Messiah-ship of Jesus Christ or to portray Him in various negative lime lights including as a homosexual.

Based on the notion that many dramatists and playwrights abound, who act and it looks very real, the question cropped up: 'Couldn't it have been that Jesus Christ in His silent and early years studied and mastered the Scriptures and then decided to *act* the role of the Messiah whom the Jews were expecting, entering the *stage* at the earliest opportunity which presented itself as recorded in the Gospel According to Luke?'

Luke 4:16-21 says, "And he came to Nazareth, where he had been brought up: and, as his custom was, he went into the synagogue on the sabbath day, and stood up for to read. [17] And there was delivered unto him the book of the prophet Esaias. And when he had opened the book, he found the place where it was written, [18] The Spirit of the Lord is upon me because he hath anointed me to preach the gospel to the poor; he hath sent me to heal the brokenhearted, to preach deliverance to the captives, and recovering of sight to the blind, to set at liberty them that are bruised,
[19] To preach the acceptable year of the Lord. [20] And he closed the book, and he gave it again to the minister, and sat down. And the eyes of all them that were in the synagogue were fastened on him. [21] And he began to say unto them, this day is this scripture fulfilled in your ears."

Many other people may still be reasoning in the same direction, and are, therefore, not sure of, or do not believe in, Jesus Christ as the Messiah. Some people have even wondered whether the Gospels were not stories made-up around one man, Jesus Christ by the authors.

The answer inferable is that Jesus Christ could not have been acting a movie script. There are many factors to be considered that lead to the conclusion that really Jesus Christ was fulfilling prophecies, being the Christ; and Jesus Christ is Lord to the glory of God the Father.

At His arrest, Jesus said to the multitude, *"Are ye come out as against a thief with swords and staves for to take me? I sat daily with you teaching in the temple, and ye laid no hold on me. [56] **But all this was done, that the scriptures of the prophets might be fulfilled**."* (Matthew 26:55-56, *emphasis added*).

The Gospels are not fiction. The events recorded therein are historical facts!

After the section on definition of some terms, this write-up studies the factors mentioned above under the main headings:

- Old Testament Prophecies About Jesus Christ and Fulfillment
- Summaries and Conclusions, and Recommendations.

1.2 Definition of Terms.

Messiah

This word transliterated from the Hebrew word מָשִׁיחַ was used to describe a person expected or foretold to be a redeemer in some religions including Judaism, Hinduism, and Islam. It is generally believed that Messianic beliefs and theories had to do with eschatological improvement of the condition of man and the world. This Hebrew word was translated in the Septuagint (LXX) into the Greek word, Χριστός (*Khristós*) which 'became the accepted Christian designation and title of Jesus of Nazareth, indicative of the principal character and function of his ministry.'[4]

Messiah, the Christ means "the anointed one." In Israel it was kings and priests that were anointed. There is little evidence from Scriptures of the anointing of prophets. During the Second Temple Period – after the rebuilding of the Temple – Israel no longer had a king on the throne hence the term was adopted for the One being expected to come and restore kingship.[5]

'Messiah' in the Old Testament

In the Old Testament the Hebrew form of this word is used in reference to the reigning king of Israel. For example, the word referred to king Saul in the following passages:

"Behold, here I am: witness against me before the Lord, and before his anointed: whose ox have I taken? or whose ass have I taken? or whom have I defrauded? whom have I oppressed? or of whose hand have I received any bribe to blind mine eyes therewith? and I will restore it you. **4** And they said, Thou hast not defrauded us, nor oppressed us, neither hast thou taken ought of any man's hand. **5** And he said unto them, The Lord is witness against you, and his anointed is witness this day, that ye have not found ought in my hand. And they answered, He is witness." (1 Sam. 12:3–5).

·Behold, this day thine eyes have seen how that the Lord had delivered thee to day into mine hand in the cave: and some bade me kill thee: but mine eye spared thee; and I said, I will not put forth mine hand against my lord; for he is the Lord's anointed." (1 Sam. 24:10).

---

[4] Wikipedia, the free encyclopedia.
[5] *The Interpreter's Dictionary of the Bible, Me – R, Vol. 4* (Nashville: Abingdon Press, 2009), 59-66.

The next reference here was to King David.

2 Sam.19:21 "But Abishai the son of Zeruiah answered and said, shall not Shimei be put to death for this, because he cursed the Lord's anointed?"

2 Chronicles 6:42 says, "O Lord God, turn not away the face of thine anointed: remember the mercies of David thy servant."

"The anointed" here refers to Solomon. The same term in the following Psalms refer to King David and kings generally.

Psalm 18:50 "Great deliverance giveth he to his king; and sheweth mercy to his anointed, to David, and to his seed for evermore."

Psalm 20:6 "Now know I that the LORD saveth his anointed; he will hear him from his holy heaven with the saving strength of his right hand."

Psalm 28: 8 "The LORD is their strength, and he is the saving strength of his anointed."

Psalm 84: 9 "Behold, O God our shield, and look upon the face of thine anointed."

Psalm 89: 38, 51 "But thou hast cast off and abhorred, thou hast been wroth with thine anointed. 51 Wherewith thine enemies have reproached, O LORD; wherewith they have reproached the footsteps of thine anointed."

Psalm 132:10, 17 "For thy servant David's sake turn not away the face of thine anointed. 17 There will I make the horn of David to bud: I have ordained a lamp for mine anointed."

It was during the Inter-testamental period (a.k.a. the silent years) - about 400 years between Malachi, the last Hebrew prophet in the Old Testament, and the beginning events in the New Testament - that the term Messiah began to refer to the King that was expected to come and redeem Israel and restore their kingdom from the empires that had oppressed Israel for many centuries.[6]

The word, Messiah or its translation to 'the Anointed One' was used by the prophet, Daniel with an eschatological connotation in Daniel 9:25–26. Notwithstanding that

---

[6] *Messiah.* Encyclopedia of Religion Second Edition Vol. 9 (USA: Macmillan Reference, 2005), 5972.

there are some scholars that tried to prove that this reference to the Messiah is not to Jesus Christ, a lot more other scholars, according to Walvoord, who accept the prophecy of Daniel as genuine also believe that the reference to 'the Messiah the Prince' in Daniel 9:25 is to Jesus Christ.[7]

Daniel 9:25–26 "Know therefore and understand, that from the going forth of the commandment to restore and to build Jerusalem unto the Messiah the Prince shall be seven weeks, and threescore and two weeks: the street shall be built again, and the wall, even in troublous times.
26 And after threescore and two weeks shall Messiah be cut off, but not for himself: and the people of the prince that shall come shall destroy the city and the sanctuary, and the end thereof shall be with a flood, and unto the end of the war desolations are determined."

'Messiah' in the New Testament

In the New Testament the Greek version of the Messiah – the Christ – is more frequently seen, except for the following two passages:

John 1:41 "He first findeth his own brother Simon, and saith unto him, we have found the Messias, which is, being interpreted, the Christ." and

John 4:25 "The woman saith unto him, I know that Messias cometh, which is called Christ: when he is come, he will tell us all things."

'The Christ' and 'Jesus Christ' appear generally in the Epistles rather than just 'Jesus' or 'the Son of Man' seen in the Gospels.

Prophecy

The message that the prophet conveys is called a prophecy. From research into many materials it appears difficult or somehow incomprehensible to define prophecy without first of all explaining who a prophet is. Evidently the two words are derived from the same root.

A Prophet

The Greek verb, **προφητευω** (prophēteuō), which translates to *prophesy* in the English language means "to speak for or on behalf of a god (deity). This implies passing to a people the mind or will of the deity. A man who does this is called a

---

[7] John F. Walvoord. *DANIEL THE KEY TO PROPHETIC REVELATION*. (Chicago: Moody Press, 1971), 229.

prophet (Greek **προφητες** – prophētes). There are many passages in the Bible, which typify the pattern of reporting by the prophets of the Old Testament: "Thus says the Lord." Examples include Exodus 7:17; 8:1; 10:3; Judges 6:8; 1 Samuel 10:18; 1 Kings 13:2; 21:19; 2 Kings 22:15–18; Isaiah 45:11, 18; Jeremiah 5:14. This implies being sent to deliver a message (prophecy) or the will of the LORD.

Exodus 7:17 "Thus saith the Lord, in this thou shalt know that I am the Lord: behold, I will smite with the rod that is in mine hand upon the waters which are in the river, and they shall be turned to blood."

Exodus 8:1 "And the Lord spoke unto Moses, Go unto Pharaoh, and say unto him, thus saith the Lord, let my people go, that they may serve me."

Exodus 10:3 "And Moses and Aaron came in unto Pharaoh, and said unto him, thus saith the Lord God of the Hebrews, how long wilt thou refuse to humble thyself before me? let my people go, that they may serve me."

Judges 6:8 "That the Lord sent a prophet unto the children of Israel, which said unto them, thus saith the Lord God of Israel, I brought you up from Egypt and brought you forth out of the house of bondage;"

1 Samuel 10:18 "And said unto the children of Israel, thus saith the Lord God of Israel, I brought up Israel out of Egypt and delivered you out of the hand of the Egyptians, and out of the hand of all kingdoms, and of them that oppressed you:"

1 Kings 13:2 "And he cried against the altar in the word of the Lord, and said, O altar, altar, thus saith the Lord; Behold, a child shall be born unto the house of David, Josiah by name; and upon thee shall he offer the priests of the high places that burn incense upon thee, and men's bones shall be burnt upon thee."

1 Kings 21:19 "And thou shalt speak unto him, saying, thus saith the Lord, Hast thou killed and also taken possession? And thou shalt speak unto him, saying, thus saith the Lord, In the place where dogs licked the blood of Naboth shall dog lick thy blood, even thine."

2 Kings 22:15-18 "And she said unto them, Thus saith the Lord God of Israel, Tell the man that sent you to me, ¹⁶ Thus saith the Lord, Behold, I will bring evil upon this place, and upon the inhabitants thereof, even all the words of the book which the king of Judah hath read: ¹⁷ Because they have forsaken me, and have burned incense unto other gods, that they might provoke me to anger with all the works of their hands; therefore my wrath shall be kindled against this place, and shall not be quenched. ¹⁸ But to the king of Judah which sent you to enquire of the Lord, thus shall ye say to him, thus saith the Lord God of Israel, As touching the words which thou hast heard;"

Isaiah 45:11 "Thus saith the Lord, the Holy One of Israel, and his Maker, Ask me of things to come concerning my sons, and concerning the work of my hand' command ye me."

Isaiah 45:18 "For thus saith the Lord that created the heavens; God himself that formed the earth and made it; he hath established it, he created it not in vain, he formed it to be inhabited: I am the Lord; and there is none else."

Jeremiah 5:14 "Wherefore thus saith the Lord God of hosts, because ye speak this word, behold, I will make my words in thy mouth fire, and this people wood, and it shall devour them."

False Prophets.

As there were true prophets, so there abound counterfeit or false prophets of GOD, who devised their own messages, which they passed to a king or the people as found in the Lamentations of Jeremiah, 1 King 22, and Ezekiel. False prophets tell the people what they want to hear, and they appeal to the people's fallen nature. The 'prophets' appeal to the flesh and the people's appetites, promising what they cannot deliver. Meanwhile, God did send warnings through Ezekiel to false prophets in the Old Testament, and in the New Testament Jesus Christ, and His apostles later, warned believers of such men in Matthew, Mark, Luke, Romans and 1Timothy.

Lamentations 2:14 "Thy prophets have seen vain and foolish things for thee: and they have not discovered thine iniquity, to turn away thy captivity; but have seen for thee false burdens and causes of banishment."

1 Kings 22:5-10 "And Jehoshaphat said unto the king of Israel, Enquire, I pray thee, at the word of the Lord to day. 6 Then the king of Israel gathered the prophets together, about four hundred men, and said unto them, Shall I go against Ramothgilead to battle, or shall I forbear? And they said, Go up; for the Lord shall deliver it into the hand of the king. 7 And Jehoshaphat said, Is there not here a prophet of the Lord besides, that we might enquire of him? 8 And the king of Israel said unto Jehoshaphat, There is yet one man, Micaiah the son of Imlah, by whom we may enquire of the Lord: but I hate him; for he doth not prophesy good concerning me, but evil. And Jehoshaphat said, Let not the king say so. 9 Then the king of Israel called an officer, and said, Hasten hither Micaiah the son of Imlah. 10 And the king of Israel and Jehoshaphat the king of Judah sat each on his throne, having put on their robes, in a void place in the entrance of the gate of Samaria; and all the prophets prophesied before them."

Ezekiel 13:2 "Son of man, prophesy against the prophets of Israel that prophesy, and say thou unto them that prophesy out of their own hearts, Hear ye the word of the Lord;"

Ezekiel 13:1-13 "And the word of the Lord came unto me, saying, ² Son of man, prophesy against the prophets of Israel that prophesy, and say thou unto them that prophesy out of their own hearts, Hear ye the word of the Lord;

³ Thus saith the Lord God; Woe unto the foolish prophets, that follow their own spirit, and have seen nothing!

⁴ O Israel, thy prophets are like the foxes in the deserts. ⁵ Ye have not gone up into the gaps, neither made up the hedge for the house of Israel to stand in the battle in the day of the Lord. ⁶ They have seen vanity and lying divination, saying, The Lord saith: and the Lord hath not sent them: and they have made others hope that they would confirm the word. ⁷ Have ye not seen a vain vision, and have ye not spoken a lying divination, whereas ye say, The Lord saith it; albeit I have not spoken?

⁸ Therefore thus saith the Lord God; Because ye have spoken vanity, and seen lies, therefore, behold, I am against you, saith the Lord God. ⁹ And mine hand shall be upon the prophets that see vanity, and that divine lies: they shall not be in the assembly of my people, neither shall they be written in the writing of the house of Israel, neither shall they enter into the land of Israel; and ye shall know that I am the Lord God. ¹⁰ Because, even because they have seduced my people, saying, Peace; and there was no peace; and one built up a wall, and, lo, others daubed it with untempered mortar: ¹¹ Say unto them which daub it with untempered mortar, that it shall fall: there shall be an overflowing shower; and ye, O great hailstones, shall fall; and a stormy wind shall rend it. ¹² Lo, when the wall is fallen, shall it not be said unto you, Where is the daubing wherewith ye have daubed it?

¹³ Therefore thus saith the Lord God; I will even rend it with a stormy wind in my fury; and there shall be an overflowing shower in mine anger, and great hailstones in my fury to consume it."

Matthew 7:15 "Beware of false prophets, which come to you in sheep's clothing, but inwardly they are ravening wolves.

Matthew 24:3-8 "And as he sat upon the mount of Olives, the disciples came unto him privately, saying, Tell us, when shall these things be? and what shall be the sign of thy coming, and of the end of the world? ⁴ And Jesus answered and said unto them, Take heed that no man deceive you. ⁵ For many shall come in my name, saying, I am Christ; and shall deceive many. ⁶ And ye shall hear of wars and rumours of wars: see that ye be not troubled: for all these things must come to pass, but the end is not yet. ⁷ For nation shall rise against nation, and kingdom against kingdom: and there shall be famines, and pestilences, and earthquakes, in divers places. ⁸ All these are the beginning of sorrows."

Mark 13:3-8 "And as he sat upon the mount of Olives over against the temple, Peter and James and John and Andrew asked him privately, 4 Tell us, when shall these things be? and what shall be the sign when all these things shall be fulfilled?
5 And Jesus answering them began to say, Take heed lest any man deceive you: 6 For many shall come in my name, saying, I am Christ; and shall deceive many. 7 And when ye shall hear of wars and rumours of wars, be ye not troubled: for such things must needs be; but the end shall not be yet. 8 For nation shall rise against nation, and kingdom against kingdom: and there shall be earthquakes in divers places, and there shall be famines and troubles: these are the beginnings of sorrows."

Luke 21:7-11 "And they asked him, saying, Master, but when shall these things be? and what sign will there be when these things shall come to pass? 8 And he said, Take heed that ye be not deceived: for many shall come in my name, saying, I am Christ; and the time draweth near: go ye not therefore after them. 9 But when ye shall hear of wars and commotions, be not terrified: for these things must first come to pass; but the end is not by and by.
10 Then said he unto them, Nation shall rise against nation, and kingdom against kingdom: 11 And great earthquakes shall be in divers places, and famines, and pestilences; and fearful sights and great signs shall there be from heaven.

Romans 16:17-20 "Now I beseech you, brethren, mark them which cause divisions and offences contrary to the doctrine which ye have learned; and avoid them. 18 For they that are such serve not our Lord Jesus Christ, but their own belly; and by good words and fair speeches deceive the hearts of the simple. 19 For your obedience is come abroad unto all men. I am glad therefore on your behalf: but yet I would have you wise unto that which is good, and simple concerning evil. 20 And the God of peace shall bruise Satan under your feet shortly. The grace of our Lord Jesus Christ be with you. Amen.

1 Timothy 4:1-3 "Now the Spirit speaketh expressly, that in the latter times some shall depart from the faith, giving heed to seducing spirits, and doctrines of devils; 2 Speaking lies in hypocrisy; having their conscience seared with a hot iron; 3 Forbidding to marry, and commanding to abstain from meats, which God hath created to be received with thanksgiving of them which believe and know the truth."

Three transliterated Hebrew words have been translated to the English word, prophet. They are *nãvî* and *hõzeh* (prophet) and *rõ eh* (seer). This implies that a prophet had the characteristics of a seer too. A prophet has been defined thus:

In religion, a **prophet**, from the Greek word προφήτης *profitis* meaning "foreteller", is an individual who is claimed to have been contacted by the supernatural or the divine, and serves as an intermediary with humanity, delivering this newfound knowledge from the supernatural entity to other people." [8]

In the Old Testament the first man to be called a prophet was Abraham, when God spoke to Abimelech, king of Gerar, in a dream, alerting him that the woman he had taken as his wife (Sarai) was actually married to a "prophet," Abram.

Genesis 20:7 "Now therefore restore the man his wife; for he is a prophet, and he shall pray for thee, and thou shalt live: and if thou restore her not, know thou that thou shalt surely die, thou, and all that are thine

From the definition above some qualifications or roles of the Old Testament prophet can be inferred. A prophet was a spokesman for God. He admonished, warned, directed, encouraged, interceded, educated and counseled. He brought the word of God to the people of God and called the people to respond. The life of Moses became a kind of benchmark or standard for all prophets of the LORD after him.

Deuteronomy 18:15–19: "The Lord thy God will raise up unto thee a Prophet from the midst of thee, of thy brethren, like unto me; unto him ye shall hearken; **16** According to all that thou desiredst of the Lord thy God in Horeb in the day of the assembly, saying, Let me not hear again the voice of the Lord my God, neither let me see this great fire any more, that I die not. **17** And the Lord said unto me, They have well spoken that which they have spoken. **18** I will raise them up a Prophet from among their brethren, like unto thee, and will put my words in his mouth; and he shall speak unto them all that I shall command him. **19** And it shall come to pass, that whosoever will not hearken unto my words which he shall speak in my name, I will require it of him."

Deuteronomy 34:10 also says: "And there arose not a prophet since in Israel like unto Moses, whom the Lord knew face to face."

The characteristics – qualifications – in Moses, which every prophet must posses are:

➢ GOD'S CALL.

God personally called Moses:

Exodus 3:7–14 " And the Lord said, I have surely seen the affliction of my people which are in Egypt, and have heard their cry by reason of their taskmasters; for I know their sorrows; **8** And I am come down to deliver them out of the hand of the Egyptians,

---

[8] Wikipedia: *Prophet.* http://www.thefreedictionary.com/prophet

and to bring them up out of that land unto a good land and a large, unto a land flowing with milk and honey; unto the place of the Canaanites, and the Hittites, and the Amorites, and the Perizzites, and the Hivites, and the Jebusites.

9 Now therefore, behold, the cry of the children of Israel is come unto me: and I have also seen the oppression wherewith the Egyptians oppress them. **10** Come now therefore, and I will send thee unto Pharaoh, that thou mayest bring forth my people the children of Israel out of Egypt.

11 And Moses said unto God, Who am I, that I should go unto Pharaoh, and that I should bring forth the children of Israel out of Egypt? **12** And he said, Certainly I will be with thee; and this shall be a token unto thee, that I have sent thee: When thou hast brought forth the people out of Egypt, ye shall serve God upon this mountain.

13 And Moses said unto God, Behold, when I come unto the children of Israel, and shall say unto them, The God of your fathers hath sent me unto you; and they shall say to me, What is his name? what shall I say unto them? **14** And God said unto Moses, I Am That I Am: and he said, Thus shalt thou say unto the children of Israel, I Am hath sent me unto you.'"

This call of Moses could be compared with the calls of Isaiah, Jeremiah, Ezekiel, of Hosea and Amos as recorded in the books that bear their names in the OT as follows.

Call of Isaiah

Isaiah 6:5-12 "Then said I, Woe is me! for I am undone; because I am a man of unclean lips, and I dwell in the midst of a people of unclean lips: for mine eyes have seen the King, the Lord of hosts. 6 Then flew one of the seraphims unto me, having a live coal in his hand, which he had taken with the tongs from off the altar: 7 And he laid it upon my mouth, and said, Lo, this hath touched thy lips; and thine iniquity is taken away, and thy sin purged.

8 Also I heard the voice of the Lord, saying, Whom shall I send, and who will go for us? Then said I, Here am I; send me. 9 And he said, Go, and tell this people, Hear ye indeed, but understand not; and see ye indeed, but perceive not. 10 Make the heart of this people fat, and make their ears heavy, and shut their eyes; lest they see with their eyes, and hear with their ears, and understand with their heart, and convert, and be healed. 11 Then said I, Lord, how long? And he answered, Until the cities be wasted without inhabitant, and the houses without man, and the land be utterly desolate, 12 And the Lord have removed men far away, and there be a great forsaking in the midst of the land.

Call of Jeremiah

Jeremiah 1:4-19 "Then the word of the Lord came unto me, saying, 5 Before I formed thee in the belly I knew thee; and before thou camest forth out of the womb I sanctified thee, and I ordained thee a prophet unto the nations. 6 Then said I, Ah, Lord God! behold, I cannot speak: for I am a child. 7 But the Lord said unto me, Say not, I am a child: for thou shalt go to all that I shall send thee, and whatsoever I command thee thou shalt speak. 8 Be not afraid of their faces: for I am with thee to deliver thee, saith the Lord. 9 Then the Lord put forth his hand, and touched my mouth. And the Lord said unto me, Behold, I have put my words in thy mouth. [10] See, I have this day set thee over the nations and over the kingdoms, to root out, and to pull down, and to destroy, and to throw down, to build, and to plant. [11] Moreover the word of the Lord came unto me, saying, Jeremiah, what seest thou? And I said, I see a rod of an almond tree. [12] Then said the Lord unto me, Thou hast well seen: for I will hasten my word to perform it.

[13] And the word of the Lord came unto me the second time, saying, What seest thou? And I said, I see a seething pot; and the face thereof is toward the north. [14] Then the Lord said unto me, Out of the north an evil shall break forth upon all the inhabitants of the land. [15] For, lo, I will call all the families of the kingdoms of the north, saith the Lord; and they shall come, and they shall set every one his throne at the entering of the gates of Jerusalem, and against all the walls thereof round about, and against all the cities of Judah. [16] And I will utter my judgments against them touching all their wickedness, who have forsaken me, and have burned incense unto other gods, and worshipped the works of their own hands.

[17] Thou therefore gird up thy loins, and arise, and speak unto them all that I command thee: be not dismayed at their faces, lest I confound thee before them. [18] For, behold, I have made thee this day a defenced city, and an iron pillar, and brasen walls against the whole land, against the kings of Judah, against the princes thereof, against the priests thereof, and against the people of the land. [19] And they shall fight against thee; but they shall not prevail against thee; for I am with thee, saith the Lord, to deliver thee. Anyone who assumed the office of prophet without an evidence of God's call on his life was a false one:

Jeremiah 14:14-16 "Then the Lord said unto me, The prophets prophesy lies in my name: I sent them not, neither have I commanded them, neither spake unto them: they prophesy unto you a false vision and divination, and a thing of nought, and the deceit of their heart.

15 Therefore thus saith the Lord concerning the prophets that prophesy in my name, and I sent them not, yet they say, Sword and famine shall not be in this land; By sword and famine shall those prophets be consumed. **16** And the people to whom they prophesy shall be cast out in the streets of Jerusalem because of the famine and the sword; and they shall have none to bury them, them, their wives, nor their sons, nor their daughters: for I will pour their wickedness upon them.; and

Jeremiah 23:21 "I have not sent these prophets, yet they ran: I have not spoken to them, yet they prophesied."

Call of Ezekiel
Ezekiel 1:1-5 "Now it came to pass in the thirtieth year, in the fourth month, in the fifth day of the month, as I was among the captives by the river of Chebar, that the heavens were opened, and I saw visions of God. [2] In the fifth day of the month, which was the fifth year of king Jehoiachin's captivity, [3] The word of the Lord came expressly unto Ezekiel the priest, the son of Buzi, in the land of the Chaldeans by the river Chebar; and the hand of the Lord was there upon him. [4] And I looked, and, behold, a whirlwind came out of the north, a great cloud, and a fire infolding itself, and a brightness was about it, and out of the midst thereof as the colour of amber, out of the

midst of the fire. 5 Also out of the midst thereof came the likeness of four living creatures. And this was their appearance; they had the likeness of a man."

Call of Hosea

Hosea 1:1-4 "The word of the Lord that came unto Hosea, the son of Beeri, in the days of Uzziah, Jotham, Ahaz, and Hezekiah, kings of Judah, and in the days of Jeroboam the son of Joash, king of Israel. 2 The beginning of the word of the Lord by Hosea. And the Lord said to Hosea, Go, take unto thee a wife of whoredoms and children of whoredoms: for the land hath committed great whoredom, departing from the Lord. 3 So he went and took Gomer the daughter of Diblaim; which conceived, and bare him a son. 4 And the Lord said unto him, Call his name Jezreel; for yet a little while, and I will avenge the blood of Jezreel upon the house of Jehu, and will cause to cease the kingdom of the house of Israel.

Call of Amos

Amos 7:12-15 "Also Amaziah said unto Amos, O thou seer, go, flee thee away into the land of Judah, and there eat bread, and prophesy there: 13 But prophesy not again any more at Bethel: for it is the king's chapel, and it is the king's court. 14 Then answered Amos, and said to Amaziah, I was no prophet, neither was I a prophet's son; but I was an herdman, and a gatherer of sycomore fruit: 15 And the Lord took me as I followed the flock, and the Lord said unto me, Go, prophesy unto my people Israel."

> USE OF SYMBOLS.

Moses sometimes used symbols to deliver God's message to His people like he did in the wilderness, raising the brazen serpent on a pole in Numbers and his uplifted hands in Exodus.

Numbers 21:8-9 "And the Lord said unto Moses, Make thee a fiery serpent, and set it upon a pole: and it shall come to pass, that every one that is bitten, when he looketh upon it, shall live. 9 And Moses made a serpent of brass, and put it upon a pole, and it came to pass, that if a serpent had bitten any man, when he beheld the serpent of brass, he lived."

Exodus 17:8-16 "Then came Amalek, and fought with Israel in Rephidim. 9 And Moses said unto Joshua, Choose us out men, and go out, fight with Amalek: to morrow I will stand on the top of the hill with the rod of God in mine hand. 10 So Joshua did as Moses had said to him, and fought with Amalek: and Moses, Aaron, and Hur went up to the top of the hill.
11 And it came to pass, when Moses held up his hand, that Israel prevailed: and when he let down his hand, Amalek prevailed. 12 But Moses hands were heavy; and they took a stone, and put it under him, and he sat thereon; and Aaron and Hur stayed up his hands, the one on the one side, and the other on the other side; and his hands were steady until the going down of the sun. 13 And Joshua discomfited Amalek and his people with the edge of the sword. 14 And the Lord said unto Moses, Write this for a

memorial in a book, and rehearse it in the ears of Joshua: for I will utterly put out the remembrance of Amalek from under heaven.

15 And Moses built an altar, and called the name of it Jehovahnissi: 16 For he said, Because the Lord hath sworn that the Lord will have war with Amalek from generation to generation."

➤   INTERCESSION.

Intercession is the act of praying on behalf of someone else to God. Praying was an important part of the prophet's roles. He knew the Lord's mind, and was in a position to pray effectively. In the light of this, Moses interceded for the people.

An example of Moses' intercessions is recorded in Exodus:

Exodus 32:11-13 "And Moses besought the Lord his God, and said, Lord, why doth thy wrath wax hot against thy people, which thou hast brought forth out of the land of Egypt with great power, and with a mighty hand?
12 Wherefore should the Egyptians speak, and say, For mischief did he bring them out, to slay them in the mountains, and to consume them from the face of the earth? Turn from thy fierce wrath, and repent of this evil against thy people.
13 Remember Abraham, Isaac, and Israel, thy servants, to whom thou swarest by thine own self, and saidst unto them, I will multiply your seed as the stars of heaven, and all this land that I have spoken of will I give unto your seed, and they shall inherit it for ever. "

Some other passages that talk about the intercession of Moses for his people include:

Numbers 11:1-2 "And when the people complained, it displeased the Lord: and the Lord heard it; and his anger was kindled; and the fire of the Lord burnt among them, and consumed them that were in the uttermost parts of the camp.
2 And the people cried unto Moses; and when Moses prayed unto the Lord, the fire was quenched."

Numbers 12:13: "And Moses cried unto the Lord, saying, Heal her now, O God, I beseech thee."

Exodus 18:19 "Hearken now unto my voice, I will give thee counsel, and God shall be with thee: Be thou for the people to God-ward, that thou mayest bring the causes unto God:"

Exodus 32:31-32 "And Moses returned unto the Lord, and said, Oh, this people have sinned a great sin, and have made them gods of gold. 32 Yet now, if thou wilt forgive their sin . . . ; and if not, blot me, I pray thee, out of thy book which thou hast written."

Numbers 14:13-19 "And Moses said unto the Lord, Then the Egyptians shall hear it, (for thou broughtest up this people in thy might from among them;) **14** And they will tell it to the inhabitants of this land: for they have heard that thou Lord art among this people, that thou Lord art seen face to face, and that thy cloud standeth over them, and that thou goest before them, by day time in a pillar of a cloud, and in a pillar of fire by night.

15 Now if thou shalt kill all this people as one man, then the nations which have heard the fame of thee will speak, saying, **16** Because the Lord was not able to bring this people into the land which he sware unto them, therefore he hath slain them in the wilderness. **17** And now, I beseech thee, let the power of my lord be great, according as thou hast spoken, saying,

18 The Lord is longsuffering, and of great mercy, forgiving iniquity and transgression, and by no means clearing the guilty, visiting the iniquity of the fathers upon the children unto the third and fourth generation. **19** Pardon, I beseech thee, the iniquity of this people according unto the greatness of thy mercy, and as thou hast forgiven this people, from Egypt even until now."

Numbers 14:19 "Pardon, I beseech thee, the iniquity of this people according unto the greatness of thy mercy, and as thou hast forgiven this people, from Egypt even until now"

Numbers 16:22 "And they fell upon their faces, and said, O God, the God of the spirits of all flesh, shall one man sin, and wilt thou be wroth with all the congregation?"

Numbers 21:9 "And Moses made a serpent of brass, and put it upon a pole, and it came to pass, that if a serpent had bitten any man, when he beheld the serpent of brass, he lived."

➢ **BRINGING GOD'S WORD TO THE PEOPLE (FORTH-TELLING).**

Moses brought the word of God – not just his passive opinion - to the people of Israel with the intention of bringing about a change to the people's situation. This is forth-telling, which may come in the form of warnings against moral irresponsibility and the like, followed by calls for repentance such as we find in the passage below.

Isaiah 30:6-9 "The burden of the beasts of the south: into the land of trouble and anguish, from whence come the young and old lion, the viper and fiery flying serpent, they will carry their riches upon the shoulders of young asses, and their treasures upon the bunches of camels, to a people that shall not profit them. **7** For the Egyptians shall help in vain, and to no purpose: therefore have I cried concerning this, Their strength is to sit still. **8** Now go, write it before them in a table, and note it in a book, that it may be for the time to come for ever and ever:

9 That this is a rebellious people, lying children, children that will not hear the law of the Lord:"

Isaiah chapters 28 and 29 constitute another example of forth-telling thus:

Isaiah 28:1-29:24
Judgment on Ephraim and Jerusalem – Impending Captivity
Woe to the crown of pride, to the drunkards of Ephraim, whose glorious beauty is a fading flower, which are on the head of the fat valleys of them that are overcome with wine! **2** Behold, the Lord hath a mighty and strong one, which as a tempest of hail and a destroying storm, as a flood of mighty waters overflowing, shall cast down to the earth with the hand. **3** The crown of pride, the drunkards of Ephraim, shall be trodden under feet: **4** And the glorious beauty, which is on the head of the fat valley, shall be a fading flower, and as the hasty fruit before the summer; which when he that looketh upon it seeth, while it is yet in his hand he eateth it up.
5 In that day shall the Lord of hosts be for a crown of glory, and for a diadem of beauty, unto the residue of his people, **6** And for a spirit of judgment to him that sitteth in judgment, and for strength to them that turn the battle to the gate. **7** But they also have erred through wine, and through strong drink are out of the way; the priest and the prophet have erred through strong drink, they are swallowed up of wine, they are out of the way through strong drink; they err in vision, they stumble in judgment. **8** For all tables are full of vomit and filthiness, so that there is no place clean. **9** Whom shall he teach knowledge? and whom shall he make to understand doctrine? them that are weaned from the milk, and drawn from the breasts. **10** For precept must be upon precept, precept upon precept; line upon line, line upon line; here a little, and there a little: **11** For with stammering lips and another tongue will he speak to this people. **12** To whom he said, This is the rest wherewith ye may cause the weary to rest; and this is the refreshing: yet they would not hear. **13** But the word of the Lord was unto them precept upon precept, precept upon precept; line upon line, line upon line; here a little, and there a little; that they might go, and fall backward, and be broken, and snared, and taken.

The Fate of Ephraim as a Warning to Judah
14 Wherefore hear the word of the Lord, ye scornful men, that rule this people which is in Jerusalem. **15** Because ye have said, We have made a covenant with death, and with hell are we at agreement; when the overflowing scourge shall pass through, it shall not come unto us: for we have made lies our refuge, and under falsehood have we hid ourselves:

A Cornerstone in Zion
16 Therefore thus saith the Lord God, Behold, I lay in Zion for a foundation a stone, a tried stone, a precious corner stone, a sure foundation: he that believeth shall not make haste. **17** Judgment also will I lay to the line, and righteousness to the plummet: and the hail shall sweep away the refuge of lies, and the waters shall overflow the hiding place. **18** And your covenant with death shall be disannulled,

and your agreement with hell shall not stand; when the overflowing scourge shall pass through, then ye shall be trodden down by it. 19 From the time that it goeth forth it shall take you: for morning by morning shall it pass over, by day and by night: and it shall be a vexation only to understand the report. 20 For the bed is shorter than that a man can stretch himself on it: and the covering narrower than that he can wrap himself in it. 21 For the Lord shall rise up as in mount Perazim, he shall be wroth as in the valley of Gibeon, that he may do his work, his strange work; and bring to pass his act, his strange act.

Heed the Teaching of God
22 Now therefore be ye not mockers, lest your bands be made strong: for I have heard from the Lord God of hosts a consumption, even determined upon the whole earth. 23 Give ye ear, and hear my voice; hearken, and hear my speech. 24 Doth the plowman plow all day to sow? doth he open and break the clods of his ground? 25 When he hath made plain the face thereof, doth he not cast abroad the fitches, and scatter the cummin, and cast in the principal wheat and the appointed barley and the rie in their place? 26 For his God doth instruct him to discretion, and doth teach him. 27 For the fitches are not threshed with a threshing instrument, neither is a cart wheel turned about upon the cummin; but the fitches are beaten out with a staff, and the cummin with a rod. 28 Bread corn is bruised; because he will not ever be threshing it, nor break it with the wheel of his cart, nor bruise it with his horsemen. 29 This also cometh forth from the Lord of hosts, which is wonderful in counsel, and excellent in working.

Warnings to Jerusalem and Judah
29 Woe to Ariel, to Ariel, the city where David dwelt! add ye year to year; let them kill sacrifices. 2 Yet I will distress Ariel, and there shall be heaviness and sorrow: and it shall be unto me as Ariel. 3 And I will camp against thee round about, and will lay siege against thee with a mount, and I will raise forts against thee. 4 And thou shalt be brought down, and shalt speak out of the ground, and thy speech shall be low out of the dust, and thy voice shall be, as of one that hath a familiar spirit, out of the ground, and thy speech shall whisper out of the dust.
5 Moreover the multitude of thy strangers shall be like small dust, and the multitude of the terrible ones shall be as chaff that passeth away: yea, it shall be at an instant suddenly. 6 Thou shalt be visited of the Lord of hosts with thunder, and with earthquake, and great noise, with storm and tempest, and the flame of devouring fire. 7 And the multitude of all the nations that fight against Ariel, even all that fight against her and her munition, and that distress her, shall be as a dream of a night vision. 8 It shall even be as when an hungry man dreameth, and, behold, he eateth; but he awaketh, and his soul is empty: or as when a thirsty man dreameth, and, behold, he drinketh; but he awaketh, and, behold, he is faint, and his soul hath appetite: so shall the multitude of all the nations be, that fight against mount Zion.

9 Stay yourselves, and wonder; cry ye out, and cry: they are drunken, but not with wine; they stagger, but not with strong drink. 10 For the Lord hath poured out upon you the spirit of deep sleep, and hath closed your eyes: the prophets and your rulers, the seers hath he covered. 11 And the vision of all is become unto you as the words of a book that is sealed, which men deliver to one that is learned, saying, Read this, I 27 thee: and he saith, I cannot; for it is sealed: 12 And the book is delivered to him that is not learned, saying, Read this, I pray thee: and he saith, I am not learned.

13 Wherefore the Lord said, Forasmuch as this people draw near me with their mouth, and with their lips do honour me, but have removed their heart far from me, and their fear toward me is taught by the precept of men: 14 Therefore, behold, I will proceed to do a marvellous work among this people, even a marvellous work and a wonder: for the wisdom of their wise men shall perish, and the understanding of their prudent men shall be hid. 15 Woe unto them that seek deep to hide their counsel from the Lord, and their works are in the dark, and they say, Who seeth us? and who knoweth us? 16 Surely your turning of things upside down shall be esteemed as the potter's clay: for shall the work say of him that made it, He made me not? or shall the thing framed say of him that framed it, He had no understanding?

Blessing Following Deliverance

17 Is it not yet a very little while, and Lebanon shall be turned into a fruitful field, and the fruitful field shall be esteemed as a forest? 18 And in that day shall the deaf hear the words of the book, and the eyes of the blind shall see out of obscurity, and out of darkness. 19 The meek also shall increase their joy in the Lord, and the poor among men shall rejoice in the Holy One of Israel. 20 For the terrible one is brought to nought, and the scorner is consumed, and all that watch for iniquity are cut off: 21 That make a man an offender for a word, and lay a snare for him that reproveth in the gate, and turn aside the just for a thing of nought.

22 Therefore thus saith the Lord, who redeemed Abraham, concerning the house of Jacob, Jacob shall not now be ashamed, neither shall his face now wax pale. 23 But when he seeth his children, the work of mine hands, in the midst of him, they shall sanctify my name, and sanctify the Holy One of Jacob, and shall fear the God of Israel. 24 They also that erred in spirit shall come to understanding, and they that murmured shall learn doctrine.

➢ FORETELLING.

To foretell is to predict an event or something that will occur at a future date. It differs from *forthtelling* that relates to the present. Moses did foretell the coming of another Prophet like him:

Deuteronomy 18:9-15 "When thou art come into the land which the Lord thy God giveth thee, thou shalt not learn to do after the abominations of those nations. 10 There shall not be found among you any one that maketh his son or his

daughter to pass through the fire, or that useth divination, or an observer of times, or an enchanter, or a witch. 11 Or a charmer, or a consulter with familiar spirits, or a wizard, or a necromancer. 12 For all that do these things are an abomination unto the Lord: and because of these abominations the Lord thy God doth drive them out from before thee. 13 Thou shalt be perfect with the Lord thy God.
14 For these nations, which thou shalt possess, hearkened unto observers of times, and unto diviners: but as for thee, the Lord thy God hath not suffered thee so to do. **15 The Lord thy God will raise up unto thee a Prophet from the midst of thee, of thy brethren, like unto me; unto him ye shall hearken;"** (Emphasis added).

Although prophecy is not always predictive, yet prediction of the future was a part of the ministry of the prophet. Most of the Old Testament prophets appeared first as foretellers. Through his fellowship with God, the prophet had access to the future. He was the seer who had insight into the plans and purposes of God.

> **PRAYING**

The prophet was prayerful. As the spokesman of GOD, the prophet must be in the presence of GOD in order to, apart from worshipping Him, know the mind of the Lord and be able to correctly say 'thus says the Lord.' For instance, Jeremiah, in his challenge to the false prophets asked:

Jeremiah 23:18–22 "For who hath stood in the counsel of the Lord, and hath perceived and heard his word? who hath marked his word, and heard it? 19 Behold, a whirlwind of the Lord is gone forth in fury, even a grievous whirlwind: it shall fall grievously upon the head of the wicked. 20 The anger of the Lord shall not return, until he have executed, and till he have performed the thoughts of his heart: in the latter days ye shall consider it perfectly. 21 I have not sent these prophets, yet they ran: I have not spoken to them, yet they prophesied. 22 But if they had stood in my counsel, and had caused my people to hear my words, then they should have turned them from their evil way, and from the evil of their doings."

Prophet Daniel also was so prayerful that that became a point for attack from his idolatrous Babylonian colleagues. For example,

Daniel 9:1–3 "In the first year of Darius the son of Ahasuerus, of the seed of the Medes, which was made king over the realm of the Chaldeans; 2 In the first year of his reign I Daniel understood by books the number of the years, whereof the word of the Lord came to Jeremiah the prophet, that he would accomplish seventy years in the desolations of Jerusalem. 3 And I set my face unto the Lord God, to seek by prayer and supplications, with fasting, and sackcloth, and ashes:"

Ezekiel also prayed. An example was:

Ezekiel 9:8–9 " And it came to pass, while they were slaying them, and I was left, that I fell upon my face, and cried, and said, Ah Lord God! wilt thou destroy all the residue of Israel in thy pouring out of thy fury upon Jerusalem? 9 Then said he unto me, The iniquity of the house of Israel and Judah is exceeding great, and the land is full of blood, and the city full of perverseness: for they say, The Lord hath forsaken the earth, and the Lord seeth not.'

One of the occasions of Samuel praying is recorded in **1 Samuel 8:6–7**:

"But the thing displeased Samuel, when they said, Give us a king to judge us. And Samuel prayed unto the Lord. 7 And the Lord said unto Samuel, Hearken unto the voice of the people in all that they say unto thee: for they have not rejected thee, but they have rejected me, that I should not reign over them."

Similarly, the other Old Testament prophets were always people of prayer.

PRIEST/PRIESTHOOD

"To be a priest is not a matter of personal achievement and dignity, but to be part of God's gracious provision to reconcile sinful humanity with the Holy God and to facilitate life and community among human beings. As liminal beings, priests stood at the boundary (Latin, *limen* – 'threshold') between holy and common, facilitating the presence of the holy God in the presence of a sinful people."[9]

Simply put by Gerald O'Collins and Edward G. Farriugia, "Members of the community set apart to offer sacrifice and mediate between God and human beings – in cultic way like the OT Levitical Priesthood (Ex. 28:1; 32:25–29; Lev. 8:1–9:24), as priest-king like Melchizedek (Gen. 14:18–20), or in a prophetic way like Ezekiel."[10]

---

[9] *The New Interpreter's Dictionary of the Bible Me – R Vol. 4*. (Nashville: Abingdon Press, 2009), 613.
[10] Gerald O'Collins, S. J., Edward G. Farrugia, S. J.' *A Concise Dictionary of Theology*. (New York/Mahwah, N.J.: Paulist Press, 2000), 212.

On the other hand Alan Richardson and John Bowden expound that according to the Hebrew Scriptures priesthood mainly referred to the lineage of the Levites and Zadokites, who practiced the Aaronic type of priesthood functions – principally to consult the "lots" to determine God's will. The prophets gradually absorbed this function, and "Priesthood gradually shifted to the functions of worship, especially cultic sacrifice." Richardson and Bowden opine that as against this Aaronic type, the Melchizedek type – priest-king, which was independent of the Levites (a.k.a. Royal Priesthood) – informed the Christian description of Jesus Christ and all who believe in Him:

Hebrews 7:26 "For such an high priest became us, who is holy, harmless, undefiled, separate from sinners, and made higher than the heavens;"

1 Peter 2:9 "But ye are a chosen generation, a royal priesthood, an holy nation, a peculiar people; that ye should shew forth the praises of him who hath called you out of darkness into his marvellous light."[11]

Jesus Christ, the only Mediator between God and men has been referred to as the Great High Priest in Hebrews, implying an office higher than the Levitical priesthood because of the nature of His final sacrifice and mediation. Believers in Christ and His finished work on the cross are baptized into His royal priesthood.

1 Timothy 2:5 "For there is one God, and one mediator between God and men, the man Christ Jesus."

Hebrews 4:14-5:10 "Seeing then that we have a great high priest, that is passed into the heavens, Jesus the Son of God, let us hold fast our profession. 15 For we have not an high priest which cannot be touched with the feeling of our infirmities; but was in all points tempted like as we are, yet without sin. 16 Let us therefore come boldly unto the throne of grace, that we may obtain mercy, and find grace to help in time of need. 5 For every high priest taken from among men is ordained for men in things pertaining to God, that he may offer both gifts and sacrifices for sins: 2 Who can have compassion on the ignorant, and on them that are out of the way; for that he himself also is compassed with infirmity.
3 And by reason hereof he ought, as for the people, so also for himself, to offer for sins. 4 And no man taketh this honour unto himself, but he that is called of God, as was Aaron. 5 So also Christ glorified not himself to be made an high priest; but he that said

---

[11] Alan Richardson and John Bowden, eds. *The Westminster Dictionary of Christian Theology.* (Philadelphia: The Westminster Press, 1983), 464.

30

unto him, Thou art my Son, to day have I begotten thee. 6 As he saith also in another place, Thou art a priest for ever after the order of Melchisedec. 7 Who in the days of his flesh, when he had offered up prayers and supplications with strong crying and tears unto him that was able to save him from death, and was heard in that he feared; 8 Though he were a Son, yet learned he obedience by the things which he suffered; 9 And being made perfect, he became the author of eternal salvation unto all them that obey him; 10 Called of God an high priest after the order of Melchisedec."

PART TWO

PROPHECIES ABOUT JESUS CHRIST AND THEIR FULFILLMENT

Many people of old at different times and different locations in the world prophesied several centuries before Jesus Christ was born, that the Messiah would come into the world scene – mainly for the purpose of delivering humanity from the clutches of the devil and everlasting damnation. These prophecies included the circumstances and place of His birth, the purpose of His coming, and a Second Coming. Some of the prophecies have double references, in which case there were instances that constituted 'types' of the actual. In the New Testament Jesus Christ also pronounced some prophecies about Himself. While many of the prophecies including His virgin birth, have been fulfilled others, especially the eschatological ones, are yet to be fully fulfilled.

Some of the prophecies, along with their fulfillment records in the New Testament, are shown below. They shall be discussed hereafter under the following six sub-titles:

- The Birth of the Messiah
- Expectation of the Messiahship
- Ministry of the Messiah
- His Rejection, Suffering and Death
- His Resurrection, Physical Appearances and Ascension
- His Future Return (Second Coming a.k.a. Second Advent).

CHAPTER 2

PROPHECIES OF THE MESSIAH'S VIRGIN BIRTH.

There are many prophecies in the Old Testament Scriptures that the Messiah would be born. Some of the prophecies, along with their corresponding New Testament references that indicate their fulfillment, are stated below.

(a) <u>A Virgin to Conceive and Give Birth</u>.

Isaiah 7:10-14 "Moreover the Lord spake again unto Ahaz, saying, [11] Ask thee a sign of the Lord thy God; ask it either in the depth, or in the height above. [12] But Ahaz said, I will not ask, neither will I tempt the Lord. [13] And he said, Hear ye now, O house of David; Is it a small thing for you to weary men, but will ye weary my God also? [14] <u>Therefore the Lord himself shall give you a sign; Behold, a virgin shall conceive, and bear a son, and shall call his name Immanuel.</u>" (Emphasis added).

This message/prophecy was from the mouth of Prophet Isaiah to King Ahaz, king of Judah, son of Jotham, the son of Uzziah, about 700 years before Christ was born. Its antecedent (Isaiah 7:1–13) was that Judah was told that Aram (Syria) had allied itself with Ephraim (former Northern Kingdom of Israel) to invade Judah, and the hearts of Ahaz and his people were terribly shaken. The LORD asked Isaiah to go with his son Shear-Jashub to Ahaz, to tell Ahaz to be careful, calm and neither be afraid nor loose heart 'because of these two smoldering stubs of firewood.'

The LORD asked that Ahaz and his people should strengthen their faith in HIM so as to stand, and to demand a sign from HIM. Although Ahaz refused to ask for sign, Isaiah gave one in the form of the prophecy of the birth.

Isaiah 7:1-13 "And it came to pass in the days of Ahaz the son of Jotham, the son of Uzziah, king of Judah, that Rezin the king of Syria, and Pekah the son of Remaliah, king of Israel, went up toward Jerusalem to war against it, but could not prevail against it. [2] And it was told the house of David, saying, Syria is confederate with Ephraim. And his heart was moved, and the heart of his people, as the trees of the wood are moved with the wind.
[3] Then said the Lord unto Isaiah, Go forth now to meet Ahaz, thou, and Shearjashub thy son, at the end of the conduit of the upper pool in the highway of the fuller's field; [4] And say unto him, Take heed, and be quiet; fear not, neither be fainthearted for the two tails of these smoking firebrands, for the fierce anger of Rezin with Syria, and of the son of Remaliah. [5] Because Syria, Ephraim, and the son of Remaliah, have taken evil counsel against thee, saying, [6] Let us go up against Judah, and vex it, and let us

make a breach therein for us, and set a king in the midst of it, even the son of Tabeal: [7] Thus saith the Lord God, It shall not stand, neither shall it come to pass. [8] For the head of Syria is Damascus, and the head of Damascus is Rezin; and within threescore and five years shall Ephraim be broken, that it be not a people. [9] And the head of Ephraim is Samaria, and the head of Samaria is Remaliah's son. If ye will not believe, surely ye shall not be established. [10] Moreover the Lord spake again unto Ahaz, saying, [11] Ask thee a sign of the Lord thy God; ask it either in the depth, or in the height above. [12] But Ahaz said, I will not ask, neither will I tempt the Lord. [13] And he said, Hear ye now, O house of David; Is it a small thing for you to weary men, but will ye weary my God also?

Fulfillment:

Notwithstanding the divided opinions of many scholars concerning the relevance of Prophet Isaiah's statement to the birth of Jesus Christ, the prophecy was fulfilled. First, in Luke's account of the birth of Jesus Christ God sent the angel Gabriel to Nazareth, a town in Galilee, to a virgin named Mary who was pledged to be married to a man named Joseph, a descendant of David, to announce to her that she would conceive and give birth to a Son, to be named Jesus.

Luke 1:26-38 "And in the sixth month the angel Gabriel was sent from God unto a city of Galilee, named Nazareth, [27] To a virgin espoused to a man whose name was Joseph, of the house of David; and the virgin's name was Mary. [28] And the angel came in unto her, and said, Hail, thou that art highly favoured, the Lord is with thee: blessed art thou among women.
[29] And when she saw him, she was troubled at his saying, and cast in her mind what manner of salutation this should be. [30] And the angel said unto her, Fear not, Mary: for thou hast found favour with God. [31] And, behold, thou shalt conceive in thy womb, and bring forth a son, and shalt call his name Jesus. [32] He shall be great, and shall be called the Son of the Highest: and the Lord God shall give unto him the throne of his father David: [33] And he shall reign over the house of Jacob for ever; and of his kingdom there shall be no end.
[34] Then said Mary unto the angel, How shall this be, seeing I know not a man? [35] And the angel answered and said unto her, The Holy Ghost shall come upon thee, and the power of the Highest shall overshadow thee: therefore also that holy thing which shall be born of thee shall be called the Son of God. [36] And, behold, thy cousin Elisabeth, she hath also conceived a son in her old age: and this is the sixth month with her, who was called barren. [37] For with God nothing shall be impossible.
[38] And Mary said, Behold the handmaid of the Lord; be it unto me according to thy word. And the angel departed from her.

Similarly, Matthew in his account noted that the Lord appeared to Joseph in a dream to reveal to him the circumstances of Mary's pregnancy and to name the Child Jesus, "because he will save his people from their sins." Matthew says:

Matthew 1:18-23 "Now the birth of Jesus Christ was on this wise: When as his mother Mary was espoused to Joseph, before they came together, she was found with child of the Holy Ghost. [19] Then Joseph her husband, being a just man, and not willing to make her a public example, was minded to put her away privily.
[20] But while he thought on these things, behold, the angel of the Lord appeared unto him in a dream, saying, Joseph, thou son of David, fear not to take unto thee Mary thy wife: for that which is conceived in her is of the Holy Ghost. [21] And she shall bring forth a son, and thou shalt call his name Jesus: for he shall save his people from their sins. [22] Now all this was done, that it might be fulfilled which was spoken of the Lord by the prophet, saying, [23] Behold, a virgin shall be with child, and shall bring forth a son, and they shall call his name Emmanuel, which being interpreted is, God with us."

Note verses 24 and 25 of chapter 1 where Matthew records that Joseph "did as the angel of the Lord had bidden him, and took unto him his wife: And knew her not till she had brought forth her firstborn son: and he called his name Jesus."

Some critics have said that it is not certain that this sign of 'Immanuel' (God with us) prophesied by Isaiah really referred to Jesus Christ, since it is not categorical who the child in the text is talking about – whether the one that was to be born shortly to the prophet, Isaiah by his pregnant wife (chapter 8 of the Book of Isaiah) or another. However, whatever their opinion, the prophecy is on record that a virgin would bear a Son, and History has it that there was an only occasion of the birth of a Son by a virgin who was not yet married but betrothed, and that virgin was Mary while the Son was Jesus Christ.

(b) Messiah's Titles.
Isaiah 9:6 "For to us a child is born, to us a son is given, and the government will be on his shoulders. And he will be called Wonderful Counselor, Mighty God, Everlasting Father, Prince of Peace."

This is one of the most profusely quoted Bible passages in Christendom regarding the prophecies of the birth of Jesus Christ. Nobody else on earth had or has ever been addressed by these titles.

[1]

(c) <u>Messiah to be Born in Bethlehem</u>

Micah 5:2 "But you, Bethlehem Ephrathah, though you are small among the clans of Judah, out of you will come for me one who will be ruler over Israel, whose origins are from of old, from ancient times."

This prophecy indicated the future birth of a King from King David's lineage and in Bethlehem. The fact that St. Matthew in his Gospel noted that King Herod inquired from the chief priests and teachers of the law where the Messiah was to be born and they told him, is an evidence of the fulfillment of the prophecy. It also disproves the claim of some Jewish scholars that the birthplace of the Messiah is unknown. The two NT passages that tell the story of the fulfillment of the prophecy of the birthplace of Jesus Christ are as follows:

Matthew 2:4-6 "And when he had gathered all the chief priests and scribes of the people together, he demanded of them where Christ should be born. 5 And they said unto him, In Bethlehem of Judaea: for thus it is written by the prophet, 6 And thou Bethlehem, in the land of Juda, art not the least among the princes of Juda: for out of thee shall come a Governor, that shall rule my people Israel.

Luke 2:1-20 "And it came to pass in those days, that there went out a decree from Caesar Augustus that all the world should be taxed. 2 (And this taxing was first made when Cyrenius was governor of Syria.) 3 And all went to be taxed, every one into his own city. 4 And Joseph also went up from Galilee, out of the city of Nazareth, into Judaea, unto the city of David, which is called Bethlehem; (because he was of the house and lineage of David:) 5 To be taxed with Mary his espoused wife, being great with child. 6 And so it was, that, while they were there, the days were accomplished that she should be delivered. 7 And she brought forth her firstborn son, and wrapped him in swaddling clothes, and laid him in a manger; because there was no room for them in the inn.
8 And there were in the same country shepherds abiding in the field, keeping watch over their flock by night. 9 And, lo, the angel of the Lord came upon them, and the glory of the Lord shone round about them: and they were sore afraid. 10 And the angel said unto them, Fear not: for, behold, I bring you good tidings of great joy, which shall be to all people. 11 For unto you is born this day in the city of David a Saviour, which is Christ the Lord. 12 And this shall be a sign unto you; Ye shall find the babe wrapped in swaddling clothes, lying in a manger.
13 And suddenly there was with the angel a multitude of the heavenly host praising God, and saying, 14 Glory to God in the highest, and on earth peace, good will toward men. 15 And it came to pass, as the angels were gone away from them into heaven, the shepherds said one to another, Let us now go even unto Bethlehem, and see this thing which is come to pass, which the Lord hath made known unto us. 16 And they came with haste, and found Mary, and Joseph, and the babe lying in a manger. 17 And when they had seen it, they made known abroad the saying which was told them concerning this child. 18 And all they that heard it wondered at those things which were told them

by the shepherds. [19] But Mary kept all these things, and pondered them in her heart. [20] And the shepherds returned, glorifying and praising God for all the things that they had heard and seen, as it was told unto them.

CHAPTER 3

PROPHECIES OF THE EXPECTATION OF THE MESSIAH

Over many centuries Before Christ (BC) many people made different prophetic statements about the 'would-be' Messiah apart from His birth and its circumstances. All these were recorded in books, which were written between 1450 and 430 BC. Fulfillment of many of the prophecies is found in various books and letters written by different people at different locations in the first Century AD (precisely between 45 and 95 AD). Some of these prophecies concerning the messiahship of Jesus Christ and the fulfillment records are produced below.

Messiah to Crush Devil's Head.

Genesis 3:15 "And I will put enmity between thee and the woman, and between thy seed and her seed; it shall bruise thy head, and thou shalt bruise his heel."

This was part of the curse that God placed on the serpent for deceiving the woman, Eve, and it implies that the Messiah would be an offspring of the woman. This we see fulfilled as recorded by Luke:

Luke 1:30–32, 34–35 "And the angel said unto her, Fear not, Mary: for thou hast found favour with God. [31] And, behold, thou shalt conceive in thy womb, and bring forth a son, and shalt call his name Jesus. [32] He shall be great, and shall be called the Son of the Highest: and the Lord God shall give unto him the throne of his father David: [34] Then said Mary unto the angel, How shall this be, seeing I know not a man? [35] And the angel answered and said unto her, The Holy Ghost shall come upon thee, and the power of the Highest shall overshadow thee: therefore also that holy thing which shall be born of thee shall be called the Son of God

Verses 30 and 31 addressed a woman, Mary. Expressly, the exclusion of a man in the conception process of the Messiah is seen in verses 34 and 35. Additionally, Paul declared to the Galatians:

Galatians 4:4 But when the fulness of the time was come, God sent forth his Son, made of a woman, made under the law.

(b) Promises to Abram

Genesis 12:1-3 Now the Lord had said unto Abram, Get thee out of thy country, and from thy kindred, and from thy father's house, unto a land that I will shew thee: [2] And I will make of thee a great nation, and I will bless thee, and make thy name great; and thou shalt be a blessing: [3] And I will bless them that bless thee, and curse him that curseth thee: and in thee shall all families of the earth be blessed.

Fulfillment:

Matthew 1:1 "The book of the generation of Jesus Christ, the son of David, the son of Abraham."

Acts 3:25 "Ye are the children of the prophets, and of the covenant which God made with our fathers, saying unto Abraham, And in thy seed shall all the kindreds of the earth be blessed.

Galatians 3:16 "Now to Abraham and his seed were the promises made. He saith not, And to seeds, as of many; but as of one, And to thy seed, which is Christ."

Messiah to be Abraham's Descendant.

Genesis 22:17-18 I will surely bless you and make your descendants as numerous as the stars in the sky and as the sand on the seashore. Your descendants will take possession of the cities of their enemies, 18 and through your offspring all nations on earth will be blessed, because you have obeyed me."

Fulfillment:

The Messiah was going to be a descendant of Abraham. The fulfillment of this prophecy (promise to Abraham by GOD) was recorded in the genealogy of Jesus Christ by Matthew and Luke.

Matthew 1:2-16 "Abraham begat Isaac; and Isaac begat Jacob; and Jacob begat Judas and his brethren; 3 and Judas begat Phares and Zara of Thamar; and Phares begat Esrom; and Esrom begat Aram; 4 and Aram begat Aminadab; and Aminadab begat Naasson; and Naasson begat Salmon; 5 and Salmon begat Booz of Rachab; and Booz begat Obed of Ruth; and Obed begat Jesse; 6 and Jesse begat David the king; and David the king begat Solomon of her *that had been the wife* of Urias; 7 and Solomon begat Roboam; and Roboam begat Abia; and Abia begat Asa; 8 and Asa begat Josaphat; and Josaphat begat Joram; and Joram begat Ozias; 9 and Ozias begat Joatham; and Joatham begat Achaz; and Achaz begat Ezekias; 10 and Ezekias begat Manasses; and Manasses begat Amon; and Amon begat Josias; 11 and Josias begat Jechonias and his brethren, about the time they were carried away to Babylon: 12 and after they were brought to Babylon, Jechonias begat Salathiel; and Salathiel begat Zorobabel; 13 and Zorobabel begat Abiud; and Abiud begat Eliakim; and Eliakim begat Azor; 14 and Azor begat Sadoc; and Sadoc begat Achim; and Achim begat Eliud; 15 and Eliud begat Eleazar; and Eleazar begat Matthan; and Matthan begat Jacob; 16 and Jacob begat Joseph the husband of Mary, of whom was born Jesus, who is called Christ."

In Matthew's Gospel, Matthew traced the genealogy of Jesus Christ from Abraham. However, in the genealogy of Jesus Christ by St Luke it was from Adam to Jesus:

Luke 3:23-34 "And Jesus himself began to be about thirty years of age, being (as was supposed) the son of Joseph, which was the son of Heli,
24 Which was the son of Matthat, which was the son of Levi, which was the son of Melchi, which was the son of Janna, which was the son of Joseph,
25 Which was the son of Mattathias, which was the son of Amos, which was the son of Naum, which was the son of Esli, which was the son of Nagge,
26 Which was the son of Maath, which was the son of Mattathias, which was the son of Semei, which was the son of Joseph, which was the son of Juda,
27 Which was the son of Joanna, which was the son of Rhesa, which was the son of Zorobabel, which was the son of Salathiel, which was the son of Neri,
28 Which was the son of Melchi, which was the son of Addi, which was the son of Cosam, which was the son of Elmodam, which was the son of Er,
29 Which was the son of Jose, which was the son of Eliezer, which was the son of Jorim, which was the son of Matthat, which was the son of Levi,
30 Which was the son of Simeon, which was the son of Juda, which was the son of Joseph, which was the son of Jonan, which was the son of Eliakim,
31 Which was the son of Melea, which was the son of Menan, which was the son of Mattatha, which was the son of Nathan, which was the son of David,
32 Which was the son of Jesse, which was the son of Obed, which was the son of Booz, which was the son of Salmon, which was the son of Naasson,
33 Which was the son of Aminadab, which was the son of Aram, which was the son of Esrom, which was the son of Phares, which was the son of Juda,
34 Which was the son of Jacob, which was the son of Isaac, which was the son of Abraham, which was the son of Thara, which was the son of Nachor,

Other records showing the fulfillment of God's promise to Abraham include the following:

Acts 3:25-26 "And you are heirs of the prophets and of the covenant God made with your fathers. He said to Abraham, 'Through your offspring all peoples on earth will be blessed.' 26 When God raised up his servant, he sent him first to you to bless you by turning each of you from your wicked ways."

Galatians 3:16 " The promises were spoken to Abraham and to his seed. The Scripture does not say "and to seeds," meaning many people, but "and to your seed," meaning one person, who is Christ."

Messiah To Come From Judah's Lineage.
Genesis 49:10 "The scepter will not depart from Judah, nor the ruler's staff from between his feet, until he comes to whom it belongs and the obedience of the nations is his."

This prophecy meant that the Messiah was going to be a descendant of Judah. Jacob pronounced it while blessing all his twelve sons by name shortly before he died in Egypt. Judah eventually became one of the 12 tribes of Israel until the revolt and break-away of 10 tribes led by Jeroboam the son of Nabat ("*So when all Israel saw that the king hearkened not unto them, the people answered the king, saying, What portion have we in David? neither have we inheritance in the son of Jesse: to your tents, O Israel: now see to thine own house, David. So Israel departed unto their tents*" (1 Kings 12:16)), while the remaining 2 tribes of Judah and Benjamin became the Southern Kingdom, Judah with Jerusalem remaining its capital. The 10 tribes continued to bear the name, Israel (Northern Kingdom), with its capital in Samaria.

Its fulfillment is recorded as part of the genealogies in Matthew and Luke thus:

Matthew 1:2–3 " Abraham was the father of Isaac, Isaac the father of Jacob, Jacob the father of Judah and his brothers, 3 Judah the father of Perez and Zerah, whose mother was Tamar, Perez the father of Hezron, Hezron the father of Ram."

Luke 3:33, 34 "The son of Amminadab, the son of Ram, the son of Hezron, the son of Perez, the son of Judah, 34 the son of Jacob, the son of Isaac, the son of Abraham, the son of Terah, the son of Nahor,'

A Star from Jacob and a Sceptre from Israel.
Numbers 24:17 "I shall see him, but not now: I shall behold him, but not nigh: there shall come a Star out of Jacob, and a Sceptre shall rise out of Israel, and shall smite the corners of Moab, and destroy all the children of Sheth.

Fulfillment:

Matthew 1:2 "Abraham begat Isaac; and Isaac begat Jacob; and Jacob begat Judas and his brethren;

Luke 3:34 "Which was the son of Jacob, which was the son of Isaac, which was the son of Abraham, which was the son of Thara, which was the son of Nachor,

God To Raise a Prophet Like Moses.

Deuteronomy 18:15-19 "The Lord thy God will raise up unto thee a Prophet from the midst of thee, of thy brethren, like unto me; unto him ye shall hearken;

¹⁶ According to all that thou desiredst of the Lord thy God in Horeb in the day of the assembly, saying, Let me not hear again the voice of the Lord my God, neither let me see this great fire any more, that I die not. ¹⁷ And the Lord said unto me, They have well spoken that which they have spoken. ¹⁸ I will raise them up a Prophet from among their brethren, like unto thee, and will put my words in his mouth; and he shall speak unto them all that I shall command him. ¹⁹ And it shall come to pass, that whosoever will not hearken unto my words which he shall speak in my name, I will require it of him."

This passage happens to be one of the earliest prophecies of the coming of the Messiah (as a Prophet). The prophecy was by Moses, while leading the people of Israel to the Promised Land. It implied that the Messiah would be a prophet like Moses. The statement was a counsel to the people to pay attention to Him. It was repeated by the voice from heaven during the transfiguration of Jesus.

NIV comment on John 1:49 says that all of Israel's messianic expectations were fulfilled by Jesus Christ.[12]

Fulfillment:

John 1:45 "Philip findeth Nathanael, and saith unto him, We have found him, of whom Moses in the law, and the prophets, did write, Jesus of Nazareth, the son of Joseph."

John 7:40 "Many of the people therefore, when they heard this saying, said, Of a truth this is the Prophet.

Luke 9:35 "And there came a voice out of the cloud, saying, This is my beloved Son: hear him " (emphasis mine).

This prophecy of Moses partly accounted for why the Jews expected the Prophet, as confirmed by the following three occasions, the first being that the Jews sent a delegation to John the Baptist to inquire whether he was the expected Messiah.

John 1:19-22 " And this is the record of John, when the Jews sent priests and Levites from Jerusalem to ask him, Who art thou? 20 And he confessed, and denied not; but confessed, I am not the Christ. 21 And they asked him, What then? Art thou Elias? And he saith, I am not. Art thou that prophet? And he answered, No. 22 Then said they unto him, Who art thou? that we may give an answer to them that sent us. What sayest thou of thyself?"

---

[12] Disciple's Study Bible, NIV, 1317.

The second occasion was when Peter expressed the fulfillment of the prophecy of Moses to the hearing of the Jews after Pentecost. In Acts of the Apostles we find the apostle telling the people that this prophecy had been fulfilled thus":

Acts 3:17-23 "And now, brethren, I wot that through ignorance ye did it, as did also your rulers. [18] But those things, which God before had shewed by the mouth of all his prophets, that Christ should suffer, he hath so fulfilled. [19] Repent ye therefore, and be converted, that your sins may be blotted out, when the times of refreshing shall come from the presence of the Lord. [20] And he shall send Jesus Christ, which before was preached unto you: [21] Whom the heaven must receive until the times of restitution of all things, which God hath spoken by the mouth of all his holy prophets since the world began. [22] For Moses truly said unto the fathers, A prophet shall the Lord your God raise up unto you of your brethren, like unto me; him shall ye hear in all things whatsoever he shall say unto you. [23] And it shall come to pass, that every soul, which will not hear that prophet, shall be destroyed from among the people.

It is note worthy, however, that some scholars have the opinion[13] that interprets the above prophecy of Moses to also[14] mean that "the prophetic office is to be filled by a succession of prophets notwithstanding that Moses said a prophet."

As a Prophet Jesus Christ prophesied in the cause of His ministry:

A. He spoke-forth in His teachings and in rebuking. For instance:

When Jesus Healed a Centurion's Servant
Matthew 8:5-13 "And when Jesus was entered into Capernaum, there came unto him a centurion, beseeching him, [6] And saying, Lord, my servant lieth at home sick of the palsy, grievously tormented. [7] And Jesus saith unto him, I will come and heal him. [8] The centurion answered and said, Lord, I am not worthy that thou shouldest come under my roof: but speak the word only, and my servant shall be healed. [9] For I am a man under authority, having soldiers under me: and I say to this man, Go, and he goeth; and to another, Come, and he cometh; and to my servant, Do this, and he doeth it. [10] When Jesus heard it, he marvelled, and said to them that followed, Verily I say unto you, I have not found so great faith, no, not in Israel. [11] And I say unto you, That many shall come from the east and west, and shall sit down with Abraham, and Isaac, and Jacob, in the kingdom of heaven. [12] But the children of the kingdom shall be cast out into outer darkness: there shall be weeping

---

[13] Charles M. Laymon, ed. *The Interpreter's One-Volume Commentary on the Bible* (Nashville: Abingdon Press, 1971), 112.

[14] G. J. Wenham, J. A. Motyer, D. A. Carso, R. T. France, eds. *New Bible Commentary, 21st Century Edition* (Downers Gove; Leicester: Inter-Varsity Press, 1994), 217

and gnashing of teeth. [13] And Jesus said unto the centurion, Go thy way; and as thou hast believed, so be it done unto thee. And his servant was healed in the selfsame hour.

On Following Him

Matthew 8:18-22 "Now when Jesus saw great multitudes about him, he gave commandment to depart unto the other side.[19] And a certain scribe came, and said unto him, Master, I will follow thee whithersoever thou goest. [20] And Jesus saith unto him, The foxes have holes, and the birds of the air have nests; but the Son of man hath not where to lay his head. [21] And another of his disciples said unto him, Lord, suffer me first to go and bury my father. [22] But Jesus said unto him, Follow me; and let the dead bury their dead.

While Rebuking Disciples for Fearfulness

Matthew 8:23-27 "And when he was entered into a ship, his disciples followed him. [24] And, behold, there arose a great tempest in the sea, insomuch that the ship was covered with the waves: but he was asleep. [25] And his disciples came to him, and awoke him, saying, Lord, save us: we perish. [26] And he saith unto them, Why are ye fearful, O ye of little faith? Then he arose, and rebuked the winds and the sea; and there was a great calm. [27] But the men marvelled, saying, What manner of man is this, that even the winds and the sea obey him!

On the Hypocrisy of the Scribes and Pharisees

Matthew 16:6-8 "Then Jesus said unto them, Take heed and beware of the leaven of the Pharisees and of the Sadducees. [7] And they reasoned among themselves, saying, It is because we have taken no bread. [8] Which when Jesus perceived, he said unto them, O ye of little faith, why reason ye among yourselves, because ye have brought no bread?"

On Faithlessness
Luke 9:37-41 "And it came to pass, that on the next day, when they were come down from the hill, much people met him. [38] And, behold, a man of the company cried out, saying, Master, I beseech thee, look upon my son: for he is mine only child. [39] And, lo, a spirit taketh him, and he suddenly crieth out; and it teareth him that he foameth again, and bruising him hardly departeth from him. [40] And I besought thy disciples to cast him out; and they could not. [41] And Jesus answering said, O faithless and perverse generation, how long shall I be with you, and suffer you? Bring thy son hither."

Luke 9:41-42 "And Jesus answering said, O faithless and perverse generation, how long shall I be with you, and suffer you? Bring thy son hither. [42] And as he was yet a coming, the devil threw him down, and tare him. And Jesus rebuked the unclean spirit, and healed the child, and delivered him again to his father."

For Lack of Understanding

Luke 9:43-45 "And they were all amazed at the mighty power of God. But while they wondered every one at all things which Jesus did, he said unto his disciples, 44 Let these sayings sink down into your ears: for the Son of man shall be delivered into the hands of men. 45 But they understood not this saying, and it was hid from them, that they perceived it not: and they feared to ask him of that saying."

Regarding Pride and Power Tussle

Luke 9:46-48 "Then there arose a reasoning among them, which of them should be greatest. 47 And Jesus, perceiving the thought of their heart, took a child, and set him by him, 48 And said unto them, Whosoever shall receive this child in my name receiveth me: and whosoever shall receive me receiveth him that sent me: for he that is least among you all, the same shall be great."

Intolerance

Luke 9:49-50 "And John answered and said, Master, we saw one casting out devils in thy name; and we forbad him, because he followeth not with us. 50 And Jesus said unto him, Forbid him not: for he that is not against us is for us."

Racial Intolerance

Luke 9:51-56 "And it came to pass, when the time was come that he should be received up, he stedfastly set his face to go to Jerusalem, 52 And sent messengers before his face: and they went, and entered into a village of the Samaritans, to make ready for him. 53 And they did not receive him, because his face was as though he would go to Jerusalem. 54 And when his disciples James and John saw this, they said, Lord, wilt thou that we command fire to come down from heaven, and consume them, even as Elias did? 55 But he turned, and rebuked them, and said, Ye know not what manner of spirit ye are of. 56 For the Son of man is not come to destroy men's lives, but to save them. And they went to another village.

Busyness About All But Christ

Luke 10:41-42 "And Jesus answered and said unto her, Martha, Martha, thou art careful and troubled about many things: 42 But one thing is needful: and Mary hath chosen that good part, which shall not be taken away from her."

Perishing for Non-repentance

Luke 13:1-5 "There were present at that season some that told him of the Galilaeans, whose blood Pilate had mingled with their sacrifices. 2 And Jesus answering said unto them, Suppose ye that these Galilaeans were sinners above all the Galilaeans, because they suffered such things? 3 I tell you, Nay: but, except ye repent, ye shall all likewise perish. 4 Or those eighteen, upon whom the tower in Siloam fell, and slew them, think ye that they were sinners above all men that dwelt in Jerusalem? [5] I tell you, Nay: but, except ye repent, ye shall all likewise perish."

B. He foretold His impending death and resurrection, His second coming, the destruction of the Temple at Jerusalem and the city of Jerusalem, etc.

Matthew 16:21 "From that time forth began Jesus to shew unto his disciples, how that he must go unto Jerusalem, and suffer many things of the elders and chief priests and scribes, and be killed, and be raised again the third day."

Mark 8:31 "And he began to teach them, that the Son of man must suffer many things, and be rejected of the elders, and of the chief priests, and scribes, and be killed, and after three days rise again."

Luke 9:22 "Saying, The Son of man must suffer many things, and be rejected of the elders and chief priests and scribes, and be slain, and be raised the third day."

Mark 9:30-32 "And they departed thence, and passed through Galilee; and he would not that any man should know it. [31] For he taught his disciples, and said unto them, The Son of man is delivered into the hands of men, and they shall kill him; and after that he is killed, he shall rise the third day. [32] But they understood not that saying, and were afraid to ask him."

Luke 9:43-45 "And they were all amazed at the mighty power of God. But while they wondered every one at all things which Jesus did, he said unto his disciples, [44] Let these sayings sink down into your ears: for the Son of man shall be delivered into the hands of men. [45] But they understood not this saying, and it was hid from them, that they perceived it not: and they feared to ask him of that saying.

Matthew 20:17-19 "And Jesus going up to Jerusalem took the twelve disciples apart in the way, and said unto them, [18] Behold, we go up to Jerusalem; and the Son of man shall be betrayed unto the chief priests and unto the scribes, and they shall condemn him to death, [19] And shall deliver him to the Gentiles to mock, and to scourge, and to crucify him: and the third day he shall rise again.

The Sign of Jonah

Matthew 12:39-40 "But he answered and said unto them, An evil and adulterous generation seeketh after a sign; and there shall no sign be given to it, but the sign of the prophet Jonas: [40] For as Jonas was three days and three nights in the whale's belly; so shall the Son of man be three days and three nights in the heart of the earth.

Matthew 16:4 "A wicked and adulterous generation seeketh after a sign; and there shall no sign be given unto it, but the sign of the prophet Jonas. And he left them, and departed."

Luke 11:29-30 "And when the people were gathered thick together, he began to say, This is an evil generation: they seek a sign; and there shall no sign be given it, but the sign of Jonas the prophet. 30 For as Jonas was a sign unto the Ninevites, so shall also the Son of man be to this generation.

Luke 18:31-33 "Then he took unto him the twelve, and said unto them, Behold, we go up to Jerusalem, and all things that are written by the prophets concerning the Son of man shall be accomplished. 32 For he shall be delivered unto the Gentiles, and shall be mocked, and spitefully entreated, and spitted on: 33 And they shall scourge him, and put him to death: and the third day he shall rise again.

John 2:19-22 "Jesus answered and said unto them, Destroy this temple, and in three days I will raise it up. 20 Then said the Jews, Forty and six years was this temple in building, and wilt thou rear it up in three days? 21 But he spake of the temple of his body. 22 When therefore he was risen from the dead, his disciples remembered that he had said this unto them; and they believed the scripture, and the word which Jesus had said.

John 3:14-15 "And as Moses lifted up the serpent in the wilderness, even so must the Son of man be lifted up: 15 That whosoever believeth in him should not perish, but have eternal life."

John 7:33-36 "Then said Jesus unto them, Yet a little while am I with you, and then I go unto him that sent me. 34 Ye shall seek me, and shall not find me: and where I am, thither ye cannot come. 35 Then said the Jews among themselves, Whither will he go, that we shall not find him? will he go unto the dispersed among the Gentiles, and teach the Gentiles? 36 What manner of saying is this that he said, Ye shall seek me, and shall not find me: and where I am, thither ye cannot come?

John 8:21 "Then said Jesus again unto them, I go my way, and ye shall seek me, and shall die in your sins: whither I go, ye cannot come."

John 10:15 "As the Father knoweth me, even so know I the Father: and I lay down my life for the sheep."

John 12:23 "And Jesus answered them, saying, The hour is come, that the Son of man should be glorified."

John 12:27 "Now is my soul troubled; and what shall I say? Father, save me from this hour: but for this cause came I unto this hour."

Jesus Christ also foretold the signs of the times of the end.

The Coming of the Son of Man

Matthew 24:26-31 "Wherefore if they shall say unto you, Behold, he is in the desert; go not forth: behold, he is in the secret chambers; believe it not. [27] For as the lightning cometh out of the east, and shineth even unto the west; so shall also the coming of the Son of man be. [28] For wheresoever the carcase is, there will the eagles be gathered together.
[29] Immediately after the tribulation of those days shall the sun be darkened, and the moon shall not give her light, and the stars shall fall from heaven, and the powers of the heavens shall be shaken: [30] And then shall appear the sign of the Son of man in heaven: and then shall all the tribes of the earth mourn, and they shall see the Son of man coming in the clouds of heaven with power and great glory. [31] And he shall send his angels with a great sound of a trumpet, and they shall gather together his elect from the four winds, from one end of heaven to the other.

No One Knows the Day or Hour

Matthew 24:36-44 "But of that day and hour knoweth no man, no, not the angels of heaven, but my Father only. [37] But as the days of Noah were, so shall also the coming of the Son of man be. [38] For as in the days that were before the flood they were eating and drinking, marrying and giving in marriage, until the day that Noe entered into the ark, [39] And knew not until the flood came, and took them all away; so shall also the coming of the Son of man be. [40] Then shall two be in the field; the one shall be taken, and the other left. [41] Two women shall be grinding at the mill; the one shall be taken, and the other left. [42] Watch therefore: for ye know not what hour your Lord doth come. [43] But know this, that if the goodman of the house had known in what watch the thief would come, he would have watched, and would not have suffered his house to be broken up. [44] Therefore be ye also ready: for in such an hour as ye think not the Son of man cometh.

Mark 13:32-37 "But of that day and that hour knoweth no man, no, not the angels which are in heaven, neither the Son, but the Father. [33] Take ye heed, watch and pray: for ye know not when the time is. [34] For the Son of Man is as a man taking a far journey, who left his house, and gave authority to his servants, and to every man his work, and commanded the porter to watch. [35] Watch ye therefore: for ye know not when the master of the house cometh, at even, or at midnight, or at the cockcrowing, or in the morning: [36] Lest coming suddenly he find you sleeping. [37] And what I say unto you I say unto all, Watch

Parable of the Ten Virgins

Matthew 25:1-13 "Then shall the kingdom of heaven be likened unto ten virgins, which took their lamps, and went forth to meet the bridegroom. [2] And five of them were wise, and five were foolish. 3 They that were foolish took their lamps, and took no oil with them: 4 But the wise took oil in their vessels with their lamps. 5 While the bridegroom tarried, they all slumbered and slept. 6 And at midnight there was a cry made, Behold, the bridegroom cometh; go ye out to meet him. 7 Then all those virgins arose, and trimmed their lamps. 8 And the foolish said unto the wise, Give us of your oil; for our lamps are gone out. 9 But the wise answered, saying, Not so; lest there be not enough for us and you: but go ye rather to them that sell, and buy for yourselves. 10 And while they went to buy, the bridegroom came; and they that were ready went in with him to the marriage: and the door was shut. 11 Afterward came also the other virgins, saying, Lord, Lord, open to us. 12 But he answered and said, Verily I say unto you, I know you not. 13 Watch therefore, for ye know neither the day nor the hour wherein the Son of man cometh.

By the parables above Jesus Christ taught about preparedness of the saints for His future return.

The Son of Man Will Judge the Nations

Matthew 25:31-46 "When the Son of man shall come in his glory, and all the holy angels with him, then shall he sit upon the throne of his glory: 32 And before him shall be gathered all nations: and he shall separate them one from another, as a shepherd divideth his sheep from the goats: 33 And he shall set the sheep on his right hand, but the goats on the left. 34 Then shall the King say unto them on his right hand, Come, ye blessed of my Father, inherit the kingdom prepared for you from the foundation of the world: 35 For I was an hungred, and ye gave me meat: I was thirsty, and ye gave me drink: I was a stranger, and ye took me in: 36 Naked, and ye clothed me: I was sick, and ye visited me: I was in prison, and ye came unto me.

37 Then shall the righteous answer him, saying, Lord, when saw we thee an hungred, and fed thee? or thirsty, and gave thee drink? 38 When saw we thee a stranger, and took thee in? or naked, and clothed thee? 39 Or when saw we thee sick, or in prison, and came unto thee? 40 And the King shall answer and say unto them, Verily I say unto you, Inasmuch as ye have done it unto one of the least of these my brethren, ye have done it unto me.

41 Then shall he say also unto them on the left hand, Depart from me, ye cursed, into everlasting fire, prepared for the devil and his angels: 42 For I was an hungred, and ye gave me no meat: I was thirsty, and ye gave me no drink: 43 I was a stranger, and ye took me not in: naked, and ye clothed me not: sick, and in prison, and ye visited me not. 44 Then shall they also answer him, saying, Lord, when saw we thee an hungred, or athirst, or a stranger, or naked, or sick, or in prison, and did not minister unto thee? 45 Then shall he answer them, saying, Verily I say unto you, Inasmuch as ye did it not to one of the least of these, ye did it not to me. 46 And these shall go away into everlasting punishment: but the righteous into life eternal.

The third occasion that indicated that the Jews were actually expecting a Prophet like Moses was when John the Baptist, while suffering in prison, sent his disciples to Jesus

Christ with the question in the following passage.

Matthew 11:1-3 "And it came to pass, when Jesus had made an end of commanding his twelve disciples, he departed thence to teach and to preach in their cities. 2 Now when John had heard in the prison the works of Christ, he sent two of his disciples, 3 And said unto him, Art thou he that should come, or do we look for another?"

Messiah To Be God's Son.

Psalm 2:7–8 "I will declare the decree: the Lord hath said unto me, Thou art my Son; this day have I begotten thee. 8 Ask of me, and I shall give thee the heathen for thine inheritance, and the uttermost parts of the earth for thy possession.

Fulfillment
The Messiah was going to be the Son of GOD. The fulfillment is found recorded in all

three Synoptic Gospels of Matthew, Mark and Luke – being a heavenly voice following

Jesus Chris's baptism in the Jordan River:

Matthew 3:16-17 "And Jesus, when he was baptized, went up straightway out of the water: and, lo, the heavens were opened unto him, and he saw the Spirit of God descending like a dove, and lighting upon him: 17 And lo a voice from heaven, saying, This is my beloved Son, in whom I am well pleased."

Mark 1:9-11 "And it came to pass in those days, that Jesus came from Nazareth of Galilee, and was baptized of John in Jordan. 10 And straightway coming up out of the water, he saw the heavens opened, and the Spirit like a dove descending upon him: 11 And there came a voice from heaven, saying, Thou art my beloved Son, in whom I am well pleased.

Luke 3:21-22 "Now when all the people were baptized, it came to pass, that Jesus also being baptized, and praying, the heaven was opened, 22 And the Holy Ghost descended in a bodily shape like a dove upon him, and a voice came from heaven, which said, Thou art my beloved Son; in thee I am well pleased.

Great Kings to Bow Before Him.

There were prophecies that the Messiah would be paid homage and worshipped by great kings, and served by all nations:

Psalms 72:9–11 "They that dwell in the wilderness shall bow before him; and his enemies shall lick the dust. 10 The kings of Tarshish and of the isles shall bring presents: the kings of Sheba and Seba shall offer gifts. 11 Yea, all kings shall fall down before him: all nations shall serve him."

Psalm 86:9 "All nations whom thou hast made shall come and worship before thee, O Lord; and shall glorify thy name."

Zechariah 14:16 "And it shall come to pass, that every one that is left of all the nations which came against Jerusalem shall even go up from year to year to worship the King, the Lord of hosts, and to keep the feast of tabernacles."

The apostle Paul says, "[9] Wherefore God also hath highly exalted him, and given him a name which is above every name: [10] That at the name of Jesus every knee should bow, of things in heaven, and things in earth, and things under the earth; [11] And that every tongue should confess that Jesus Christ is Lord, to the glory of God the Father" (Philippians 2:9-11). Already all persons that have accepted Jesus Christ as personal Lord and Savior, who are scattered in many nations of the world, do worship Him. Worshipping Jesus Christ began during His First Advent with the Magi, shortly after His birth.

The gospel by Matthew has the story of the visit of the Magi to the Baby Jesus, giving Him gifts and bowing in worship to Him; the worship by all nations (at least where the Gospel has been preached) has begun, but will blossom at the Second Advent.

Matthew 2:1–11 "Now when Jesus was born in Bethlehem of Judaea in the days of Herod the king, behold, there came wise men from the east to Jerusalem, [2] Saying, Where is he that is born King of the Jews? for we have seen his star in the east, and are come to worship him. [3] When Herod the king had heard these things, he was troubled, and all Jerusalem with him. [4] And when he had gathered all the chief priests and scribes of the people together, he demanded of them where Christ should be born. [5] And they said unto him, In Bethlehem of Judaea: for thus it is written by the prophet, [6] And thou Bethlehem, in the land of Juda, art not the least among the princes of Juda: for out of thee shall come a Governor, that shall rule my people Israel. [7] Then Herod, when he had privily called the wise men, enquired of them diligently what time the star appeared. [8] And he sent them to Bethlehem, and said, Go and search diligently for the young child; and when ye have found him, bring me word again, that I may come and worship him also. [9] When they had heard the king, they departed; and, lo, the star, which they saw in the east, went before them, till it came and stood over where the young child was. [10] When they saw the star, they rejoiced with exceeding great joy. [11] And when they were come into the house, they saw the young child with Mary his mother, and fell down, and worshipped him: and when they had opened their treasures, they presented unto him gifts; gold, and frankincense and myrrh.

Messiah coming to be the Righteous Judge

Psalm 96:13 "Before the Lord: for he cometh, for he cometh to judge the earth: he shall judge the world with righteousness, and the people with his truth."

Jeremiah 23:5-6 "Behold, the days come, saith the Lord, that I will raise unto David a righteous Branch, and a King shall reign and prosper, and shall execute judgment and justice in the earth. 6 In his days Judah shall be saved, and Israel shall dwell safely: and this is his name whereby he shall be called, The Lord Our Righteousness.

This prophecy is still for a future fulfillment at the Second Advent of Jesus Christ.

However, other Bible passages that report the worship of Jesus Christ during the First

Advent include the following:

Matthew 14:33 "Then they that were in the ship came and worshipped him, saying, Of a truth thou art the Son of God."

Matthew 28:9 "And as they went to tell his disciples, behold, Jesus met them, saying, All hail. And they came and held him by the feet, and worshipped him."

Messiah To Be David's Descendant.

2 Samuel 7:12-16 "And when thy days be fulfilled, and thou shalt sleep with thy fathers, I will set up thy seed after thee, which shall proceed out of thy bowels, and I will establish his kingdom. 13 He shall build an house for my name, and I will stablish the throne of his kingdom for ever. 14 I will be his father, and he shall be my son. If he commit iniquity, I will chasten him with the rod of men, and with the stripes of the children of men: 15 But my mercy shall not depart away from him, as I took it from Saul, whom I put away before thee. 16 And thine house and thy kingdom shall be established for ever before thee: thy throne shall be established for ever.

Psalms 132:11 "The Lord hath sworn in truth unto David; he will not turn from it; Of the fruit of thy body will I set upon thy throne."

Isaiah 11:1, 10 "And there shall come forth a rod out of the stem of Jesse, and a Branch shall grow out of his roots: 10 And in that day there shall be a root of Jesse, which shall stand for an ensign of the people; to it shall the Gentiles seek: and his rest shall be glorious."

Jeremiah 33:15-16 "In those days, and at that time, will I cause the Branch of righteousness to grow up unto David; and he shall execute judgment and righteousness in the land. 16 In those days shall Judah be saved, and Jerusalem shall dwell safely: and this is the name wherewith she shall be called, The Lord our righteousness."

These three passages are records of the prophecy that the Messiah would be a descendant of king David. And record of the fulfillment of the prophecy is found in the genealogy as per Matthew and Luke as detailed earlier. Remember that the angel Gabriel repeated the above prophecies to Mary while announcing the conception of Jesus Christ.

Luke 1:31-33 And, behold, thou shalt conceive in thy womb, and bring forth a son, and shalt call his name Jesus. [32] He shall be great, and shall be called the Son of the Highest: and the Lord God shall give unto him the throne of his father David: [33] And he shall reign over the house of Jacob for ever; and of his kingdom there shall be no end."

Messiah to be Part of The Everlasting Covenant.
Isaiah 55:3-4 "Incline your ear, and come unto me: hear, and your soul shall live; and I will make an everlasting covenant with you, even the sure mercies of David. [4] Behold, I have given him for a witness to the people, a leader and commander to the people."

Jeremiah 31:31-34 "Behold, the days come, saith the Lord, that I will make a new covenant with the house of Israel, and with the house of Judah: [32] Not according to the covenant that I made with their fathers in the day that I took them by the hand to bring them out of the land of Egypt; which my covenant they brake, although I was an husband unto them, saith the Lord: [33] But this shall be the covenant that I will make with the house of Israel; After those days, saith the Lord, I will put my law in their inward parts, and write it in their hearts; and will be their God, and they shall be my people. [34] And they shall teach no more every man his neighbour, and every man his brother, saying, Know the Lord: for they shall all know me, from the least of them unto the greatest of them, saith the Lord: for I will forgive their iniquity, and I will remember their sin no more."

That the Messiah was going to be part of the everlasting covenant is the summary of the above two prophecy records in Isaiah and Jeremiah. The fulfillment of the prophecies in the NT is found in the following passages:

Matthew 26:28 "For this is my blood of the new testament, which is shed for many for the remission of sins."

Mark 14: 24 "And he said unto them, This is my blood of the new testament, which is shed for many."

Luke 22:20 "Likewise also the cup after supper, saying, This cup is the new testament in my blood, which is shed for you."

Hebrews 8:6-13 "But now hath he obtained a more excellent ministry, by how much also he is the mediator of a better covenant, which was established upon better promises. [7] For if that first covenant had been faultless, then should no place have been sought for the second. [8] For finding fault with them, he saith, Behold, the days come, saith the Lord, when I will make a new covenant with the house of Israel and with the house of Judah: [9] Not according to the covenant that I made with their fathers in the day when I took them by the hand to lead them out of the land of Egypt; because they continued not in my covenant, and I regarded them not, saith the Lord.

[10] For this is the covenant that I will make with the house of Israel after those days, saith the Lord; I will put my laws into their mind, and write them in their hearts: and I will be to them a God, and they shall be to me a people: [11] And they shall not teach every man his neighbour, and every man his brother, saying, Know the Lord: for all shall know me, from the least to the greatest. [12] For I will be merciful to their unrighteousness, and their sins and their iniquities will I remember no more. [13] In that he saith, A new covenant, he hath made the first old. Now that which decayeth and waxeth old is ready to vanish away.

Messiah's Early Ministry To Be in Galilee.

Isaiah 9: 1–2 Nevertheless the dimness shall not be such as was in her vexation, when at the first he lightly afflicted the land of Zebulun and the land of Naphtali, and afterward did more grievously afflict her by the way of the sea, beyond Jordan, in Galilee of the nations [2] The people that walked in darkness have seen a great light: they that dwell in the land of the shadow of death, upon them hath the light shined.

The prophecy here refers to the commencement of the spiritual ministry of the Messiah in Galilee. The fulfillment of the prophecy is recorded in Matthew's Gospel as follows:

Jesus Starts His Ministry in Galilee

Matthew 4:12-16 "Now when Jesus had heard that John was cast into prison, he departed into Galilee; [13] And leaving Nazareth, he came and dwelt in Capernaum, which is upon the sea coast, in the borders of Zabulon and Nephthalim: [14] That it might be fulfilled which was spoken by Esaias the prophet, saying, [15] The land of Zabulon, and the land of Nephthalim, by the way of the sea, beyond Jordan, Galilee of the Gentiles; [16] The people which sat in darkness saw great light; and to them which sat in the region and shadow of death light is sprung up.

The Messiah Will Do Miraculous Healing

Isaiah 35:5–6 "Then the eyes of the blind shall be opened, and the ears of the deaf shall be unstopped. [6] Then shall the lame man leap as an hart, and the tongue of the dumb sing: for in the wilderness shall waters break out, and streams in the desert."

It was prophesied that the Messiah would restore the sight of the blind, the hearing of the deaf, make the dumb speak, the lame walk, and so on. Various writers of the New Testament books, including the following, recorded the fulfillment of this prophecy:

Matthew 4:23-25 "And Jesus went about all Galilee, teaching in their synagogues, and preaching the gospel of the kingdom, and healing all manner of sickness and all manner of disease among the people. 24 And his fame went throughout all Syria: and they brought unto him all sick people that were taken with divers diseases and torments, and those which were possessed with devils, and those which were lunatick, and those that had the palsy; and he healed them. 25 And there followed him great multitudes of people from Galilee, and from Decapolis, and from Jerusalem, and from Judaea, and from beyond Jordan

Matthew 9:35 "And Jesus went about all the cities and villages, teaching in their synagogues, and preaching the gospel of the kingdom, and healing every sickness and every disease among the people.

Matthew 11:2-6 "Now when John had heard in the prison the works of Christ, he sent two of his disciples, 3 And said unto him, Art thou he that should come, or do we look for another? 4 Jesus answered and said unto them, Go and shew John again those things which ye do hear and see: 5 The blind receive their sight, and the lame walk, the lepers are cleansed, and the deaf hear, the dead are raised up, and the poor have the gospel preached to them. 6 And blessed is he, whosoever shall not be offended in me.

Some instances of the miraculous healing Jesus Christ did with regard to the blind,

deaf, lame, leprous, etc.:

Mark 7:34-35 "And looking up to heaven, he sighed, and saith unto him, Ephphatha, that is, Be opened. 35 And straightway his ears were opened, and the string of his tongue was loosed, and he spake plain."

Luke 7:21-22 "And in that same hour he cured many of their infirmities and plagues, and of evil spirits; and unto many that were blind he gave sight. 22 Then Jesus answering said unto them, Go your way, and tell John what things ye have seen and heard; how that the blind see, the lame walk, the lepers are cleansed, the deaf hear, the dead are raised, to the poor the gospel is preached."

John 9:4-7 "I must work the works of him that sent me, while it is day: the night cometh, when no man can work. 5 As long as I am in the world, I am the light of the world. 6 When he had thus spoken, he spat on the ground, and made clay of the spittle, and he anointed the eyes of the blind man with the clay, 7 And said unto him, Go, wash in the pool of Siloam, (which is by interpretation, Sent.) He went his way therefore, and washed, and came seeing.

Messiah To Do (Other) Miraculous Signs.

Isaiah 42:5–9 "Thus saith God the Lord, he that created the heavens, and stretched them out; he that spread forth the earth, and that which cometh out of it; he that giveth breath unto the people upon it, and spirit to them that walk therein: ⁶ I the Lord have called thee in righteousness, and will hold thine hand, and will keep thee, and give thee for a covenant of the people, for a light of the Gentiles; ⁷ To open the blind eyes, to bring out the prisoners from the prison, and them that sit in darkness out of the prison house. ⁸ I am the Lord: that is my name: and my glory will I not give to another, neither my praise to graven images. ⁹ Behold, the former things are come to pass, and new things do I declare: before they spring forth I tell you of them.

It was prophesied that the Messiah would, in addition to healing the sick and doing other miraculous signs, have as part of His mission freeing people held bound and be a light to the Gentiles. As found below, this prophecy was fulfilled.

Matthew 9:18-19, 23-38 "While he spake these things unto them, behold, there came a certain ruler, and worshipped him, saying, My daughter is even now dead: but come and lay thy hand upon her, and she shall live. ¹⁹ And Jesus arose, and followed him, and so did his disciples." **23** And when Jesus came into the ruler's house, and saw the minstrels and the people making a noise, ²⁴ He said unto them, Give place: for the maid is not dead, but sleepeth. And they laughed him to scorn. ²⁵ But when the people were put forth, he went in, and took her by the hand, and the maid arose. ²⁶ And the fame hereof went abroad into all that land.
²⁷ And when Jesus departed thence, two blind men followed him, crying, and saying, Thou son of David, have mercy on us. ²⁸ And when he was come into the house, the blind men came to him: and Jesus saith unto them, Believe ye that I am able to do this? They said unto him, Yea, Lord. ²⁹ Then touched he their eyes, saying, According to your faith be it unto you. ³⁰ And their eyes were opened; and Jesus straitly charged them, saying, See that no man know it.
³¹ But they, when they were departed, spread abroad his fame in all that country. ³² As they went out, behold, they brought to him a dumb man possessed with a devil.
³³ And when the devil was cast out, the dumb spake: and the multitudes marvelled, saying, It was never so seen in Israel. ³⁴ But the Pharisees said, He casteth out devils through the prince of the devils. ³⁵ And Jesus went about all the cities and villages, teaching in their synagogues, and preaching the gospel of the kingdom, and healing every sickness and every disease among the people. ³⁶ But when he saw the multitudes, he was moved with compassion on them, because they fainted, and were scattered abroad, as sheep having no shepherd. ³⁷ Then saith he unto his disciples, The harvest truly is plenteous, but the labourers are few; ³⁸ Pray ye therefore the Lord of the harvest, that he will send forth labourers into his harvest.

During the dedication of Jesus Christ in the temple Simeon commented in line with the prophecy that Jesus Christ would be light to the Gentiles.

Luke 2:28-32 "Then took he him up in his arms, and blessed God, and said, [29] Lord, now lettest thou thy servant depart in peace, according to thy word: [30] For mine eyes have seen thy salvation, [31] Which thou hast prepared before the face of all people; [32] A light to lighten the Gentiles, and the glory of thy people Israel.

Luke 13:22 "And he went through the cities and villages, teaching, and journeying toward Jerusalem."

Jesus Heals a Man Born Blind
John 9:1-17 "And as Jesus passed by, he saw a man which was blind from his birth. [2] And his disciples asked him, saying, Master, who did sin, this man, or his parents, that he was born blind? [3] Jesus answered, Neither hath this man sinned, nor his parents: but that the works of God should be made manifest in him. [4] I must work the works of him that sent me, while it is day: the night cometh, when no man can work. [5] As long as I am in the world, I am the light of the world. [6] When he had thus spoken, he spat on the ground, and made clay of the spittle, and he anointed the eyes of the blind man with the clay, [7] And said unto him, Go, wash in the pool of Siloam, (which is by interpretation, Sent.) He went his way therefore, and washed, and came seeing. [8] The neighbours therefore, and they which before had seen him that he was blind, said, Is not this he that sat and begged? [9] Some said, This is he: others said, He is like him: but he said, I am he. [10] Therefore said they unto him, How were thine eyes opened? [11] He answered and said, A man that is called Jesus made clay, and anointed mine eyes, and said unto me, Go to the pool of Siloam, and wash: and I went and washed, and I received sight. [12] Then said they unto him, Where is he? He said, I know not. [13] They brought to the Pharisees him that aforetime was blind. [14] And it was the sabbath day when Jesus made the clay, and opened his eyes. [15] Then again the Pharisees also asked him how he had received his sight. He said unto them, He put clay upon mine eyes, and I washed, and do see. [16] Therefore said some of the Pharisees, This man is not of God, because he keepeth not the sabbath day. Others said, How can a man that is a sinner do such miracles? And there was a division among them. [17] They say unto the blind man again, What sayest thou of him, that he hath opened thine eyes? He said, He is a prophet.

John 20:30 "And many other signs truly did Jesus in the presence of his disciples, which are not written in this book."

In his address at the home of Cornelius the apostle Peter mentioned "How God anointed Jesus of Nazareth with the Holy Ghost and with power: who went about doing good, and healing all that were oppressed of the devil; for God was with him"

(Acts 10:38).

Acts 13:46-47 "Then Paul and Barnabas waxed bold, and said, It was necessary that the word of God should first have been spoken to you: but seeing ye put it from you, and judge yourselves unworthy of everlasting life, lo, we turn to the Gentiles. ⁴⁷ For so hath the Lord commanded us, saying, I have set thee to be a light of the Gentiles, that thou shouldest be for salvation unto the ends of the earth

Acts 26:17-18 "Delivering thee from the people, and from the Gentiles, unto whom now I send thee, ¹⁸ To open their eyes, and to turn them from darkness to light, and from the power of Satan unto God, that they may receive forgiveness of sins, and inheritance among them which are sanctified by faith that is in me.

A lot more of Jesus Christ's miracles are also stated in chapter 4 of this book, under

The Ministry of the Expected Messiah.

Messiah To Preach Good News.

Isaiah 61:1–3 The Spirit of the Lord God is upon me; because the Lord hath anointed me to preach good tidings unto the meek; he hath sent me to bind up the brokenhearted, to proclaim liberty to the captives, and the opening of the prison to them that are bound; ² To proclaim the acceptable year of the Lord, and the day of vengeance of our God; to comfort all that mourn; ³ To appoint unto them that mourn in Zion, to give unto them beauty for ashes, the oil of joy for mourning, the garment of praise for the spirit of heaviness; that they might be called trees of righteousness, the planting of the Lord, that he might be glorified.

The Messiah was going to have a two-fold mission: the first encompasses healing the people, preaching the good news of the Kingdom and freeing of those under the bondage of sin and the powers of darkness (bringing salvation). The second leg of the mission was eschatological - proclaiming the day of God's vengeance on the unrighteous, and establishing His kingdom, which shall take place during His second coming.

Jesus Christ's confirmation of the fulfillment of this prophecy is found in His announcement/introduction of His ministry in the   :

Luke 4:16-21 "And he came to Nazareth, where he had been brought up: and, as his custom was, he went into the synagogue on the sabbath day, and stood up for to read. ¹⁷ And there was delivered unto him the book of the prophet Esaias. And when he had opened the book, he found the place where it was written, ¹⁸ The Spirit of the Lord is upon me, because he hath anointed me to preach the gospel to the poor; he hath sent me to heal the brokenhearted, to preach deliverance to the captives, and recovering of sight to the blind, to set at liberty them that are bruised, [19] To preach the acceptable year of the Lord. [20] And he closed the book, and he gave it again to the minister, and sat down. And the eyes of all them that were in the synagogue were fastened on him. [21] And he began to say unto them, This day is this scripture fulfilled in your ears."

It is generally believed that Jesus did not include in His quotation from Isaiah, "*and the day of vengeance of our God, ... and a garment of praise instead of a spirit of despair...*' very likely because He was not going to fulfill that until His second coming as mentioned above. He knew His mission for that period and would not exceed it.

Messiah To Come at a Specified Time.

Daniel 9:24–26 Seventy weeks are determined upon thy people and upon thy holy city, to finish the transgression, and to make an end of sins, and to make reconciliation for iniquity, and to bring in everlasting righteousness, and to seal up the vision and prophecy, and to anoint the most Holy.
25 Know therefore and understand, that from the going forth of the commandment to restore and to build Jerusalem unto the Messiah the Prince shall be seven weeks, and threescore and two weeks: the street shall be built again, and the wall, even in troublous times.
26 And after threescore and two weeks shall Messiah be cut off, but not for himself: and the people of the prince that shall come shall destroy the city and the sanctuary; and the end thereof shall be with a flood, and unto the end of the war desolations are determined."

This prophecy by Daniel proffered that the Messiah was to come at a specific time:

-   70 Weeks of the History had been decreed for the people of Israel and their Holy City (Jerusalem) to experience the following:
    (i)   "to finish the transgression;"
    (ii)   "to make an end of sins;"
    (iii)   "to make reconciliation [atonement] for iniquity" by the unblemished blood of the Lamb of God – the Messiah;
    (iv)   "to bring in everlasting righteousness" (which is available only in the Messiah);
    (v)   "to seal up the vision and prophecy;"
    (vi)   "to anoint the most Holy (place)."
-   The period from the authorization of the rebuilding of Jerusalem and its

temple (Nehemiah's times) to the coming of a "Messiah the Prince" would be 69 Weeks. After 62 Weeks the Messiah would [appear on the scene and] be crucified; and the agents of the prince (the emperor) shall destroy the city and the temple.

In the NT the apostle Paul mentioned that the birth of the Messiah was specified in his letters to the Galatians and the Ephesians:

Galatians 4:4–5 "But when the fulness of the time was come, God sent forth his Son, made of a woman, made under the law, 5 To redeem them that were under the law, that we might receive the adoption of sons.

Ephesians 1:7-10 "In whom we have redemption through his blood, the forgiveness of sins, according to the riches of his grace; 8 Wherein he hath abounded toward us in all wisdom and prudence; 9 Having made known unto us the mystery of his will, according to his good pleasure which he hath purposed in himself: 10 That in the dispensation of the fulness of times he might gather together in one all things in Christ, both which are in heaven, and which are on earth; even in him"

Messiah's Triumphant Entry To Jerusalem.
Zechariah 9: 9 "Rejoice greatly, O daughter of Zion; shout, O daughter of Jerusalem: behold, thy King cometh unto thee: he is just, and having salvation; lowly, and riding upon an ass, and upon a colt the foal of an ass."

The Messiah would ultimately enter Jerusalem triumphantly, though humbly on a donkey rather than a horse or chariot. Entering on a horse or a chariot would have portrayed Him as a conquering Messiah as expected by the Jews. The fulfillment of this prophecy is found in Matthew, Mark, Luke and John detailed as Jesus Christ's Triumphal Entry are as follows:

Matthew 21:1-11 "And when they drew nigh unto Jerusalem, and were come to Bethphage, unto the mount of Olives, then sent Jesus two disciples, 2 Saying unto them, Go into the village over against you, and straightway ye shall find an ass tied, and a colt with her: loose them, and bring them unto me. 3 And if any man say ought unto you, ye shall say, The Lord hath need of them; and straightway he will send them. 4 All this was done, that it might be fulfilled which was spoken by the prophet, saying, 5 Tell ye the daughter of Sion, Behold, thy King cometh unto thee, meek, and sitting upon an ass, and a colt the foal of an ass. 6 And the disciples went, and did as Jesus commanded them, 7 And brought the ass, and the colt, and put on them their clothes, and they set him thereon. 8 And a very great multitude spread their garments in the way; others cut down branches from the trees, and strawed them in the way. 9 And the multitudes that went before, and that followed, cried, saying, Hosanna to the son of David: Blessed is he that cometh in the name of the Lord; Hosanna in the highest. [10] And when he was come into Jerusalem, all the city was moved, saying, Who is this? [11] And the multitude said, This is Jesus the prophet of Nazareth of Galilee."

Mark 11:1-10 "And when they came nigh to Jerusalem, unto Bethphage and Bethany, at the mount of Olives, he sendeth forth two of his disciples, [2] And saith unto them, Go your way into the village over against you: and as soon as ye be entered into it, ye shall find a colt tied, whereon never man sat; loose him, and bring him. [3] And if any man say unto you, Why do ye this? say ye that the Lord hath need of him; and straightway he will send him hither. [4] And they went their way, and found the colt tied by the door without in a place where two ways met; and they loose him. [5] And certain of them that stood there said unto them, What do ye, loosing the colt? [6] And they said unto them even as Jesus had commanded: and they let them go. [7] And they brought the colt to Jesus, and cast their garments on him; and he sat upon him.
[8] And many spread their garments in the way: and others cut down branches off the trees, and strawed them in the way. [9] And they that went before, and they that followed, cried, saying, Hosanna; Blessed is he that cometh in the name of the Lord: [10] Blessed be the kingdom of our father David, that cometh in the name of the Lord: Hosanna in the highest.

Luke 19:29-38 "And it came to pass, when he was come nigh to Bethphage and Bethany, at the mount called the mount of Olives, he sent two of his disciples, [30] Saying, Go ye into the village over against you; in the which at your entering ye shall find a colt tied, whereon yet never man sat: loose him, and bring him hither.
[31] And if any man ask you, Why do ye loose him? thus shall ye say unto him, Because the Lord hath need of him. [32] And they that were sent went their way, and found even as he had said unto them. [33] And as they were loosing the colt, the owners thereof said unto them, Why loose ye the colt? [34] And they said, The Lord hath need of him. [35] And they brought him to Jesus: and they cast their garments upon the colt, and they set Jesus thereon. [36] And as he went, they spread their clothes in the way.
[37] And when he was come nigh, even now at the descent of the mount of Olives, the whole multitude of the disciples began to rejoice and praise God with a loud voice for all the mighty works that they had seen; [38] Saying, Blessed be the King that cometh in the name of the Lord: peace in heaven, and glory in the highest."

John 12:12-15 "On the next day much people that were come to the feast, when they heard that Jesus was coming to Jerusalem, [13] Took branches of palm trees, and went forth to meet him, and cried, Hosanna: Blessed is the King of Israel that cometh in the name of the Lord. [14] And Jesus, when he had found a young ass, sat thereon; as it is written, [15] Fear not, daughter of Sion: behold, thy King cometh, sitting on an ass's colt.

The significance of this entry into Jerusalem, by which Jesus Christ showed Himself publicly as the expected Messiah, is in the subsequent cleansing of the temple.

The Messiah Will Cleanse The Temple.

Malachi 3:1 Behold, I will send my messenger, and he shall prepare the way before me: and the Lord, whom ye seek, shall suddenly come to his temple, even the messenger of the covenant, whom ye delight in: behold, he shall come, saith the Lord of hosts.

This prophecy of Malachi talked about the special entry of the Messiah into the Temple with authority. Matthew, Mark and Luke recorded the fulfillment of the prophecy:

Matthew 21:12-15 "And Jesus went into the temple of God, and cast out all them that sold and bought in the temple, and overthrew the tables of the moneychangers, and the seats of them that sold doves, 13 And said unto them, It is written, My house shall be called the house of prayer; but ye have made it a den of thieves. 14 And the blind and the lame came to him in the temple; and he healed them. 15 And when the chief priests and scribes saw the wonderful things that he did, and the children crying in the temple, and saying, Hosanna to the son of David; they were sore displeased."

Mark 11:12–19 "And on the morrow, when they were come from Bethany, he was hungry: 13 And seeing a fig tree afar off having leaves, he came, if haply he might find any thing thereon: and when he came to it, he found nothing but leaves; for the time of figs was not yet. 14 And Jesus answered and said unto it, No man eat fruit of thee hereafter for ever. And his disciples heard it. 15 And they come to Jerusalem: and Jesus went into the temple, and began to cast out them that sold and bought in the temple, and overthrew the tables of the moneychangers, and the seats of them that sold doves; 16 And would not suffer that any man should carry any vessel through the temple. 17 And he taught, saying unto them, Is it not written, My house shall be called of all nations the house of prayer? but ye have made it a den of thieves.
18 And the scribes and chief priests heard it, and sought how they might destroy him: for they feared him, because all the people was astonished at his doctrine. 19 And when even was come, he went out of the city.

Luke 19:45-48 "And he went into the temple, and began to cast out them that sold therein, and them that bought; 46 Saying unto them, It is written, My house is the house of prayer: but ye have made it a den of thieves. 47 And he taught daily in the temple. But the chief priests and the scribes and the chief of the people sought to destroy him, 48 And could not find what they might do: for all the people were very attentive to hear him."

CHAPTER 4
THE MINISTRY OF THE EXPECTED MESSIAH

The Messiah that the Jews expected should be a great man of war, Saul-like[15] in appearance, with the function of delivering the Jews from their political oppressors (various nations and kingdoms which have kept Israel from living and thriving as a sovereign nation over the centuries). But the Messiah of God's model had an agenda different from the above role. He should play a role that is more spiritual than political as the prophet Isaiah foretold it:

<u>Messiah to Preach Good News and do Miracles.</u>

Isaiah 61:1-4 "The Spirit of the Lord God is upon me; because the Lord hath anointed me to preach good tidings unto the meek; he hath sent me to bind up the brokenhearted, to proclaim liberty to the captives, and the opening of the prison to them that are bound; 2 To proclaim the acceptable year of the Lord, and the day of vengeance of our God; to comfort all that mourn; 3 To appoint unto them that mourn in Zion, to give unto them beauty for ashes, the oil of joy for mourning, the garment of praise for the spirit of heaviness; that they might be called trees of righteousness, the planting of the Lord, that he might be glorified. 4 And they shall build the old wastes, they shall raise up the former desolations, and they shall repair the waste cities, the desolations of many generations."

As mentioned in chapter 3 above, it was expected that the Messiah would do miraculous signs, and preach the good news as foretold by Prophet Isaiah (quoted

---

[15] Saul was the first king of Israel after God had ruled Israel through judges before Israel demanded a king in order to be like other nations (ruled by human kings). Saul is described in the Bible as follows:

1 Samuel 9:1-2 "Now there was a man of Benjamin, whose name was Kish, the son of Abiel, the son of Zeror, the son of Bechorath, the son of Aphiah, a Benjamite, a mighty man of power. 2 And he had a son, whose name was Saul, a choice young man, and a goodly: and there was not among the children of Israel a goodlier person than he: from his shoulders and upward he was higher than any of the people.

1 Samuel 10:23-24 "And they ran and fetched him thence: and when he stood among the people, he was higher than any of the people from his shoulders and upward. 24 And Samuel said to all the people, See ye him whom the Lord hath chosen, that there is none like him among all the people? And all the people shouted, and said, God save the king.

above). This chapter, therefore, is meant to submit that Jesus Christ performed, and met, all the expectations of the "expected Messiah" as far as His ministry was concerned during the nearly three-and-a-half years of His earthly ministry.

In consonance with the prophecy of Isaiah stated above, according to the Gospel by Matthew, Jesus Christ went about preaching the good news about the kingdom of God, teaching and doing miracles thereby fulfilling His ministry before He was "cut off" (using the words of Prophet Daniel 9:26).

Matthew 4:23-24 says, "And Jesus went about all Galilee, teaching in their synagogues, and preaching the gospel of the kingdom, and healing all manner of sickness and all manner of disease among the people. 24 And his fame went throughout all Syria: and they brought unto him all sick people that were taken with divers diseases and torments, and those which were possessed with devils, and those which were lunatick, and those that had the palsy; and he healed them."

Some of the teachings and miracles are stated or described below.

Jesus Christ Did Miracles That Supported His Ministry.

I. He performed miracles that showed that Jesus Christ had power over sicknesses, diseases and evil spirit, by healing the following: -

(1) A leper

Matthew 8:1-4 "When he was come down from the mountain, great multitudes followed him. 2 And, behold, there came a leper and worshipped him, saying, Lord, if thou wilt, thou canst make me clean.
3 And Jesus put forth his hand, and touched him, saying, I will; be thou clean. And immediately his leprosy was cleansed. 4 And Jesus saith unto him, See thou tell no man; but go thy way, shew thyself to the priest, and offer the gift that Moses commanded, for a testimony unto them.

Mark 1:40-44 "And there came a leper to him, beseeching him, and kneeling down to him, and saying unto him, If thou wilt, thou canst make me clean. 41 And Jesus, moved with compassion, put forth his hand, and touched him, and saith unto him, I will; be thou clean. 42 And as soon as he had spoken, immediately the leprosy departed from him, and he was cleansed. 43 And he straitly charged him, and forthwith sent him away; 44 And saith unto him, See thou say nothing to any man: but go thy way, shew thyself to the priest, and offer for thy cleansing those things which Moses commanded, for a testimony unto them.

Luke 5:12-14 "And it came to pass, when he was in a certain city, behold a man full of leprosy: who seeing Jesus fell on his face, and besought him, saying, Lord, if thou wilt, thou canst make me clean. 13 And he put forth his hand, and touched him, saying, I will: be thou clean. And immediately the leprosy departed from him. 14 And he charged him to tell no man: but go, and shew thyself to the priest, and offer for thy cleansing, according as Moses commanded, for a testimony unto them.

(2) A Centurion's Servant from a distance and without contact or meeting the servant.

Matthew 8:5-10 "And when Jesus was entered into Capernaum, there came unto him a centurion, beseeching him, 6 And saying, Lord, my servant lieth at home sick of the palsy, grievously tormented. 7 And Jesus saith unto him, I will come and heal him. 8 The centurion answered and said, Lord, I am not worthy that thou shouldest come under my roof: but speak the word only, and my servant shall be healed. 9 For I am a man under authority, having soldiers under me: and I say to this man, Go, and he goeth; and to another, Come, and he cometh; and to my servant, Do this, and he doeth it. 10 When Jesus heard it, he marvelled, and said to them that followed, Verily I say unto you, I have not found so great faith, no, not in Israel.

Luke 7:1-10 "Now when he had ended all his sayings in the audience of the people, he entered into Capernaum. 2 And a certain centurion's servant, who was dear unto him, was sick, and ready to die. 3 And when he heard of Jesus, he sent unto him the elders of the Jews, beseeching him that he would come and heal his servant. 4 And when they came to Jesus, they besought him instantly, saying, That he was worthy for whom he should do this: 5 For he loveth our nation, and he hath built us a synagogue. 6 Then Jesus went with them. And when he was now not far from the house, the centurion sent friends to him, saying unto him, Lord, trouble not thyself: for I am not worthy that thou shouldest enter under my roof: 7 Wherefore neither thought I myself worthy to come unto thee: but say in a word, and my servant shall be healed. 8 For I also am a man set under authority, having under me soldiers, and I say unto one, Go, and he goeth; and to another, Come, and he cometh; and to my servant, Do this, and he doeth it. 9 When Jesus heard these things, he marvelled at him, and turned him about, and said unto the people that followed him, I say unto you, I have not found so great faith, no, not in Israel. 10 And they that were sent, returning to the house, found the servant whole that had been sick.

(3) The Mother-In-Law of Peter

Matthew 8:14-15 "And when Jesus was come into Peter's house, he saw his wife's mother laid, and sick of a fever. 15 And he touched her hand, and the fever left her: and she arose, and ministered unto them."

Mark 1:29-31 "And forthwith, when they were come out of the synagogue, they entered into the house of Simon and Andrew, with James and John. 30 But Simon's wife's mother lay sick of a fever, and anon they tell him of her. 31 And he came and took her by the hand, and lifted her up; and immediately the fever left her, and she ministered unto them."

Luke 4:38-39 "And he arose out of the synagogue, and entered into Simon's house. And Simon's wife's mother was taken with a great fever; and they besought him for her. 39 And he stood over her, and rebuked the fever; and it left her: and immediately she arose and ministered unto them."

(4) The Man Sick of Palsy
Matthew 9:1-8 "And he entered into a ship, and passed over, and came into his own city. 2 And, behold, they brought to him a man sick of the palsy, lying on a bed: and Jesus seeing their faith said unto the sick of the palsy; Son, be of good cheer; thy sins be forgiven thee. 3 And, behold, certain of the scribes said within themselves, This man blasphemeth.
4 And Jesus knowing their thoughts said, Wherefore think ye evil in your hearts? 5 For whether is easier, to say, Thy sins be forgiven thee; or to say, Arise, and walk?
6 But that ye may know that the Son of man hath power on earth to forgive sins, (then saith he to the sick of the palsy,) Arise, take up thy bed, and go unto thine house. 7 And he arose, and departed to his house. 8 But when the multitudes saw it, they marvelled, and glorified God, which had given such power unto men."

Mark 2:1-12 "And again he entered into Capernaum after some days; and it was noised that he was in the house. 2 And straightway many were gathered together, insomuch that there was no room to receive them, no, not so much as about the door: and he preached the word unto them. 3 And they come unto him, bringing one sick of the palsy, which was borne of four. 4 And when they could not come nigh unto him for the press, they uncovered the roof where he was: and when they had broken it up, they let down the bed wherein the sick of the palsy lay.
5 When Jesus saw their faith, he said unto the sick of the palsy, Son, thy sins be forgiven thee. 6 But there was certain of the scribes sitting there, and reasoning in their hearts, 7 Why doth this man thus speak blasphemies? who can forgive sins but God only? 8 And immediately when Jesus perceived in his spirit that they so reasoned within themselves, he said unto them, Why reason ye these things in your hearts? 9 Whether is it easier to say to the sick of the palsy, Thy sins be forgiven thee; or to say, Arise, and take up thy bed, and walk? 10 But that ye may know that the Son of man hath power on earth to forgive sins, (he saith to the sick of the palsy,)
11 I say unto thee, Arise, and take up thy bed, and go thy way into thine house. 12 And immediately he arose, took up the bed, and went forth before them all; insomuch that they were all amazed, and glorified God, saying, We never saw it on this fashion."

Luke 5:17-26 "And it came to pass on a certain day, as he was teaching, that there were Pharisees and doctors of the law sitting by, which were come out of every town of Galilee, and Judaea, and Jerusalem: and the power of the Lord was present to heal them. 18 And, behold, men brought in a bed a man which was taken with a palsy: and they sought means to bring him in, and to lay him before him. 19 And when they could not find by what way they might bring him in because of the multitude, they went upon the housetop, and let him down through the tiling with his couch into the midst before Jesus.

20 And when he saw their faith, he said unto him, Man, thy sins are forgiven thee. 21 And the scribes and the Pharisees began to reason, saying, Who is this which speaketh blasphemies? Who can forgive sins, but God alone? 22 But when Jesus perceived their thoughts, he answering said unto them, What reason ye in your hearts? 23 Whether is easier, to say, Thy sins be forgiven thee; or to say, Rise up and walk? 4 But that ye may know that the Son of man hath power upon earth to forgive sins, (he said unto the sick of the palsy,) I say unto thee, Arise, and take up thy couch, and go into thine house.
25 And immediately he rose up before them, and took up that whereon he lay, and departed to his own house, glorifying God. 26 And they were all amazed, and they glorified God, and were filled with fear, saying, We have seen strange things to day."

(5) The Gadarene Demoniac.

Matthew 8:28-34 "And when he was come to the other side into the country of the Gergesenes, there met him two possessed with devils, coming out of the tombs, exceeding fierce, so that no man might pass by that way. 29 And, behold, they cried out, saying, What have we to do with thee, Jesus, thou Son of God? art thou come hither to torment us before the time? 30 And there was a good way off from them an herd of many swine feeding. 31 So the devils besought him, saying, If thou cast us out, suffer us to go away into the herd of swine.
32 And he said unto them, Go. And when they were come out, they went into the herd of swine: and, behold, the whole herd of swine ran violently down a steep place into the sea, and perished in the waters. 33 And they that kept them fled, and went their ways into the city, and told every thing, and what was befallen to the possessed of the devils. 34 And, behold, the whole city came out to meet Jesus: and when they saw him, they besought him that he would depart out of their coasts."

Mark 5:1-20 "And they came over unto the other side of the sea, into the country of the Gadarenes. 2 And when he was come out of the ship, immediately there met him out of the tombs a man with an unclean spirit, 3 Who had his dwelling among the tombs; and no man could bind him, no, not with chains: 4 Because that he had been often bound with fetters and chains, and the chains had been plucked asunder by him, and the fetters broken in pieces: neither could any man tame him. 5 And always, night and day, he was in the mountains, and in the tombs, crying, and cutting himself with stones. 6 But when he saw Jesus afar off, he ran and worshipped him, 7 And cried with a loud voice, and said, What have I to do with thee, Jesus, thou Son of the most high God? I adjure thee by God, that thou torment me not. 8 For he said unto him, Come out of the man, thou unclean spirit. 9 And he asked him, What is thy name? And he answered, saying, My name is Legion: for we are many. 10 And he besought him much that he would not send them away out of the country.
11 Now there was there nigh unto the mountains a great herd of swine feeding. 12 And all the devils besought him, saying, Send us into the swine, that we may enter into them. 13 And forthwith Jesus gave them leave. And the unclean spirits went out, and entered into the swine: and the herd ran violently down a steep place into the sea, (they were about two thousand;) and were choked in the sea. 14 And they that fed the swine fled, and told it in the city, and in the country. And they went out to see what it

was that was done. 15 And they come to Jesus, and see him that was possessed with the devil, and had the legion, sitting, and clothed, and in his right mind: and they were afraid. 16 And they that saw it told them how it befell to him that was possessed with the devil, and also concerning the swine. 17 And they began to pray him to depart out of their coasts.

18 And when he was come into the ship, he that had been possessed with the devil prayed him that he might be with him. 19 Howbeit Jesus suffered him not, but saith unto him, Go home to thy friends, and tell them how great things the Lord hath done for thee, and hath had compassion on thee. 20 And he departed, and began to publish in Decapolis how great things Jesus had done for him: and all men did marvel."

Luke 8:26-39 "And they arrived at the country of the Gadarenes, which is over against Galilee. 27 And when he went forth to land, there met him out of the city a certain man, which had devils long time, and ware no clothes, neither abode in any house, but in the tombs.

28 When he saw Jesus, he cried out, and fell down before him, and with a loud voice said, What have I to do with thee, Jesus, thou Son of God most high? I beseech thee, torment me not. 29 (For he had commanded the unclean spirit to come out of the man. For oftentimes it had caught him: and he was kept bound with chains and in fetters; and he brake the bands, and was driven of the devil into the wilderness.)

30 And Jesus asked him, saying, What is thy name? And he said, Legion: because many devils were entered into him. 31 And they besought him that he would not command them to go out into the deep.

32 And there was there an herd of many swine feeding on the mountain: and they besought him that he would suffer them to enter into them. And he suffered them.

33 Then went the devils out of the man, and entered into the swine: and the herd ran violently down a steep place into the lake, and were choked. 34 When they that fed them saw what was done, they fled, and went and told it in the city and in the country. 35 Then they went out to see what was done; and came to Jesus, and found the man, out of whom the devils were departed, sitting at the feet of Jesus, clothed, and in his right mind: and they were afraid. 36 They also which saw it told them by what means he that was possessed of the devils was healed.

37 Then the whole multitude of the country of the Gadarenes round about besought him to depart from them; for they were taken with great fear: and he went up into the ship, and returned back again. 38 Now the man out of whom the devils were departed besought him that he might be with him: but Jesus sent him away, saying,

39 Return to thine own house, and shew how great things God hath done unto thee. And he went his way, and published throughout the whole city how great things Jesus had done unto him."

(6) A Woman Having Chronic Hemorrhage.
Matthew 9:20-22 "And, behold, a woman, which was diseased with an issue of blood twelve years, came behind him, and touched the hem of his garment: 21 For she said within herself, If I may but touch his garment, I shall be whole. 22 But Jesus turned him

about, and when he saw her, he said, Daughter, be of good comfort; thy faith hath made thee whole. And the woman was made whole from that hour."

Mark 5:25-34 "And a certain woman, which had an issue of blood twelve years, 26 And had suffered many things of many physicians, and had spent all that she had, and was nothing bettered, but rather grew worse, 27 When she had heard of Jesus, came in the press behind, and touched his garment. 28 For she said, If I may touch but his clothes, I shall be whole. 29 And straightway the fountain of her blood was dried up; and she felt in her body that she was healed of that plague.
30 And Jesus, immediately knowing in himself that virtue had gone out of him, turned him about in the press, and said, Who touched my clothes? 31 And his disciples said unto him, Thou seest the multitude thronging thee, and sayest thou, Who touched me? 32 And he looked round about to see her that had done this thing.
33 But the woman fearing and trembling, knowing what was done in her, came and fell down before him, and told him all the truth. 34 And he said unto her, Daughter, thy faith hath made thee whole; go in peace, and be whole of thy plague."

Luke 8:43-48 "And a woman having an issue of blood twelve years, which had spent all her living upon physicians, neither could be healed of any, 44 Came behind him, and touched the border of his garment: and immediately her issue of blood stanched. 45 And Jesus said, Who touched me? When all denied, Peter and they that were with him said, Master, the multitude throng thee and press thee, and sayest thou, Who touched me? 46 And Jesus said, Somebody hath touched me: for I perceive that virtue is gone out of me.
47 And when the woman saw that she was not hid, she came trembling, and falling down before him, she declared unto him before all the people for what cause she had touched him, and how she was healed immediately. 48 And he said unto her, Daughter, be of good comfort: thy faith hath made thee whole; go in peace.

(7) Two Blind Men.
Matthew 9:27-31 "And when Jesus departed thence, two blind men followed him, crying, and saying, Thou son of David, have mercy on us. 28 And when he was come into the house, the blind men came to him: and Jesus saith unto them, Believe ye that I am able to do this? They said unto him, Yea, Lord. 29 Then touched he their eyes, saying, According to your faith be it unto you. 30 And their eyes were opened; and Jesus straitly charged them, saying, See that no man know it. 31 But they, when they were departed, spread abroad his fame in all that country.

(8) The Demon-Possessed Man.
Matthew 9:32-33 "As they went out, behold, they brought to him a dumb man possessed with a devil. 33 And when the devil was cast out, the dumb spake: and the multitudes marvelled, saying, It was never so seen in Israel.

(9) The Man With Withered Hand.
Matthew 12:9-13 "And when he was departed thence, he went into their synagogue: 10 And, behold, there was a man which had his hand withered. And they asked him,

saying, Is it lawful to heal on the sabbath days? that they might accuse him. 11 And he said unto them, What man shall there be among you, that shall have one sheep, and if it fall into a pit on the sabbath day, will he not lay hold on it, and lift it out? 12 How much then is a man better than a sheep? Wherefore it is lawful to do well on the sabbath days. 13 Then saith he to the man, Stretch forth thine hand. And he stretched it forth; and it was restored whole, like as the other.

Mark 3:1-5 "And he entered again into the synagogue; and there was a man there which had a withered hand. 2 And they watched him, whether he would heal him on the sabbath day; that they might accuse him. 3 And he saith unto the man which had the withered hand, Stand forth. 4 And he saith unto them, Is it lawful to do good on the sabbath days, or to do evil? to save life, or to kill? But they held their peace. 5 And when he had looked round about on them with anger, being grieved for the hardness of their hearts, he saith unto the man, Stretch forth thine hand. And he stretched it out: and his hand was restored whole as the other.

Luke 6:6-11 "And it came to pass also on another sabbath, that he entered into the synagogue and taught: and there was a man whose right hand was withered. 7 And the scribes and Pharisees watched him, whether he would heal on the sabbath day; that they might find an accusation against him. 8 But he knew their thoughts, and said to the man which had the withered hand, Rise up, and stand forth in the midst. And he arose and stood forth.
9 Then said Jesus unto them, I will ask you one thing; Is it lawful on the sabbath days to do good, or to do evil? to save life, or to destroy it? 10 And looking round about upon them all, he said unto the man, Stretch forth thy hand. And he did so: and his hand was restored whole as the other. 11 And they were filled with madness; and communed one with another what they might do to Jesus."

Mark 9:14-29 "And when he came to his disciples, he saw a great multitude about them, and the scribes questioning with them. 15 And straightway all the people, when they beheld him, were greatly amazed, and running to him saluted him. 16 And he asked the scribes, What question ye with them? 17 And one of the multitude answered and said, Master, I have brought unto thee my son, which hath a dumb spirit; 18 And wheresoever he taketh him, he teareth him: and he foameth, and gnasheth with his teeth, and pineth away: and I spake to thy disciples that they should cast him out; and they could not.
19 He answereth him, and saith, O faithless generation, how long shall I be with you? how long shall I suffer you? bring him unto me. 20 And they brought him unto him: and when he saw him, straightway the spirit tare him; and he fell on the ground, and wallowed foaming. 21 And he asked his father, How long is it ago since this came unto him? And he said, Of a child. 22 And ofttimes it hath cast him into the fire, and into the waters, to destroy him: but if thou canst do any thing, have compassion on us, and help us.
23 Jesus said unto him, If thou canst believe, all things are possible to him that believeth. 24 And straightway the father of the child cried out, and said with tears, Lord, I believe; help thou mine unbelief. 25 When Jesus saw that the people came

running together, he rebuked the foul spirit, saying unto him, Thou dumb and deaf spirit, I charge thee, come out of him, and enter no more into him. 26 And the spirit cried, and rent him sore, and came out of him: and he was as one dead; insomuch that many said, He is dead.

27 But Jesus took him by the hand, and lifted him up; and he arose. 28 And when he was come into the house, his disciples asked him privately, Why could not we cast him out? 29 And he said unto them, This kind can come forth by nothing, but by prayer and fasting."

(10) An Epileptic.

Matthew 17:14-21 "And when they were come to the multitude, there came to him a certain man, kneeling down to him, and saying, 5 Lord, have mercy on my son: for he is lunatick, and sore vexed: for ofttimes he falleth into the fire, and oft into the water. 16 And I brought him to thy disciples, and they could not cure him.

17 Then Jesus answered and said, O faithless and perverse generation, how long shall I be with you? how long shall I suffer you? bring him hither to me. 18 And Jesus rebuked the devil; and he departed out of him: and the child was cured from that very hour. 19 Then came the disciples to Jesus apart, and said, Why could not we cast him out? 20 And Jesus said unto them, Because of your unbelief: for verily I say unto you, If ye have faith as a grain of mustard seed, ye shall say unto this mountain, Remove hence to yonder place; and it shall remove; and nothing shall be impossible unto you. 21 Howbeit this kind goeth not out but by prayer and fasting."

Mark 9:14-29 "And when he came to his disciples, he saw a great multitude about them, and the scribes questioning with them. 15 And straightway all the people, when they beheld him, were greatly amazed, and running to him saluted him.

16 And he asked the scribes, What question ye with them? 17 And one of the multitude answered and said, Master, I have brought unto thee my son, which hath a dumb spirit; 18 And wheresoever he taketh him, he teareth him: and he foameth, and gnasheth with his teeth, and pineth away: and I spake to thy disciples that they should cast him out; and they could not.

19 He answereth him, and saith, O faithless generation, how long shall I be with you? how long shall I suffer you? bring him unto me. 20 And they brought him unto him: and when he saw him, straightway the spirit tare him; and he fell on the ground, and wallowed foaming. 21 And he asked his father, How long is it ago since this came unto him? And he said, Of a child. 22 And ofttimes it hath cast him into the fire, and into the waters, to destroy him: but if thou canst do any thing, have compassion on us, and help us.

23 Jesus said unto him, If thou canst believe, all things are possible to him that believeth. 24 And straightway the father of the child cried out, and said with tears, Lord, I believe; help thou mine unbelief. 25 When Jesus saw that the people came running together, he rebuked the foul spirit, saying unto him, Thou dumb and deaf spirit, I charge thee, come out of him, and enter no more into him. 26 And the spirit cried, and rent him sore, and came out of him: and he was as one dead; insomuch that many said, He is dead. 27 But Jesus took him by the hand, and lifted him up; and he arose. 28 And when he was come into the house, his disciples asked him privately, Why

could not we cast him out? 29 And he said unto them, This kind can come forth by nothing, but by prayer and fasting."

Luke 9:37-42 "And it came to pass, that on the next day, when they were come down from the hill, much people met him. 38 And, behold, a man of the company cried out, saying, Master, I beseech thee, look upon my son: for he is mine only child.
39 And, lo, a spirit taketh him, and he suddenly crieth out; and it teareth him that he foameth again, and bruising him hardly departeth from him. 40 And I besought thy disciples to cast him out; and they could not.
41 And Jesus answering said, O faithless and perverse generation, how long shall I be with you, and suffer you? Bring thy son hither. 42 And as he was yet a coming, the devil threw him down, and tare him. And Jesus rebuked the unclean spirit, and healed the child, and delivered him again to his father."

(11) Two Blind Men Outside Jericho.
Matthew 20:29-34 "And as they departed from Jericho, a great multitude followed him. 30 And, behold, two blind men sitting by the way side, when they heard that Jesus passed by, cried out, saying, Have mercy on us, O Lord, thou son of David. 31 And the multitude rebuked them, because they should hold their peace: but they cried the more, saying, Have mercy on us, O Lord, thou son of David. 32 And Jesus stood still, and called them, and said, What will ye that I shall do unto you? 33 They say unto him, Lord, that our eyes may be opened. 34 So Jesus had compassion on them, and touched their eyes: and immediately their eyes received sight, and they followed him."

(12) A Man With Unclean Spirit.
Mark 1:23-27 "And there was in their synagogue a man with an unclean spirit; and he cried out, 24 Saying, Let us alone; what have we to do with thee, thou Jesus of Nazareth? art thou come to destroy us? I know thee who thou art, the Holy One of God.
25 And Jesus rebuked him, saying, Hold thy peace, and come out of him. 26 And when the unclean spirit had torn him, and cried with a loud voice, he came out of him. 27 And they were all amazed, insomuch that they questioned among themselves, saying, What thing is this? what new doctrine is this? for with authority commandeth he even the unclean spirits, and they do obey him."

Luke 4:33-36 "And in the synagogue there was a man, which had a spirit of an unclean devil, and cried out with a loud voice, 34 Saying, Let us alone; what have we to do with thee, thou Jesus of Nazareth? art thou come to destroy us? I know thee who thou art; the Holy One of God. 35 And Jesus rebuked him, saying, Hold thy peace, and come out of him. And when the devil had thrown him in the midst, he came out of him, and hurt him not.
36 And they were all amazed, and spake among themselves, saying, What a word is this! for with authority and power he commandeth the unclean spirits, and they come out."

(13) A Deaf And Dumb Man.

Mark 7:31-37 "And again, departing from the coasts of Tyre and Sidon, he came unto the sea of Galilee, through the midst of the coasts of Decapolis. 32 And they bring unto him one that was deaf, and had an impediment in his speech; and they beseech him to put his hand upon him.

33 And he took him aside from the multitude, and put his fingers into his ears, and he spit, and touched his tongue; 34 And looking up to heaven, he sighed, and saith unto him, Ephphatha, that is, Be opened. 35 And straightway his ears were opened, and the string of his tongue was loosed, and he spake plain.

36 And he charged them that they should tell no man: but the more he charged them, so much the more a great deal they published it; 37 And were beyond measure astonished, saying, He hath done all things well: he maketh both the deaf to hear, and the dumb to speak."

(14) A Blind Man At Bethesda.

Mark 8:22-26 "And he cometh to Bethsaida; and they bring a blind man unto him, and besought him to touch him. 23 And he took the blind man by the hand, and led him out of the town; and when he had spit on his eyes, and put his hands upon him, he asked him if he saw ought. 24 And he looked up, and said, I see men as trees, walking. 25 After that he put his hands again upon his eyes, and made him look up: and he was restored, and saw every man clearly. 26 And he sent him away to his house, saying, Neither go into the town, nor tell it to any in the town."

(15) Blind Bartimaeus.

Mark 10:46-52 "And they came to Jericho: and as he went out of Jericho with his disciples and a great number of people, blind Bartimaeus, the son of Timaeus, sat by the highway side begging. 47 And when he heard that it was Jesus of Nazareth, he began to cry out, and say, Jesus, thou son of David, have mercy on me. 48 And many charged him that he should hold his peace: but he cried the more a great deal, Thou son of David, have mercy on me.

49 And Jesus stood still, and commanded him to be called. And they call the blind man, saying unto him, Be of good comfort, rise; he calleth thee. 50 And he, casting away his garment, rose, and came to Jesus. 51 And Jesus answered and said unto him, What wilt thou that I should do unto thee? The blind man said unto him, Lord, that I might receive my sight. 52 And Jesus said unto him, Go thy way; thy faith hath made thee whole. And immediately he received his sight, and followed Jesus in the way."

Luke 18:35-43 "And it came to pass, that as he was come nigh unto Jericho, a certain blind man sat by the way side begging: 36 And hearing the multitude pass by, he asked what it meant. 37 And they told him, that Jesus of Nazareth passeth by. 38 And he cried, saying, Jesus, thou son of David, have mercy on me. 39 And they which went before rebuked him, that he should hold his peace: but he cried so much the more, Thou son of David, have mercy on me.

40 And Jesus stood, and commanded him to be brought unto him: and when he was come near, he asked him, 41 Saying, What wilt thou that I shall do unto thee? And he said, Lord, that I may receive my sight. 42 And Jesus said unto him, Receive thy sight:

thy faith hath saved thee. [43] And immediately he received his sight, and followed him, glorifying God: and all the people, when they saw it, gave praise unto God."

(16) A Stooped (Crippled) Woman
Luke 13:10-17 "And he was teaching in one of the synagogues on the sabbath. [11] And, behold, there was a woman which had a spirit of infirmity eighteen years, and was bowed together, and could in no wise lift up herself. [12] And when Jesus saw her, he called her to him, and said unto her, Woman, thou art loosed from thine infirmity. [13] And he laid his hands on her: and immediately she was made straight, and glorified God. [14] And the ruler of the synagogue answered with indignation, because that Jesus had healed on the sabbath day, and said unto the people, There are six days in which men ought to work: in them therefore come and be healed, and not on the sabbath day.

[15] The Lord then answered him, and said, Thou hypocrite, doth not each one of you on the sabbath loose his ox or his ass from the stall, and lead him away to watering?

[16] And ought not this woman, being a daughter of Abraham, whom Satan hath bound, lo, these eighteen years, be loosed from this bond on the sabbath day? [17] And when he had said these things, all his adversaries were ashamed: and all the people rejoiced for all the glorious things that were done by him."

(17) A Man With Dropsy
Luke 14:1-6 " And it came to pass, as he went into the house of one of the chief Pharisees to eat bread on the sabbath day, that they watched him. [2] And, behold, there was a certain man before him which had the dropsy.

[3] And Jesus answering spake unto the lawyers and Pharisees, saying, Is it lawful to heal on the sabbath day? [4] And they held their peace. And he took him, and healed him, and let him go; [5] And answered them, saying, Which of you shall have an ass or an ox fallen into a pit, and will not straightway pull him out on the sabbath day? [6] And they could not answer him again to these things."

(18) Ten Lepers.
Luke 17:11-19 "And it came to pass, as he went to Jerusalem, that he passed through the midst of Samaria and Galilee. [12] And as he entered into a certain village, there met him ten men that were lepers, which stood afar off: [13] And they lifted up their voices, and said, Jesus, Master, have mercy on us. [14] And when he saw them, he said unto them, Go shew yourselves unto the priests. And it came to pass, that, as they went, they were cleansed. [15] And one of them, when he saw that he was healed, turned back, and with a loud voice glorified God, [16] And fell down on his face at his feet, giving him thanks: and he was a Samaritan.

[17] And Jesus answering said, Were there not ten cleansed? but where are the nine?

[18] There are not found that returned to give glory to God, save this stranger. [19] And he said unto him, Arise, go thy way: thy faith hath made thee whole."

(19) The Ear of Malchus.
Luke 22:49-51 "When they which were about him saw what would follow, they said unto him, Lord, shall we smite with the sword? [50] And one of them smote the servant

of the high priest, and cut off his right ear. ⁵¹ And Jesus answered and said, Suffer ye thus far. And he touched his ear, and healed him."

(20) The Son of a Royal Officer.

John 4:46-54 "So Jesus came again into Cana of Galilee, where he made the water wine. And there was a certain nobleman, whose son was sick at Capernaum. ⁴⁷ When he heard that Jesus was come out of Judaea into Galilee, he went unto him, and besought him that he would come down, and heal his son: for he was at the point of death.
⁴⁸ Then said Jesus unto him, Except ye see signs and wonders, ye will not believe. ⁴⁹ The nobleman saith unto him, Sir, come down ere my child die. ⁰ Jesus saith unto him, Go thy way; thy son liveth. And the man believed the word that Jesus had spoken unto him, and he went his way. ⁵¹ And as he was now going down, his servants met him, and told him, saying, Thy son liveth. ⁵² Then enquired he of them the hour when he began to amend. And they said unto him, Yesterday at the seventh hour the fever left him. ⁵³ So the father knew that it was at the same hour, in the which Jesus said unto him, Thy son liveth: and himself believed, and his whole house. ⁵⁴ This is again the second miracle that Jesus did, when he was come out of Judaea into Galilee."

(21) A Lame Man At Bethesda.

John 5:1-16 "After this there was a feast of the Jews; and Jesus went up to Jerusalem. ² Now there is at Jerusalem by the sheep market a pool, which is called in the Hebrew tongue Bethesda, having five porches. ³ In these lay a great multitude of impotent folk, of blind, halt, withered, waiting for the moving of the water. ⁴ For an angel went down at a certain season into the pool, and troubled the water: whosoever then first after the troubling of the water stepped in was made whole of whatsoever disease he had. ⁵ And a certain man was there, which had an infirmity thirty and eight years. ⁶ When Jesus saw him lie, and knew that he had been now a long time in that case, he saith unto him, Wilt thou be made whole? ⁷ The impotent man answered him, Sir, I have no man, when the water is troubled, to put me into the pool: but while I am coming, another steppeth down before me. ⁸ Jesus saith unto him, Rise, take up thy bed, and walk. ⁹ And immediately the man was made whole, and took up his bed, and walked: and on the same day was the sabbath.
¹⁰ The Jews therefore said unto him that was cured, It is the sabbath day: it is not lawful for thee to carry thy bed. ¹¹ He answered them, He that made me whole, the same said unto me, Take up thy bed, and walk. ¹² Then asked they him, What man is that which said unto thee, Take up thy bed, and walk? ¹³ And he that was healed wist not who it was: for Jesus had conveyed himself away, a multitude being in that place. ¹⁴ Afterward Jesus findeth him in the temple, and said unto him, Behold, thou art made whole: sin no more, lest a worse thing come unto thee. ¹⁵ The man departed, and told the Jews that it was Jesus, which had made him whole. ¹⁶ And therefore did the Jews persecute Jesus, and sought to slay him, because he had done these things on the sabbath day."

(22) A Man Born Blind.

John 9:1-7 "And as Jesus passed by, he saw a man which was blind from his birth.

2 And his disciples asked him, saying, Master, who did sin, this man, or his parents, that he was born blind? 3 Jesus answered, Neither hath this man sinned, nor his parents: but that the works of God should be made manifest in him. 4 I must work the works of him that sent me, while it is day: the night cometh, when no man can work. 5 As long as I am in the world, I am the light of the world. 6 When he had thus spoken, he spat on the ground, and made clay of the spittle, and he anointed the eyes of the blind man with the clay, 7 And said unto him, Go, wash in the pool of Siloam, (which is by interpretation, Sent.) He went his way therefore, and washed, and came seeing."

II. Miracles That Showed That Jesus Christ Had Power Over Death.

(a) He Raised The Only Son of a Woman.
Luke 7:11-16 "And it came to pass the day after, that he went into a city called Nain; and many of his disciples went with him, and much people. 12 Now when he came nigh to the gate of the city, behold, there was a dead man carried out, the only son of his mother, and she was a widow: and much people of the city was with her. 13 And when the Lord saw her, he had compassion on her, and said unto her, Weep not. 14 And he came and touched the bier: and they that bare him stood still. And he said, Young man, I say unto thee, Arise. 15 And he that was dead sat up, and began to speak. And he delivered him to his mother. 16 And there came a fear on all: and they glorified God, saying, That a great prophet is risen up among us; and, That God hath visited his people.

(b) He Raised The Daughter Of Jairus.
Matthew 9:23-26 "And when Jesus came into the ruler's house, and saw the minstrels and the people making a noise, 24 He said unto them, Give place: for the maid is not dead, but sleepeth. And they laughed him to scorn. 25 But when the people were put forth, he went in, and took her by the hand, and the maid arose.
26 And the fame hereof went abroad into all that land.

Mark 5:22-24 "And, behold, there cometh one of the rulers of the synagogue, Jairus by name; and when he saw him, he fell at his feet, 23 And besought him greatly, saying, My little daughter lieth at the point of death: I pray thee, come and lay thy hands on her, that she may be healed; and she shall live. 24 And Jesus went with him; and much people followed him, and thronged him.

Luke 8:41-42 "And, behold, there came a man named Jairus, and he was a ruler of the synagogue: and he fell down at Jesus' feet, and besought him that he would come into his house: 42 For he had one only daughter, about twelve years of age, and she lay a dying. But as he went the people thronged him.

Luke 8:49-56 "While he yet spake, there cometh one from the ruler of the synagogue's house, saying to him, Thy daughter is dead; trouble not the Master.
50 But when Jesus heard it, he answered him, saying, Fear not: believe only, and she shall be made whole. 51 And when he came into the house, he suffered no man to go in, save Peter, and James, and John, and the father and the mother of the maiden.

52 And all wept, and bewailed her: but he said, Weep not; she is not dead, but sleepeth. 53 And they laughed him to scorn, knowing that she was dead. 54 And he put them all out, and took her by the hand, and called, saying, Maid, arise. 55 And her spirit came again, and she arose straightway: and he commanded to give her meat. 56 And her parents were astonished: but he charged them that they should tell no man what was done.

(c) He Raised Lazarus.

John 11:38-45 "Jesus therefore again groaning in himself cometh to the grave. It was a cave, and a stone lay upon it. 39 Jesus said, Take ye away the stone. Martha, the sister of him that was dead, saith unto him, Lord, by this time he stinketh: for he hath been dead four days.

40 Jesus saith unto her, Said I not unto thee, that, if thou wouldest believe, thou shouldest see the glory of God? 41 Then they took away the stone from the place where the dead was laid. And Jesus lifted up his eyes, and said, Father, I thank thee that thou hast heard me. 42 And I knew that thou hearest me always: but because of the people which stand by I said it, that they may believe that thou hast sent me. 43 And when he thus had spoken, he cried with a loud voice, Lazarus, come forth. 44 And he that was dead came forth, bound hand and foot with graveclothes: and his face was bound about with a napkin. Jesus saith unto them, Loose him, and let him go. 45 Then many of the Jews which came to Mary, and had seen the things which Jesus did, believed on him.

(d) He Arose From The Dead After Three Days And Nights.

Matthew 28:1-7 "In the end of the sabbath, as it began to dawn toward the first day of the week, came Mary Magdalene and the other Mary to see the sepulchre. 2 And, behold, there was a great earthquake: for the angel of the Lord descended from heaven, and came and rolled back the stone from the door, and sat upon it. 3 His countenance was like lightning, and his raiment white as snow: 4 And for fear of him the keepers did shake, and became as dead men. 5 And the angel answered and said unto the women, Fear not ye: for I know that ye seek Jesus, which was crucified. 6 He is not here: for he is risen, as he said. Come, see the place where the Lord lay. 7 And go quickly, and tell his disciples that he is risen from the dead; and, behold, he goeth before you into Galilee; there shall ye see him: lo, I have told you.

Mark 16:1-8 "And when the sabbath was past, Mary Magdalene, and Mary the mother of James, and Salome, had bought sweet spices, that they might come and anoint him. 2 And very early in the morning the first day of the week, they came unto the sepulchre at the rising of the sun. 3 And they said among themselves, Who shall roll us away the stone from the door of the sepulchre? 4 And when they looked, they saw that the stone was rolled away: for it was very great. 5 And entering into the sepulchre, they saw a young man sitting on the right side, clothed in a long white garment; and they were affrighted.

6 And he saith unto them, Be not affrighted: Ye seek Jesus of Nazareth, which was crucified: he is risen; he is not here: behold the place where they laid him. 7 But go your way, tell his disciples and Peter that he goeth before you into Galilee: there shall

ye see him, as he said unto you. [8] And they went out quickly, and fled from the sepulchre; for they trembled and were amazed: neither said they any thing to any man; for they were afraid.

Luke 24:1-12 "Now upon the first day of the week, very early in the morning, they came unto the sepulchre, bringing the spices which they had prepared, and certain others with them. [2] And they found the stone rolled away from the sepulchre. [3] And they entered in, and found not the body of the Lord Jesus. [4] And it came to pass, as they were much perplexed thereabout, behold, two men stood by them in shining garments: [5] And as they were afraid, and bowed down their faces to the earth, they said unto them, Why seek ye the living among the dead? [6] He is not here, but is risen: remember how he spake unto you when he was yet in Galilee, [7] Saying, The Son of man must be delivered into the hands of sinful men, and be crucified, and the third day rise again. [8] And they remembered his words,
[9] And returned from the sepulchre, and told all these things unto the eleven, and to all the rest. [10] It was Mary Magdalene and Joanna, and Mary the mother of James, and other women that were with them, which told these things unto the apostles. [11] And their words seemed to them as idle tales, and they believed them not. [12] Then arose Peter, and ran unto the sepulchre; and stooping down, he beheld the linen clothes laid by themselves, and departed, wondering in himself at that which was come to pass.

John 20:1-9 "The first day of the week cometh Mary Magdalene early, when it was yet dark, unto the sepulchre, and seeth the stone taken away from the sepulchre. [2] Then she runneth, and cometh to Simon Peter, and to the other disciple, whom Jesus loved, and saith unto them, They have taken away the Lord out of the sepulchre, and we know not where they have laid him.
[3] Peter therefore went forth, and that other disciple, and came to the sepulchre. [4] So they ran both together: and the other disciple did outrun Peter, and came first to the sepulchre. [5] And he stooping down, and looking in, saw the linen clothes lying; yet went he not in. [6] Then cometh Simon Peter following him, and went into the sepulchre, and seeth the linen clothes lie, [7] And the napkin, that was about his head, not lying with the linen clothes, but wrapped together in a place by itself. [8] Then went in also that other disciple, which came first to the sepulchre, and he saw, and believed. [9] For as yet they knew not the scripture, that he must rise again from the dead.

III. Miracles That Showed That Jesus Christ Had Power Over Elements of Nature.

(i) Jesus Turned Water Into Wine.
John 2:1-11 "And the third day there was a marriage in Cana of Galilee; and the mother of Jesus was there: [2] And both Jesus was called, and his disciples, to the marriage. [3] And when they wanted wine, the mother of Jesus saith unto him, They have no wine. [4] Jesus saith unto her, Woman, what have I to do with thee? mine hour is not yet come. [5] His mother saith unto the servants, Whatsoever he saith unto you, do it.
[6] And there were set there six waterpots of stone, after the manner of the purifying of the Jews, containing two or three firkins apiece. [7] Jesus saith unto them, Fill the

waterpots with water. And they filled them up to the brim. [8] And he saith unto them, Draw out now, and bear unto the governor of the feast. And they bare it.

[9] When the ruler of the feast had tasted the water that was made wine, and knew not whence it was: (but the servants which drew the water knew;) the governor of the feast called the bridegroom, [10] And saith unto him, Every man at the beginning doth set forth good wine; and when men have well drunk, then that which is worse: but thou hast kept the good wine until now. [11] This beginning of miracles did Jesus in Cana of Galilee, and manifested forth his glory; and his disciples believed on him.

(ii) He Calmed The Sea Storm.

Matthew 8:23-27 "And when he was entered into a ship, his disciples followed him. [24] And, behold, there arose a great tempest in the sea, insomuch that the ship was covered with the waves: but he was asleep. [25] And his disciples came to him, and awoke him, saying, Lord, save us: we perish. [26] And he saith unto them, Why are ye fearful, O ye of little faith? Then he arose, and rebuked the winds and the sea; and there was a great calm. [27] But the men marvelled, saying, What manner of man is this, that even the winds and the sea obey him!

Mark 4:35-41 "And the same day, when the even was come, he saith unto them, Let us pass over unto the other side. [36] And when they had sent away the multitude, they took him even as he was in the ship. And there were also with him other little ships. [37] And there arose a great storm of wind, and the waves beat into the ship, so that it was now full. [38] And he was in the hinder part of the ship, asleep on a pillow: and they awake him, and say unto him, Master, carest thou not that we perish?

[39] And he arose, and rebuked the wind, and said unto the sea, Peace, be still. And the wind ceased, and there was a great calm. [40] And he said unto them, Why are ye so fearful? how is it that ye have no faith? [41] And they feared exceedingly, and said one to another, What manner of man is this, that even the wind and the sea obey him?

Luke 8:22-25 "Now it came to pass on a certain day, that he went into a ship with his disciples: and he said unto them, Let us go over unto the other side of the lake. And they launched forth. [23] But as they sailed he fell asleep: and there came down a storm of wind on the lake; and they were filled with water, and were in jeopardy. [24] And they came to him, and awoke him, saying, Master, master, we perish. Then he arose, and rebuked the wind and the raging of the water: and they ceased, and there was a calm. [25] And he said unto them, Where is your faith? And they being afraid wondered, saying one to another, What manner of man is this! for he commandeth even the winds and water, and they obey him.

(iii) He Fed Five Thousand Men With Five Barley Loaves And Two Fishes.

Matthew 14:15-21 "And when it was evening, his disciples came to him, saying, This is a desert place, and the time is now past; send the multitude away, that they may go into the villages, and buy themselves victuals. [16] But Jesus said unto them, They need not depart; give ye them to eat. [17] And they say unto him, We have here but five loaves, and two fishes.

[18] He said, Bring them hither to me. [19] And he commanded the multitude to sit down on the grass, and took the five loaves, and the two fishes, and looking up to heaven, he blessed, and brake, and gave the loaves to his disciples, and the disciples to the multitude. [20] And they did all eat, and were filled: and they took up of the fragments that remained twelve baskets full. [21] And they that had eaten were about five thousand men, beside women and children.

Mark 6:35-44 "And when the day was now far spent, his disciples came unto him, and said, This is a desert place, and now the time is far passed: [36] Send them away, that they may go into the country round about, and into the villages, and buy themselves bread: for they have nothing to eat.
[37] He answered and said unto them, Give ye them to eat. And they say unto him, Shall we go and buy two hundred pennyworth of bread, and give them to eat? [38] He saith unto them, How many loaves have ye? go and see. And when they knew, they say, Five, and two fishes. [39] And he commanded them to make all sit down by companies upon the green grass. [40] And they sat down in ranks, by hundreds, and by fifties.
[41] And when he had taken the five loaves and the two fishes, he looked up to heaven, and blessed, and brake the loaves, and gave them to his disciples to set before them; and the two fishes divided he among them all. [42] And they did all eat, and were filled. [43] And they took up twelve baskets full of the fragments, and of the fishes. [44] And they that did eat of the loaves were about five thousand men.

Luke 9:12-17 "And when the day began to wear away, then came the twelve, and said unto him, Send the multitude away, that they may go into the towns and country round about, and lodge, and get victuals: for we are here in a desert place.
[13] But he said unto them, Give ye them to eat. And they said, We have no more but five loaves and two fishes; except we should go and buy meat for all this people. [14] For they were about five thousand men. And he said to his disciples, Make them sit down by fifties in a company. [15] And they did so, and made them all sit down. [16] Then he took the five loaves and the two fishes, and looking up to heaven, he blessed them, and brake, and gave to the disciples to set before the multitude. [17] And they did eat, and were all filled: and there was taken up of fragments that remained to them twelve baskets.

John 6:5-14 "When Jesus then lifted up his eyes, and saw a great company come unto him, he saith unto Philip, Whence shall we buy bread, that these may eat?
[6] And this he said to prove him: for he himself knew what he would do. [7] Philip answered him, Two hundred pennyworth of bread is not sufficient for them, that every one of them may take a little. [8] One of his disciples, Andrew, Simon Peter's brother, saith unto him, [9] There is a lad here, which hath five barley loaves, and two small fishes: but what are they among so many?
[10] And Jesus said, Make the men sit down. Now there was much grass in the place. So the men sat down, in number about five thousand. [11] And Jesus took the loaves; and when he had given thanks, he distributed to the disciples, and the disciples to them that were set down; and likewise of the fishes as much as they would.

12 When they were filled, he said unto his disciples, Gather up the fragments that remain, that nothing be lost. 13 Therefore they gathered them together, and filled twelve baskets with the fragments of the five barley loaves, which remained over and above unto them that had eaten. 14 Then those men, when they had seen the miracle that Jesus did, said, This is of a truth that prophet that should come into the world.

(iv) Jesus Walked On The Sea – on Water.
Matthew 14:22-33 "And straightway Jesus constrained his disciples to get into a ship, and to go before him unto the other side, while he sent the multitudes away.
23 And when he had sent the multitudes away, he went up into a mountain apart to pray: and when the evening was come, he was there alone. 24 But the ship was now in the midst of the sea, tossed with waves: for the wind was contrary. 25 And in the fourth watch of the night Jesus went unto them, walking on the sea. 26 And when the disciples saw him walking on the sea, they were troubled, saying, It is a spirit; and they cried out for fear. 27 But straightway Jesus spake unto them, saying, Be of good cheer; it is I; be not afraid.
28 And Peter answered him and said, Lord, if it be thou, bid me come unto thee on the water. 29 And he said, Come. And when Peter was come down out of the ship, he walked on the water, to go to Jesus. 30 But when he saw the wind boisterous, he was afraid; and beginning to sink, he cried, saying, Lord, save me. 31 And immediately Jesus stretched forth his hand, and caught him, and said unto him, O thou of little faith, wherefore didst thou doubt? 32 And when they were come into the ship, the wind ceased. 33 Then they that were in the ship came

Mark 6:45-52 "And straightway he constrained his disciples to get into the ship, and to go to the other side before unto Bethsaida, while he sent away the people. 46 And when he had sent them away, he departed into a mountain to pray. 47 And when even was come, the ship was in the midst of the sea, and he alone on the land.
48 And he saw them toiling in rowing; for the wind was contrary unto them: and about the fourth watch of the night he cometh unto them, walking upon the sea, and would have passed by them. 49 But when they saw him walking upon the sea, they supposed it had been a spirit, and cried out: 50 For they all saw him, and were troubled. And immediately he talked with them, and saith unto them, Be of good cheer: it is I; be not afraid. 51 And he went up unto them into the ship; and the wind ceased: and they were sore amazed in themselves beyond measure, and wondered. 52 For they considered not the miracle of the loaves: for their heart was hardened.

John 6:16-21 "And when even was now come, his disciples went down unto the sea, 17 And entered into a ship, and went over the sea toward Capernaum. And it was now dark, and Jesus was not come to them. 18 And the sea arose by reason of a great wind that blew. 19 So when they had rowed about five and twenty or thirty furlongs, they see Jesus walking on the sea, and drawing nigh unto the ship: and they were afraid. 20 But he saith unto them, It is I; be not afraid. 21 Then they willingly received him into the ship: and immediately the ship was at the land whither they went.

(v) <u>He Fed Four Thousand Men With Seven Loaves And A Few Fish.</u>

Matthew 15:32-38 "Then Jesus called his disciples unto him, and said, I have compassion on the multitude, because they continue with me now three days, and have nothing to eat: and I will not send them away fasting, lest they faint in the way. ³³ And his disciples say unto him, Whence should we have so much bread in the wilderness, as to fill so great a multitude? ³⁴ And Jesus saith unto them, How many loaves have ye? And they said, Seven, and a few little fishes. ³⁵ And he commanded the multitude to sit down on the ground.

³⁶ And he took the seven loaves and the fishes, and gave thanks, and brake them, and gave to his disciples, and the disciples to the multitude. ³⁷ And they did all eat, and were filled: and they took up of the broken meat that was left seven baskets full. ³⁸ And they that did eat were four thousand men, beside women and children.

Mark 8:1-9 "In those days the multitude being very great, and having nothing to eat, Jesus called his disciples unto him, and saith unto them, ² I have compassion on the multitude, because they have now been with me three days, and have nothing to eat: ³ And if I send them away fasting to their own houses, they will faint by the way: for divers of them came from far. ⁴ And his disciples answered him, From whence can a man satisfy these men with bread here in the wilderness? ⁵ And he asked them, How many loaves have ye? And they said, Seven.

⁶ And he commanded the people to sit down on the ground: and he took the seven loaves, and gave thanks, and brake, and gave to his disciples to set before them; and they did set them before the people. ⁷ And they had a few small fishes: and he blessed, and commanded to set them also before them. ⁸ So they did eat, and were filled: and they took up of the broken meat that was left seven baskets. ⁹ And they that had eaten were about four thousand: and he sent them away.

(vi) <u>He Cursed The Fig Tree And It Withered.</u>

Matthew 21:18-22 "Now in the morning as he returned into the city, he hungered. ¹⁹ And when he saw a fig tree in the way, he came to it, and found nothing thereon, but leaves only, and said unto it, Let no fruit grow on thee henceforward for ever. And presently the fig tree withered away. ²⁰ And when the disciples saw it, they marvelled, saying, How soon is the fig tree withered away!

²¹ Jesus answered and said unto them, Verily I say unto you, If ye have faith, and doubt not, ye shall not only do this which is done to the fig tree, but also if ye shall say unto this mountain, Be thou removed, and be thou cast into the sea; it shall be done. ²² And all things, whatsoever ye shall ask in prayer, believing, ye shall receive.

Mark 11:12-14, 20-24 "And on the morrow, when they were come from Bethany, he was hungry: ¹³ And seeing a fig tree afar off having leaves, he came, if haply he might find any thing thereon: and when he came to it, he found nothing but leaves; for the time of figs was not yet. ¹⁴ And Jesus answered and said unto it, No man eat fruit of thee hereafter for ever. And his disciples heard it.

²⁰ And in the morning, as they passed by, they saw the fig tree dried up from the roots. ²¹ And Peter calling to remembrance saith unto him, Master, behold, the fig tree which thou cursedst is withered away. ²² And Jesus answering saith unto them, Have faith in God. ²³ For verily I say unto you, That whosoever shall say unto this

mountain, Be thou removed, and be thou cast into the sea; and shall not doubt in his heart, but shall believe that those things which he saith shall come to pass; he shall have whatsoever he saith. 24 Therefore I say unto you, What things soever ye desire, when ye pray, believe that ye receive them, and ye shall have them.

Jesus Christ Preached The Good News And Taught Life-Changing Lessons.

As was expected of the expected Messiah, Jesus Christ went about, in addition to healing the sick and doing other miracles (shown above), preaching the good news of the kingdom of God and teaching His disciples and other people that cared important, life-changing lessons.

Matthew 4:17, 23
17 From that time Jesus began to preach, and to say, Repent: for the kingdom of heaven is at hand. 23 And Jesus went about all Galilee, teaching in their synagogues, and preaching the gospel of the kingdom, and healing all manner of sickness and all manner of disease among the people.

Matthew 9:35 "And Jesus went about all the cities and villages, teaching in their synagogues, and preaching the gospel of the kingdom, and healing every sickness and every disease among the people.

Luke 4:15 "And he taught in their synagogues, being glorified of all."
Jesus taught many lessons about the kingdom of God plainly and in parables; He taught about heaven and hell as well as the principles of the kingdom in His 'Sermon on the Mount' (Matt. 5, 6 and 7). Some of these lessons are also found in Luke 6.

Sermon On The Mount.

Matthew 5:1-48
The Beatitudes
And seeing the multitudes, he went up into a mountain: and when he was set, his disciples came unto him:
2 And he opened his mouth, and taught them, saying,
3 Blessed are the poor in spirit: for theirs is the kingdom of heaven.
4 Blessed are they that mourn: for they shall be comforted.
5 Blessed are the meek: for they shall inherit the earth.
6 Blessed are they which do hunger and thirst after righteousness: for they shall be filled.
7 Blessed are the merciful: for they shall obtain mercy.
8 Blessed are the pure in heart: for they shall see God.
9 Blessed are the peacemakers: for they shall be called the children of God.

83

¹⁰ Blessed are they which are persecuted for righteousness' sake: for theirs is the kingdom of heaven.

¹¹ Blessed are ye, when men shall revile you, and persecute you, and shall say all manner of evil against you falsely, for my sake.

¹² Rejoice, and be exceeding glad: for great is your reward in heaven: for so persecuted they the prophets which were before you.

Salt of the Earth and Light of the World

¹³ Ye are the salt of the earth: but if the salt have lost his savour, wherewith shall it be salted? it is thenceforth good for nothing, but to be cast out, and to be trodden under foot of men. ¹⁴ Ye are the light of the world. A city that is set on an hill cannot be hid. ¹⁵ Neither do men light a candle, and put it under a bushel, but on a candlestick; and it giveth light unto all that are in the house. ¹⁶ Let your light so shine before men, that they may see your good works, and glorify your Father which is in heaven.

Messiah Came to Fulfill the Law.

¹⁷ Think not that I am come to destroy the law, or the prophets: I am not come to destroy, but to fulfil. ¹⁸ For verily I say unto you, Till heaven and earth pass, one jot or one tittle shall in no wise pass from the law, till all be fulfilled. ¹⁹ Whosoever therefore shall break one of these least commandments, and shall teach men so, he shall be called the least in the kingdom of heaven: but whosoever shall do and teach them, the same shall be called great in the kingdom of heaven.

²⁰ For I say unto you, That except your righteousness shall exceed the righteousness of the scribes and Pharisees, ye shall in no case enter into the kingdom of heaven.

Anger and Lust

²¹ Ye have heard that it was said of them of old time, Thou shalt not kill; and whosoever shall kill shall be in danger of the judgment: ²² But I say unto you, That whosoever is angry with his brother without a cause shall be in danger of the judgment: and whosoever shall say to his brother, Raca, shall be in danger of the council: but whosoever shall say, Thou fool, shall be in danger of hell fire. ²³ Therefore if thou bring thy gift to the altar, and there rememberest that thy brother hath ought against thee; ²⁴ Leave there thy gift before the altar, and go thy way; first be reconciled to thy brother, and then come and offer thy gift. ²⁵ Agree with thine adversary quickly, whiles thou art in the way with him; lest at any time the adversary deliver thee to the judge, and the judge deliver thee to the officer, and thou be cast into prison. ²⁶ Verily I say unto thee, Thou shalt by no means come out thence, till thou hast paid the uttermost farthing.

²⁷ Ye have heard that it was said by them of old time, Thou shalt not commit adultery: ²⁸ But I say unto you, That whosoever looketh on a woman to lust after her hath committed adultery with her already in his heart. ²⁹ And if thy right eye offend thee, pluck it out, and cast it from thee: for it is profitable for thee that one of thy members should perish, and not that thy whole body should be cast into hell. ³⁰ And if thy right hand offend thee, cut it off, and cast it from thee: for it is profitable for thee that one of thy members should perish, and not that thy whole body should be cast into hell.

Divorce

31 It hath been said, Whosoever shall put away his wife, let him give her a writing of divorcement: 32 But I say unto you, That whosoever shall put away his wife, saving for the cause of fornication, causeth her to commit adultery: and whosoever shall marry her that is divorced committeth adultery.

Swearing

33 Again, ye have heard that it hath been said by them of old time, Thou shalt not forswear thyself, but shalt perform unto the Lord thine oaths: 34 But I say unto you, Swear not at all; neither by heaven; for it is God's throne: 35 Nor by the earth; for it is his footstool: neither by Jerusalem; for it is the city of the great King. 36 Neither shalt thou swear by thy head, because thou canst not make one hair white or black. 37 But let your communication be, Yea, yea; Nay, nay: for whatsoever is more than these cometh of evil.

Revenge

38 Ye have heard that it hath been said, An eye for an eye, and a tooth for a tooth: 39 But I say unto you, That ye resist not evil: but whosoever shall smite thee on thy right cheek, turn to him the other also. 40 And if any man will sue thee at the law, and take away thy coat, let him have thy cloak also. 41 And whosoever shall compel thee to go a mile, go with him twain 42 Give to him that asketh thee, and from him that would borrow of thee turn not thou away.

Loving Your Enemy

43 Ye have heard that it hath been said, Thou shalt love thy neighbour, and hate thine enemy. 44 But I say unto you, Love your enemies, bless them that curse you, do good to them that hate you, and pray for them which despitefully use you, and persecute you; 45 That ye may be the children of your Father which is in heaven: for he maketh his sun to rise on the evil and on the good, and sendeth rain on the just and on the unjust. 46 For if ye love them which love you, what reward have ye? do not even the publicans the same? 47 And if ye salute your brethren only, what do ye more than others? do not even the publicans so? 48 Be ye therefore perfect, even as your Father which is in heaven is perfect.

Matthew 6:1-34
Giving Alms and Praying Privately

Take heed that ye do not your alms before men, to be seen of them: otherwise ye have no reward of your Father which is in heaven. 2 Therefore when thou doest thine alms, do not sound a trumpet before thee, as the hypocrites do in the synagogues and in the streets, that they may have glory of men. Verily I say unto you, They have their reward. 3 But when thou doest alms, let not thy left hand know what thy right hand doeth: 4 That thine alms may be in secret: and thy Father which seeth in secret himself shall reward thee openly. 5 And when thou prayest, thou shalt not be as the hypocrites are: for they love to pray standing in the synagogues and in the corners of the streets, that they may be seen of men. Verily I say unto you, They have their reward.

Prayer Format

6 But thou, when thou prayest, enter into thy closet, and when thou hast shut thy door, pray to thy Father which is in secret; and thy Father which seeth in secret shall reward thee openly. 7 But when ye pray, use not vain repetitions, as the heathen do: for they think that they shall be heard for their much speaking. 8 Be not ye therefore like unto them: for your Father knoweth what things ye have need of, before ye ask him.

9 After this manner therefore pray ye: Our Father which art in heaven, Hallowed be thy name.

10 Thy kingdom come, Thy will be done in earth, as it is in heaven.

11 Give us this day our daily bread.

12 And forgive us our debts, as we forgive our debtors.

13 And lead us not into temptation, but deliver us from evil: For thine is the kingdom, and the power, and the glory, for ever. Amen.

14 For if ye forgive men their trespasses, your heavenly Father will also forgive you: 15 But if ye forgive not men their trespasses, neither will your Father forgive your trespasses.

Fasting

16 Moreover when ye fast, be not, as the hypocrites, of a sad countenance: for they disfigure their faces, that they may appear unto men to fast. Verily I say unto you, They have their reward. 17 But thou, when thou fastest, anoint thine head, and wash thy face; 18 That thou appear not unto men to fast, but unto thy Father which is in secret: and thy Father, which seeth in secret, shall reward thee openly.

Investing in Heaven

19 Lay not up for yourselves treasures upon earth, where moth and rust doth corrupt, and where thieves break through and steal: 20 But lay up for yourselves treasures in heaven, where neither moth nor rust doth corrupt, and where thieves do not break through nor steal: 21 For where your treasure is, there will your heart be also. 22 The light of the body is the eye: if therefore thine eye be single, thy whole body shall be full of light. 23 But if thine eye be evil, thy whole body shall be full of darkness. If therefore the light that is in thee be darkness, how great is that darkness! 24 No man can serve two masters: for either he will hate the one, and love the other; or else he will hold to the one, and despise the other. Ye cannot serve God and mammon.

Don't Be Anxious About the Future

25 Therefore I say unto you, Take no thought for your life, what ye shall eat, or what ye shall drink; nor yet for your body, what ye shall put on. Is not the life more than meat, and the body than raiment? 26 Behold the fowls of the air: for they sow not, neither do they reap, nor gather into barns; yet your heavenly Father feedeth them. Are ye not much better than they? 27 Which of you by taking thought can add one cubit unto his stature? 28 And why take ye thought for raiment? Consider the lilies of the field, how they grow; they toil not, neither do they spin: 29 And yet I say unto you, That even Solomon in all his glory was not arrayed like one of these. 30 Wherefore, if God so clothe the grass of the field, which to day is, and to morrow is cast into the oven, shall he not much more clothe you, O ye of little faith? 31 Therefore take no thought,

saying, What shall we eat? or, What shall we drink? or, Wherewithal shall we be clothed? [32] (For after all these things do the Gentiles seek:) for your heavenly Father knoweth that ye have need of all these things. [33] But seek ye first the kingdom of God, and his righteousness; and all these things shall be added unto you. [34] Take therefore no thought for the morrow: for the morrow shall take thought for the things of itself. Sufficient unto the day is the evil thereof.

Matthew 7: 1-29
Judging Others
Judge not, that ye be not judged. [2] For with what judgment ye judge, ye shall be judged: and with what measure ye mete, it shall be measured to you again. [3] And why beholdest thou the mote that is in thy brother's eye, but considerest not the beam that is in thine own eye? [4] Or how wilt thou say to thy brother, Let me pull out the mote out of thine eye; and, behold, a beam is in thine own eye? [5] Thou hypocrite, first cast out the beam out of thine own eye; and then shalt thou see clearly to cast out the mote out of thy brother's eye. [6] Give not that which is holy unto the dogs, neither cast ye your pearls before swine, lest they trample them under their feet, and turn again and rend you.

Asking and Receiving
[7] Ask, and it shall be given you; seek, and ye shall find; knock, and it shall be opened unto you: [8] For every one that asketh receiveth; and he that seeketh findeth; and to him that knocketh it shall be opened. [9] Or what man is there of you, whom if his son ask bread, will he give him a stone? [10] Or if he ask a fish, will he give him a serpent? [11] If ye then, being evil, know how to give good gifts unto your children, how much more shall your Father which is in heaven give good things to them that ask him?

The Golden Rule and The Narrow Gate
[12] Therefore all things whatsoever ye would that men should do to you, do ye even so to them: for this is the law and the prophets. [13] Enter ye in at the strait gate: for wide is the gate, and broad is the way, that leadeth to destruction, and many there be which go in thereat: [14] Because strait is the gate, and narrow is the way, which leadeth unto life, and few there be that find it.

Caution on False Prophets
[15] Beware of false prophets, which come to you in sheep's clothing, but inwardly they are ravening wolves. [16] Ye shall know them by their fruits. Do men gather grapes of thorns, or figs of thistles? [17] Even so every good tree bringeth forth good fruit; but a corrupt tree bringeth forth evil fruit. [18] A good tree cannot bring forth evil fruit, neither can a corrupt tree bring forth good fruit. [19] Every tree that bringeth not forth good fruit is hewn down, and cast into the fire. [20] Wherefore by their fruits ye shall know them.

Profession Without Faith
[21] Not every one that saith unto me, Lord, Lord, shall enter into the kingdom of heaven; but he that doeth the will of my Father which is in heaven. [22] Many will say to

me in that day, Lord, Lord, have we not prophesied in thy name? and in thy name have cast out 88s? and in thy name done many wonderful works? 23 And then will I profess unto them, I never knew you: depart from me, ye that work iniquity.

Building on the Sand or on the Rock
24 Therefore whosoever heareth these sayings of mine, and doeth them, I will liken him unto a wise man, which built his house upon a rock: 25 And the rain descended, and the floods came, and the winds blew, and beat upon that house; and it fell not: for it was founded upon a rock. 26 And every one that heareth these sayings of mine, and doeth them not, shall be likened unto a foolish man, which built his house upon the sand: 27 And the rain descended, and the floods came, and the winds blew, and beat upon that house; and it fell: and great was the fall of it. 28 And it came to pass, when Jesus had ended these sayings, the people were astonished at his doctrine: 29 For he taught them as one having authority, and not as the scribes.

The parables that Jesus Christ spoke are as follows: -

1. Building On The Solid Rock Or On Sand.
Matthew 7:24-27 "Therefore whosoever heareth these sayings of mine, and doeth them, I will liken him unto a wise man, which built his house upon a rock: 25 And the rain descended, and the floods came, and the winds blew, and beat upon that house; and it fell not: for it was founded upon a rock. 26 And every one that heareth these sayings of mine, and doeth them not, shall be likened unto a foolish man, which built his house upon the sand: 27 And the rain descended, and the floods came, and the winds blew, and beat upon that house; and it fell: and great was the fall of it"

Luke 6:47-49 "Whosoever cometh to me, and heareth my sayings, and doeth them, I will shew you to whom he is like: 48 He is like a man which built an house, and digged deep, and laid the foundation on a rock: and when the flood arose, the stream beat vehemently upon that house, and could not shake it: for it was founded upon a rock. 49 But he that heareth, and doeth not, is like a man that without a foundation built an house upon the earth; against which the stream did beat vehemently, and immediately it fell; and the ruin of that house was great.

2. The Sower And His Different Soils
Matthew 13:3-8 "And when much people were gathered together, and were come to him out of every city, he spake by a parable: 5 A sower went out to sow his seed: and as he sowed, some fell by the way side; and it was trodden down, and the fowls of the air devoured it. 6 And some fell upon a rock; and as soon as it was sprung up, it withered away, because it lacked moisture. 7 And some fell among thorns; and the thorns sprang up with it, and choked it. 8 And other fell on good ground, and sprang up, and bare fruit an hundredfold. And when he had said these things, he cried, He that hath ears to hear, let him hear.
11 Now the parable is this: The seed is the word of God. 12 Those by the way side are they that hear; then cometh the devil, and taketh away the word out of their hearts,

lest they should believe and be saved. [13] They on the rock are they, which, when they hear, receive the word with joy; and these have no root, which for a while believe, and in time of temptation fall away.

[14] And that which fell among thorns are they, which, when they have heard, go forth, and are choked with cares and riches and pleasures of this life, and bring no fruit to perfection. [15] But that on the good ground are they, which in an honest and good heart, having heard the word, keep it, and bring forth fruit with patience."

Mark 4:3-8 "Hearken; Behold, there went out a sower to sow: [4] And it came to pass, as he sowed, some fell by the way side, and the fowls of the air came and devoured it up. [5] And some fell on stony ground, where it had not much earth; and immediately it sprang up, because it had no depth of earth: [6] But when the sun was up, it was scorched; and because it had no root, it withered away. [7] And some fell among thorns, and the thorns grew up, and choked it, and it yielded no fruit. [8] And other fell on good ground, and did yield fruit that sprang up and increased; and brought forth, some thirty, and some sixty, and some an hundred.

Luke 8:4-8, 11-15 "And when much people were gathered together, and were come to him out of every city, he spake by a parable: [5] A sower went out to sow his seed: and as he sowed, some fell by the way side; and it was trodden down, and the fowls of the air devoured it. [6] And some fell upon a rock; and as soon as it was sprung up, it withered away, because it lacked moisture. [7] And some fell among thorns; and the thorns sprang up with it, and choked it. [8] And other fell on good ground, and sprang up, and bare fruit an hundredfold. And when he had said these things, he cried, He that hath ears to hear, let him hear.

[11] Now the parable is this: The seed is the word of God. [12] Those by the way side are they that hear; then cometh the devil, and taketh away the word out of their hearts, lest they should believe and be saved. [13] They on the rock are they, which, when they hear, receive the word with joy; and these have no root, which for a while believe, and in time of temptation fall away. [14] And that which fell among thorns are they, which, when they have heard, go forth, and are choked with cares and riches and pleasures of this life, and bring no fruit to perfection. [15] But that on the good ground are they, which in an honest and good heart, having heard the word, keep it, and bring forth fruit with patience

3 The Wheat And The Weeds
Matthew 13:24-30 "Another parable put he forth unto them, saying, The kingdom of heaven is likened unto a man which sowed good seed in his field: [25] But while men slept, his enemy came and sowed tares among the wheat, and went his way. [26] But when the blade was sprung up, and brought forth fruit, then appeared the tares also. [27] So the servants of the householder came and said unto him, Sir, didst not thou sow good seed in thy field? from whence then hath it tares?

[28] He said unto them, An enemy hath done this. The servants said unto him, Wilt thou then that we go and gather them up? [29] But he said, Nay; lest while ye gather up the tares, ye root up also the wheat with them. [30] Let both grow together until the harvest:

and in the time of harvest I will say to the reapers, Gather ye together first the tares, and bind them in bundles to burn them: but gather the wheat into my barn.

Mark 4:26-29 "And he said, So is the kingdom of God, as if a man should cast seed into the ground; 27 And should sleep, and rise night and day, and the seed should spring and grow up, he knoweth not how. 28 For the earth bringeth forth fruit of herself; first the blade, then the ear, after that the full corn in the ear. 29 But when the fruit is brought forth, immediately he putteth in the sickle, because the harvest is come.

4 The Mustard Seed.
Matthew 13:31-32 "Another parable put he forth unto them, saying, The kingdom of heaven is like to a grain of mustard seed, which a man took, and sowed in his field: 32 Which indeed is the least of all seeds: but when it is grown, it is the greatest among herbs, and becometh a tree, so that the birds of the air come and lodge in the branches thereof.

Mark 4:30-32 "And he said, Whereunto shall we liken the kingdom of God? or with what comparison shall we compare it? 31 It is like a grain of mustard seed, which, when it is sown in the earth, is less than all the seeds that be in the earth: 32 But when it is sown, it groweth up, and becometh greater than all herbs, and shooteth out great branches; so that the fowls of the air may lodge under the shadow of it.

Luke 13:18-19 "Then said he, Unto what is the kingdom of God like? and whereunto shall I resemble it? 19 It is like a grain of mustard seed, which a man took, and cast into his garden; and it grew, and waxed a great tree; and the fowls of the air lodged in the branches of it.

5 The Impact of the Leaven.
Matthew 13:33 "Another parable spake he unto them; The kingdom of heaven is like unto leaven, which a woman took, and hid in three measures of meal, till the whole was leavened.

Luke 13:20 "And again he said, Whereunto shall I liken the kingdom of God?"

6 The Hidden Treasure In A Field.
Matthew 13:44 "Again, the kingdom of heaven is like unto treasure hid in a field; the which when a man hath found, he hideth, and for joy thereof goeth and selleth all that he hath, and buyeth that field.

7 The Priceless Pearl.
Matthew 13:45-46 "Again, the kingdom of heaven is like unto a merchant man, seeking goodly pearls: 46 Who, when he had found one pearl of great price, went and sold all that he had, and bought it.

8 The Dragnet and the Separation of its Content.

Matthew 13:47-50 "Again, the kingdom of heaven is like unto a net, that was cast into the sea, and gathered of every kind: [48] Which, when it was full, they drew to shore, and sat down, and gathered the good into vessels, but cast the bad away. [49] So shall it be at the end of the world: the angels shall come forth, and sever the wicked from among the just, [50] And shall cast them into the furnace of fire: there shall be wailing and gnashing of teeth.

9 The Unmerciful Servant and His Unforgiveness.

Matthew 18:23-35 "Therefore is the kingdom of heaven likened unto a certain king, which would take account of his servants. [24] And when he had begun to reckon, one was brought unto him, which owed him ten thousand talents. [25] But forasmuch as he had not to pay, his lord commanded him to be sold, and his wife, and children, and all that he had, and payment to be made.
[26] The servant therefore fell down, and worshipped him, saying, Lord, have patience with me, and I will pay thee all. [27] Then the lord of that servant was moved with compassion, and loosed him, and forgave him the debt. [28] But the same servant went out, and found one of his fellowservants, which owed him an hundred pence: and he laid hands on him, and took him by the throat, saying, Pay me that thou owest. [29] And his fellowservant fell down at his feet, and besought him, saying, Have patience with me, and I will pay thee all. [30] And he would not: but went and cast him into prison, till he should pay the debt.
[31] So when his fellowservants saw what was done, they were very sorry, and came and told unto their lord all that was done. [32] Then his lord, after that he had called him, said unto him, O thou wicked servant, I forgave thee all that debt, because thou desiredst me: [33] Shouldest not thou also have had compassion on thy fellowservant, even as I had pity on thee? [34] And his lord was wroth, and delivered him to the tormentors, till he should pay all that was due unto him. [35] So likewise shall my heavenly Father do also unto you, if ye from your hearts forgive not every one his brother their trespasses.

10 Rewarding The Workers In The Vineyard.

Matthew 20:1-16 "For the kingdom of heaven is like unto a man that is an householder, which went out early in the morning to hire labourers into his vineyard. [2] And when he had agreed with the labourers for a penny a day, he sent them into his vineyard. [3] And he went out about the third hour, and saw others standing idle in the marketplace, [4] And said unto them; Go ye also into the vineyard, and whatsoever is right I will give you. And they went their way. [5] Again he went out about the sixth and ninth hour, and did likewise.
[6] And about the eleventh hour he went out, and found others standing idle, and saith unto them, Why stand ye here all the day idle? [7] They say unto him, Because no man hath hired us. He saith unto them, Go ye also into the vineyard; and whatsoever is right, that shall ye receive. [8] So when even was come, the lord of the vineyard saith unto his steward, Call the labourers, and give them their hire, beginning from the last unto the first. [9] And when they came that were hired about the eleventh hour, they received every man a penny.

¹⁰ But when the first came, they supposed that they should have received more; and they likewise received every man a penny. ¹¹ And when they had received it, they murmured against the goodman of the house, ¹² Saying, These last have wrought but one hour, and thou hast made them equal unto us, which have borne the burden and heat of the day. ¹³ But he answered one of them, and said, Friend, I do thee no wrong: didst not thou agree with me for a penny? ¹⁴ Take that thine is, and go thy way: I will give unto this last, even as unto thee. ¹⁵ Is it not lawful for me to do what I will with mine own? Is thine eye evil, because I am good? ¹⁶ So the last shall be first, and the first last: for many be called, but few chosen.

11 The Two Sons and Their Responses to Their Father's Bidding.

Matthew 21:28-32 "But what think ye? A certain man had two sons; and he came to the first, and said, Son, go work to day in my vineyard. ²⁹ He answered and said, I will not: but afterward he repented, and went. ³⁰ And he came to the second, and said likewise. And he answered and said, I go, sir: and went not. ³¹ Whether of them twain did the will of his father? They say unto him, The first. Jesus saith unto them, Verily I say unto you, That the publicans and the harlots go into the kingdom of God before you. ³² For John came unto you in the way of righteousness, and ye believed him not: but the publicans and the harlots believed him: and ye, when ye had seen it, repented not afterward, that ye might believe him.

12 The Wicked Vine Growers and Their End.

Matthew 21:33-40 "Hear another parable: There was a certain householder, which planted a vineyard, and hedged it round about, and digged a winepress in it, and built a tower, and let it out to husbandmen, and went into a far country:
³⁴ And when the time of the fruit drew near, he sent his servants to the husbandmen, that they might receive the fruits of it. ³⁵ And the husbandmen took his servants, and beat one, and killed another, and stoned another. ³⁶ Again, he sent other servants more than the first: and they did unto them likewise. ³⁷ But last of all he sent unto them his son, saying, They will reverence my son.
³⁸ But when the husbandmen saw the son, they said among themselves, This is the heir; come, let us kill him, and let us seize on his inheritance. ³⁹ And they caught him, and cast him out of the vineyard, and slew him. ⁴⁰ When the lord therefore of the vineyard cometh, what will he do unto those husbandmen?

Mark 12:1-9 "And he began to speak unto them by parables. A certain man planted a vineyard, and set an hedge about it, and digged a place for the winefat, and built a tower, and let it out to husbandmen, and went into a far country. ² And at the season he sent to the husbandmen a servant, that he might receive from the husbandmen of the fruit of the vineyard. ³ And they caught him, and beat him, and sent him away empty. ⁴ And again he sent unto them another servant; and at him they cast stones, and wounded him in the head, and sent him away shamefully handled. ⁵ And again he sent another; and him they killed, and many others; beating some, and killing some.
⁶ Having yet therefore one son, his wellbeloved, he sent him also last unto them, saying, They will reverence my son. ⁷ But those husbandmen said among themselves, This is the heir; come, let us kill him, and the inheritance shall be ours.' ⁸ And they

took him, and killed him, and cast him out of the vineyard. 9 What shall therefore the lord of the vineyard do? he will come and destroy the husbandmen, and will give the vineyard unto others.

Luke 20:9-16 "Then began he to speak to the people this parable; A certain man planted a vineyard, and let it forth to husbandmen, and went into a far country for a long time. 10 And at the season he sent a servant to the husbandmen, that they should give him of the fruit of the vineyard: but the husbandmen beat him, and sent him away empty. 11 And again he sent another servant: and they beat him also, and entreated him shamefully, and sent him away empty. 12 And again he sent a third: and they wounded him also, and cast him out.
13 Then said the lord of the vineyard, What shall I do? I will send my beloved son: it may be they will reverence him when they see him. 14 But when the husbandmen saw him, they reasoned among themselves, saying, This is the heir: come, let us kill him, that the inheritance may be ours. 15 So they cast him out of the vineyard, and killed him. What therefore shall the lord of the vineyard do unto them? 16 He shall come and destroy these husbandmen, and shall give the vineyard to others. And when they heard it, they said, God forbid.

13 The Guests to Wedding Feast.

Matthew 22:1-14 "And Jesus answered and spake unto them again by parables, and said, 2 The kingdom of heaven is like unto a certain king, which made a marriage for his son, 3 And sent forth his servants to call them that were bidden to the wedding: and they would not come.
4 Again, he sent forth other servants, saying, Tell them which are bidden, Behold, I have prepared my dinner: my oxen and my fatlings are killed, and all things are ready: come unto the marriage. 5 But they made light of it, and went their ways, one to his farm, another to his merchandise: 6 And the remnant took his servants, and entreated them spitefully, and slew them. 7 But when the king heard thereof, he was wroth: and he sent forth his armies, and destroyed those murderers, and burned up their city.
8 Then saith he to his servants, The wedding is ready, but they which were bidden were not worthy. 9 Go ye therefore into the highways, and as many as ye shall find, bid to the marriage. 10 So those servants went out into the highways, and gathered together all as many as they found, both bad and good: and the wedding was furnished with guests.
11 And when the king came in to see the guests, he saw there a man which had not on a wedding garment: 12 And he saith unto him, Friend, how camest thou in hither not having a wedding garment? And he was speechless. 13 Then said the king to the servants, Bind him hand and foot, and take him away, and cast him into outer darkness, there shall be weeping and gnashing of teeth. 14 For many are called, but few are chosen.

The Great Banquet.

Luke 14:16-24 "Then said he unto him, A certain man made a great supper, and bade many: 17 And sent his servant at supper time to say to them that were bidden, Come; for all things are now ready. 18 And they all with one consent began to make excuse.

The first said unto him, I have bought a piece of ground, and I must needs go and see it: I pray thee have me excused.

¹⁹ And another said, I have bought five yoke of oxen, and I go to prove them: I pray thee have me excused. ²⁰ And another said, I have married a wife, and therefore I cannot come. ²¹ So that servant came, and shewed his lord these things. Then the master of the house being angry said to his servant, Go out quickly into the streets and lanes of the city, and bring in hither the poor, and the maimed, and the halt, and the blind.

²² And the servant said, Lord, it is done as thou hast commanded, and yet there is room. ²³ And the lord said unto the servant, Go out into the highways and hedges, and compel them to come in, that my house may be filled. ²⁴ For I say unto you, That none of those men which were bidden shall taste of my supper."

14 The Budding Fig Tree.

Matthew 24:32-33 "Now learn a parable of the fig tree; When his branch is yet tender, and putteth forth leaves, ye know that summer is nigh: ³³ So likewise ye, when ye shall see all these things, know that it is near, even at the doors.

Luke 21:20-31 "And when ye shall see Jerusalem compassed with armies, then know that the desolation thereof is nigh. ²¹ Then let them which are in Judaea flee to the mountains; and let them which are in the midst of it depart out; and let not them that are in the countries enter thereinto. ²² For these be the days of vengeance, that all things which are written may be fulfilled. ²³ But woe unto them that are with child, and to them that give suck, in those days! for there shall be great distress in the land, and wrath upon this people.

²⁴ And they shall fall by the edge of the sword, and shall be led away captive into all nations: and Jerusalem shall be trodden down of the Gentiles, until the times of the Gentiles be fulfilled. ²⁵ And there shall be signs in the sun, and in the moon, and in the stars; and upon the earth distress of nations, with perplexity; the sea and the waves roaring; ²⁶ Men's hearts failing them for fear, and for looking after those things which are coming on the earth: for the powers of heaven shall be shaken. ²⁷ And then shall they see the Son of man coming in a cloud with power and great glory. ²⁸ And when these things begin to come to pass, then look up, and lift up your heads; for your redemption draweth nigh. ²⁹ And he spake to them a parable; Behold the fig tree, and all the trees; ³⁰ When they now shoot forth, ye see and know of your own selves that summer is now nigh at hand. ³¹ So likewise ye, when ye see these things come to pass, know ye that the kingdom of God is nigh at hand.

15 The Wise and Faithful Servant – Readiness For The Lord's Return

Matthew 24:45-51 "Who then is a faithful and wise servant, whom his lord hath made ruler over his household, to give them meat in due season? ⁴⁶ Blessed is that servant, whom his lord when he cometh shall find so doing. ⁴⁷ Verily I say unto you, That he shall make him ruler over all his goods. ⁴⁸ But and if that evil servant shall say in his heart, My lord delayeth his coming; ⁴⁹ And shall begin to smite his fellowservants, and to eat and drink with the drunken;

50 The lord of that servant shall come in a day when he looketh not for him, and in an hour that he is not aware of, 51 And shall cut him asunder, and appoint him his portion with the hypocrites: there shall be weeping and gnashing of teeth.

Luke 12:42-48 "And the Lord said, Who then is that faithful and wise steward, whom his lord shall make ruler over his household, to give them their portion of meat in due season? 43 Blessed is that servant, whom his lord when he cometh shall find so doing. 44 Of a truth I say unto you, that he will make him ruler over all that he hath. 45 But and if that servant say in his heart, My lord delayeth his coming; and shall begin to beat the menservants and maidens, and to eat and drink, and to be drunken;
46 The lord of that servant will come in a day when he looketh not for him, and at an hour when he is not aware, and will cut him in sunder, and will appoint him his portion with the unbelievers. 47 And that servant, which knew his lord's will, and prepared not himself, neither did according to his will, shall be beaten with many stripes.
48 But he that knew not, and did commit things worthy of stripes, shall be beaten with few stripes. For unto whomsoever much is given, of him shall be much required: and to whom men have committed much, of him they will ask the more.

16 <u>The Ten Virgins – Readiness For The Lord's Return</u>
Matthew 25:1-13 "Then shall the kingdom of heaven be likened unto ten virgins, which took their lamps, and went forth to meet the bridegroom. 2 And five of them were wise, and five were foolish. 3 They that were foolish took their lamps, and took no oil with them: 4 But the wise took oil in their vessels with their lamps. 5 While the bridegroom tarried, they all slumbered and slept. 6 And at midnight there was a cry made, Behold, the bridegroom cometh; go ye out to meet him. 7 Then all those virgins arose, and trimmed their lamps.
8 And the foolish said unto the wise, Give us of your oil; for our lamps are gone out.
9 But the wise answered, saying, Not so; lest there be not enough for us and you: but go ye rather to them that sell, and buy for yourselves. 10 And while they went to buy, the bridegroom came; and they that were ready went in with him to the marriage: and the door was shut. 11 Afterward came also the other virgins, saying, Lord, Lord, open to us. 12 But he answered and said, Verily I say unto you, I know you not. 13 Watch therefore, for ye know neither the day nor the hour wherein the Son of man cometh.

17 <u>The Talents</u> <u>Preparing For The Lord's Return</u>
Matthew 25:14-30 "For the kingdom of heaven is as a man travelling into a far country, who called his own servants, and delivered unto them his goods. 15 And unto one he gave five talents, to another two, and to another one; to every man according to his several ability; and straightway took his journey.
16 Then he that had received the five talents went and traded with the same, and made them other five talents. 17 And likewise he that had received two, he also gained other two. 18 But he that had received one went and digged in the earth, and hid his lord's money. 19 After a long time the lord of those servants cometh, and reckoneth with them.

20 And so he that had received five talents came and brought other five talents, saying, Lord, thou deliveredst unto me five talents: behold, I have gained beside them five talents more. 21 His lord said unto him, Well done, thou good and faithful servant: thou hast been faithful over a few things, I will make thee ruler over many things: enter thou into the joy of thy lord.

22 He also that had received two talents came and said, Lord, thou deliveredst unto me two talents: behold, I have gained two other talents beside them. 23 His lord said unto him, Well done, good and faithful servant; thou hast been faithful over a few things, I will make thee ruler over many things: enter thou into the joy of thy lord. 24 Then he which had received the one talent came and said, Lord, I knew thee that thou art an hard man, reaping where thou hast not sown, and gathering where thou hast not strawed: 25 And I was afraid, and went and hid thy talent in the earth: lo, there thou hast that is thine. 26 His lord answered and said unto him, Thou wicked and slothful servant, thou knewest that I reap where I sowed not, and gather where I have not strawed: 27 Thou oughtest therefore to have put my money to the exchangers, and then at my coming I should have received mine own with usury.

28 Take therefore the talent from him, and give it unto him which hath ten talents.

29 For unto every one that hath shall be given, and he shall have abundance: but from him that hath not shall be taken away even that which he hath. 30 And cast ye the unprofitable servant into outer darkness: there shall be weeping and gnashing of teeth."

Luke 19:11-27 "And as they heard these things, he added and spake a parable, because he was nigh to Jerusalem, and because they thought that the kingdom of God should immediately appear. 12 He said therefore, A certain nobleman went into a far country to receive for himself a kingdom, and to return. 13 And he called his ten servants, and delivered them ten pounds, and said unto them, Occupy till I come. 14 But his citizens hated him, and sent a message after him, saying, We will not have this man to reign over us. 15 And it came to pass, that when he was returned, having received the kingdom, then he commanded these servants to be called unto him, to whom he had given the money, that he might know how much every man had gained by trading.

16 Then came the first, saying, Lord, thy pound hath gained ten pounds.

17 And he said unto him, Well, thou good servant: because thou hast been faithful in a very little, have thou authority over ten cities. 18 And the second came, saying, Lord, thy pound hath gained five pounds. 19 And he said likewise to him, Be thou also over five cities. 20 And another came, saying, Lord, behold, here is thy pound, which I have kept laid up in a napkin: 21 For I feared thee, because thou art an austere man: thou takest up that thou layedst not down, and reapest that thou didst not sow. 22 And he saith unto him, Out of thine own mouth will I judge thee, thou wicked servant. Thou knewest that I was an austere man, taking up that I laid not down, and reaping that I did not sow: 23 Wherefore then gavest not thou my money into the bank, that at my coming I might have required mine own with usury? 24 And he said unto them that stood by, Take from him the pound, and give it to him that hath ten pounds. 25 (And they said unto him, Lord, he hath ten pounds.)

26 For I say unto you, That unto every one which hath shall be given; and from him that hath not, even that he hath shall be taken away from him. 27 But those mine enemies, which would not that I should reign over them, bring hither, and slay them before me.

18 The Travelling House Owner – Anticipating The Lord's Return

Mark 13:34-37 "For the Son of Man is as a man taking a far journey, who left his house, and gave authority to his servants, and to every man his work, and commanded the porter to watch. 35 Watch ye therefore: for ye know not when the master of the house cometh, at even, or at midnight, or at the cockcrowing, or in the morning: 36 Lest coming suddenly he find you sleeping. 37 And what I say unto you I say unto all, Watch."

19 The Good Samaritan – Love in Action

Luke 10:30-37 "And Jesus answering said, A certain man went down from Jerusalem to Jericho, and fell among thieves, which stripped him of his raiment, and wounded him, and departed, leaving him half dead. 31 And by chance there came down a certain priest that way: and when he saw him, he passed by on the other side. 32 And likewise a Levite, when he was at the place, came and looked on him, and passed by on the other side. 33 But a certain Samaritan, as he journeyed, came where he was: and when he saw him, he had compassion on him, 34 And went to him, and bound up his wounds, pouring in oil and wine, and set him on his own beast, and brought him to an inn, and took care of him.

35 And on the morrow when he departed, he took out two pence, and gave them to the host, and said unto him, Take care of him; and whatsoever thou spendest more, when I come again, I will repay thee. 36 Which now of these three, thinkest thou, was neighbour unto him that fell among the thieves? 37 And he said, He that shewed mercy on him. Then said Jesus unto him, Go, and do thou likewise."

20 The Rich Fool.

Luke 12:13-21 "And one of the company said unto him, Master, speak to my brother, that he divide the inheritance with me. 14 And he said unto him, Man, who made me a judge or a divider over you? 15 And he said unto them, Take heed, and beware of covetousness: for a man's life consisteth not in the abundance of the things which he possesseth.

16 And he spake a parable unto them, saying, The ground of a certain rich man brought forth plentifully: 17 And he thought within himself, saying, What shall I do, because I have no room where to bestow my fruits? 18 And he said, This will I do: I will pull down my barns, and build greater; and there will I bestow all my fruits and my goods. 19 And I will say to my soul, Soul, thou hast much goods laid up for many years; take thine ease, eat, drink, and be merry. 20 But God said unto him, Thou fool, this night thy soul shall be required of thee: then whose shall those things be, which thou hast provided? 21 So is he that layeth up treasure for himself, and is not rich toward God."

21 The Fruitless Fig Tree.

Luke 13:6-9 "He spake also this parable; A certain man had a fig tree planted in his vineyard; and he came and sought fruit thereon, and found none. 7 Then said he unto the dresser of his vineyard, Behold, these three years I come seeking fruit on this fig tree, and find none: cut it down; why cumbereth it the ground? 8 And he answering said unto him, Lord, let it alone this year also, till I shall dig about it, and dung it: 9 And if it bear fruit, well: and if not, then after that thou shalt cut it down.

22 Counting The Cost.

Luke 14:25-33 "And there went great multitudes with him: and he turned, and said unto them, 26 If any man come to me, and hate not his father, and mother, and wife, and children, and brethren, and sisters, yea, and his own life also, he cannot be my disciple. 27 And whosoever doth not bear his cross, and come after me, cannot be my disciple.

28 For which of you, intending to build a tower, sitteth not down first, and counteth the cost, whether he have sufficient to finish it? 29 Lest haply, after he hath laid the foundation, and is not able to finish it, all that behold it begin to mock him, 30 Saying, This man began to build, and was not able to finish.

31 Or what king, going to make war against another king, sitteth not down first, and consulteth whether he be able with ten thousand to meet him that cometh against him with twenty thousand? 32 Or else, while the other is yet a great way off, he sendeth an ambassage, and desireth conditions of peace. 33 So likewise, whosoever he be of you that forsaketh not all that he hath, he cannot be my disciple."

23 The Lost Sheep.

Matthew 18:12-14 "How think ye? if a man have an hundred sheep, and one of them be gone astray, doth he not leave the ninety and nine, and goeth into the mountains, and seeketh that which is gone astray? 13 And if so be that he find it, verily I say unto you, he rejoiceth more of that sheep, than of the ninety and nine which went not astray. 14 Even so it is not the will of your Father which is in heaven, that one of these little ones should perish."

Luke 15:3 "And he spake this parable unto them, saying,"

24 The Lost Coin.

Luke 15:8-10 "Either what woman having ten pieces of silver, if she lose one piece, doth not light a candle, and sweep the house, and seek diligently till she find it? 9 And when she hath found it, she calleth her friends and her neighbours together, saying, Rejoice with me; for I have found the piece which I had lost. 10 Likewise, I say unto you, there is joy in the presence of the angels of God over one sinner that repenteth."

[16] This parable has always been titled "The Prodigal Son." But a close study reveals that Jesus Christ's emphasis tilted more on the large-hearted father of the prodigal son, who was looking out to seeing the lost son return one day, and his readiness to receive the son back to himself. This typified

Luke 15:11-32 "And he said, A certain man had two sons: 12 And the younger of them said to his father, Father, give me the portion of goods that falleth to me. And he divided unto them his living. 13 And not many days after the younger son gathered all together, and took his journey into a far country, and there wasted his substance with riotous living. 14 And when he had spent all, there arose a mighty famine in that land; and he began to be in want. 15 And he went and joined himself to a citizen of that country; and he sent him into his fields to feed swine. 16 And he would fain have filled his belly with the husks that the swine did eat: and no man gave unto him.
17 And when he came to himself, he said, How many hired servants of my father's have bread enough and to spare, and I perish with hunger! 18 I will arise and go to my father, and will say unto him, Father, I have sinned against heaven, and before thee, 19 And am no more worthy to be called thy son: make me as one of thy hired servants. 20 And he arose, and came to his father. But when he was yet a great way off, his father saw him, and had compassion, and ran, and fell on his neck, and kissed him. 21 And the son said unto him, Father, I have sinned against heaven, and in thy sight, and am no more worthy to be called thy son. 22 But the father said to his servants, Bring forth the best robe, and put it on him; and put a ring on his hand, and shoes on his feet:
23 And bring hither the fatted calf, and kill it; and let us eat, and be merry: 24 For this my son was dead, and is alive again; he was lost, and is found. And they began to be merry. 25 Now his elder son was in the field: and as he came and drew nigh to the house, he heard musick and dancing. 26 And he called one of the servants, and asked what these things meant. 27 And he said unto him, Thy brother is come; and thy father hath killed the fatted calf, because he hath received him safe and sound.
28 And he was angry, and would not go in: therefore came his father out, and intreated him. 29 And he answering said to his father, Lo, these many years do I serve thee, neither transgressed I at any time thy commandment: and yet thou never gavest me a kid, that I might make merry with my friends: 30 But as soon as this thy son was come, which hath devoured thy living with harlots, thou hast killed for him the fatted calf. 31 And he said unto him, Son, thou art ever with me, and all that I have is thine. 32 It was meet that we should make merry, and be glad: for this thy brother was dead, and is alive again; and was lost, and is found."

26 The Shrewd Servant.
Luke 16:1-13 "And he said also unto his disciples, There was a certain rich man, which had a steward; and the same was accused unto him that he had wasted his goods. 2 And he called him, and said unto him, How is it that I hear this of thee? give an account of thy stewardship; for thou mayest be no longer steward.
3 Then the steward said within himself, What shall I do? for my lord taketh away from me the stewardship: I cannot dig; to beg I am ashamed. 4 I am resolved what to do, that, when I am put out of the stewardship, they may receive me into their houses.
5 So he called every one of his lord's debtors unto him, and said unto the first, How much owest thou unto my lord? 6 And he said, An hundred measures of oil. And he said unto him, Take thy bill, and sit down quickly, and write fifty. 7 Then said he to

our heavenly Father that is willing and ready to welcome any sinner that repents and returns to Him in Christ Jesus.

another, And how much owest thou? And he said, An hundred measures of wheat. And he said unto him, Take thy bill, and write fourscore.

8 And the lord commended the unjust steward, because he had done wisely: for the children of this world are in their generation wiser than the children of light. 9 And I say unto you, Make to yourselves friends of the mammon of unrighteousness; that, when ye fail, they may receive you into everlasting habitations. 10 He that is faithful in that which is least is faithful also in much: and he that is unjust in the least is unjust also in much.

11 If therefore ye have not been faithful in the unrighteous mammon, who will commit to your trust the true riches? 12 And if ye have not been faithful in that which is another man's, who shall give you that which is your own? 13 No servant can serve two masters: for either he will hate the one, and love the other; or else he will hold to the one, and despise the other. Ye cannot serve God and mammon.

27 The Rich Man And Lazarus.

Luke 16:19-31 "There was a certain rich man, which was clothed in purple and fine linen, and fared sumptuously every day: 20 And there was a certain beggar named Lazarus, which was laid at his gate, full of sores, 21 And desiring to be fed with the crumbs which fell from the rich man's table: moreover the dogs came and licked his sores.

22 And it came to pass, that the beggar died, and was carried by the angels into Abraham's bosom: the rich man also died, and was buried; 23 And in hell he lift up his eyes, being in torments, and seeth Abraham afar off, and Lazarus in his bosom.

24 And he cried and said, Father Abraham, have mercy on me, and send Lazarus, that he may dip the tip of his finger in water, and cool my tongue; for I am tormented in this flame.

25 But Abraham said, Son, remember that thou in thy lifetime receivedst thy good things, and likewise Lazarus evil things: but now he is comforted, and thou art tormented. 26 And beside all this, between us and you there is a great gulf fixed: so that they which would pass from hence to you cannot; neither can they pass to us, that would come from thence.

27 Then he said, I pray thee therefore, father, that thou wouldest send him to my father's house: 28 For I have five brethren; that he may testify unto them, lest they also come into this place of torment. 29 Abraham saith unto him, They have Moses and the prophets; let them hear them. 30 And he said, Nay, father Abraham: but if one went unto them from the dead, they will repent. 31 And he said unto him, If they hear not Moses and the prophets, neither will they be persuaded, though one rose from the dead.

28 The Persistent Widow And The Reluctant Judge.

Luke 18:1-8 " And he spake a parable unto them to this end, that men ought always to pray, and not to faint; 2 Saying, There was in a city a judge, which feared not God, neither regarded man: 3 And there was a widow in that city; and she came unto him, saying, Avenge me of mine adversary.

4 And he would not for a while: but afterward he said within himself, Though I fear not God, nor regard man;5 Yet because this widow troubleth me, I will avenge her, lest

by her continual coming she weary me.[6] And the Lord said, Hear what the unjust judge saith. [7] And shall not God avenge his own elect, which cry day and night unto him, though he bear long with them? [8] I tell you that he will avenge them speedily. Nevertheless when the Son of man cometh, shall he find faith on the earth?"

29 The Pharisee And The Tax Collector.
Luke 18:10-14 "Two men went up into the temple to pray; the one a Pharisee, and the other a publican. [11] The Pharisee stood and prayed thus with himself, God, I thank thee, that I am not as other men are, extortioners, unjust, adulterers, or even as this publican. [12] I fast twice in the week, I give tithes of all that I possess.
[13] And the publican, standing afar off, would not lift up so much as his eyes unto heaven, but smote upon his breast, saying, God be merciful to me a sinner. [14] I tell you, this man went down to his house justified rather than the other: for every one that exalteth himself shall be abased; and he that humbleth himself shall be exalted

30 The Servant's Role.
Luke 17:7-10 "But which of you, having a servant plowing or feeding cattle, will say unto him by and by, when he is come from the field, Go and sit down to meat?
[8] And will not rather say unto him, Make ready wherewith I may sup, and gird thyself, and serve me, till I have eaten and drunken; and afterward thou shalt eat and drink? [9] Doth he thank that servant because he did the things that were commanded him? I trow not. [10] So likewise ye, when ye shall have done all those things which are commanded you, say, We are unprofitable servants: we have done that which was our duty to do."

31 The Friend At Midnight.
Luke 11:5-13 "And he said unto them, Which of you shall have a friend, and shall go unto him at midnight, and say unto him, Friend, lend me three loaves; [6] For a friend of mine in his journey is come to me, and I have nothing to set before him? [7] And he from within shall answer and say, Trouble me not: the door is now shut, and my children are with me in bed; I cannot rise and give thee.
[8] I say unto you, Though he will not rise and give him, because he is his friend, yet because of his importunity he will rise and give him as many as he needeth. [9] And I say unto you, Ask, and it shall be given you; seek, and ye shall find; knock, and it shall be opened unto you. [10] For every one that asketh receiveth; and he that seeketh findeth; and to him that knocketh it shall be opened. [11] If a son shall ask bread of any of you that is a father, will he give him a stone? or if he ask a fish, will he for a fish give him a serpent? [12] Or if he shall ask an egg, will he offer him a scorpion? [13] If ye then, being evil, know how to give good gifts unto your children: how much more shall your heavenly Father give the Holy Spirit to them that ask him?"

32. The Forgiven Debts.
Luke 7:41-43 "There was a certain creditor which had two debtors: the one owed five hundred pence, and the other fifty. [42] And when they had nothing to pay, he frankly forgave them both. Tell me therefore, which of them will love him most?

[43] Simon answered and said, I suppose that he, to whom he forgave most. And he said unto him, Thou hast rightly judged."

The apostle John wanted the Bible student to know that Jesus Christ performed more miracles and spoke more parables than all that the evangelists recorded. So in closing his Gospel of Jesus he stated,

"And many other signs truly did Jesus in the presence of his disciples, which are not written in this book: [31] But these are written, that ye might believe that Jesus is the Christ, the Son of God; and that believing ye might have life through his name" (John 20:30-31).

CHAPTER 5
PROPHECIES OF THE MESSIAH'S REJECTION, SUFFERING, AND DEATH

There are prophecies in the Scriptures, which say that the people would reject the Messiah, He would suffer physical assault, mental agony, and ignominious death, and be resurrected. Some of the relevant Scriptures and passages pointing to their fulfillment are produced below: -

A. Hatred of Messiah Without Cause.
Psalm 35:19 "Let not them that are mine enemies wrongfully rejoice over me: *neither* let them wink with the eye that hate me without a cause."

Psalm 69:4 "They that hate me without a cause are more than the hairs of mine head: they that would destroy me, *being* mine enemies wrongfully, are mighty: then I restored *that* which I took not away."

The psalmist prophesied that the Messiah would be hated without cause. While Jesus was addressing His disciples, He reiterated the prophecies, which turned out as a fulfillment of the prophecy. The apostle John recorded it thus:

John 15:21-25 "But all these things will they do unto you for my name's sake, because they know not him that sent me. 22 If I had not come and spoken unto them, they had not had sin: but now they have no cloke for their sin. 23 He that hateth me hateth my Father also. 24 If I had not done among them the works which none other man did, they had not had sin: but now have they both seen and hated both me and my Father. 25 But *this cometh to pass*, that the word might be fulfilled that is written in their law, They hated me without a cause."

Other New Testament passages that confirm that the Messiah was rejected are as follows:

Matthew 13:53-58 "And it came to pass, that when Jesus had finished these parables, he departed thence. 54 And when he was come into his own country, he taught them in their synagogue, insomuch that they were astonished, and said, Whence hath this man this wisdom, and these mighty works? 55 Is not this the carpenter's son? is not his mother called Mary? and his brethren, James, and Joses, and Simon, and Judas? 56 And his sisters, are they not all with us? Whence then hath this man all these things? 57 And they were offended in him. But Jesus said unto them, A prophet is not without honour, save in his own country, and in his own house. 58 And he did not many mighty works there because of their unbelief."

Matthew 15:10-20 "And he called the multitude, and said unto them, Hear, and understand: [11] Not that which goeth into the mouth defileth a man; but that which cometh out of the mouth, this defileth a man. [12] Then came his disciples, and said unto him, Knowest thou that the Pharisees were offended, after they heard this saying?
[13] But he answered and said, Every plant, which my heavenly Father hath not planted, shall be rooted up. [14] Let them alone: they be blind leaders of the blind. And if the blind lead the blind, both shall fall into the ditch. [15] Then answered Peter and said unto him, Declare unto us this parable. [16] And Jesus said, Are ye also yet without understanding? [17] Do not ye yet understand, that whatsoever entereth in at the mouth goeth into the belly, and is cast out into the draught?
[18] But those things which proceed out of the mouth come forth from the heart; and they defile the man. [19] For out of the heart proceed evil thoughts, murders, adulteries, fornications, thefts, false witness, blasphemies: [20] These are the things which defile a man: but to eat with unwashen hands defileth not a man."

Matthew 22:15-22 "Then went the Pharisees, and took counsel how they might entangle him in his talk. [16] And they sent out unto him their disciples with the Herodians, saying, Master, we know that thou art true, and teachest the way of God in truth, neither carest thou for any man: for thou regardest not the person of men.
[17] Tell us therefore, What thinkest thou? Is it lawful to give tribute unto Caesar, or not? [18] But Jesus perceived their wickedness, and said, Why tempt ye me, ye hypocrites? [19] Shew me the tribute money. And they brought unto him a penny. [20] And he saith unto them, Whose is this image and superscription? [21] They say unto him, Caesar's. Then saith he unto them, Render therefore unto Caesar the things which are Caesar's; and unto God the things that are God's. [22] When they had heard these words, they marvelled, and left him, and went their way."

John 1:10-12 "He was in the world, and the world was made by him, and the world knew him not. [11] He came unto his own, and his own received him not. [12] But as many as received him, to them gave he power to become the sons of God, even to them that 104 on his name:

Acts 4:27 "For of a truth against thy holy child Jesus, whom thou hast anointed, both Herod, and Pontius Pilate, with the Gentiles, and the people of Israel, were gathered together,

B. Messiah To Be Sneered At.
Psalm 22:7-8 "All they that see me laugh me to scorn: they shoot out the lip, they shake the head, *saying*, [8] He trusted on the Lord *that* he would deliver him: let him deliver him, seeing he delighted in him."

The psalmist here prophesied that the Messiah would be mocked and sneered at. The verse of the psalm is found as fulfilled in the accounts of Luke and Matthew.

Luke 23:11 "And Herod with his men of war set him at nought, and mocked *him*, and arrayed him in a gorgeous robe, and sent him again to Pilate."

Luke 23:35-39 "And the people stood beholding. And the rulers also with them derided *him*, saying, He saved others; let him save himself, if he be Christ, the chosen of God. 36 And the soldiers also mocked him, coming to him, and offering him vinegar, 37 and saying, If thou be the king of the Jews, save thyself. 38 And a superscription also was written over him in letters of Greek, and Latin, and Hebrew, THIS IS THE KING OF THE JEWS. 39 And one of the malefactors which were hanged railed on him, saying, If thou be Christ, save thyself and us."

Matthew 27:39-44 "And they that passed by reviled him, wagging their heads, 40 and saying, Thou that destroyest the temple, and buildest *it* in three days, save thyself. If thou be the Son of God, come down from the cross. 41 Likewise also the chief priests mocking *him*, with the scribes and elders, said, 42 He saved others; himself he cannot save. If he be the King of Israel, let him now come down from the cross, and we will believe him. 43 He trusted in God; let him deliver him now, if he will have him: for he said, I am the Son of God. 44 The thieves also, which were crucified with him, cast the same in his teeth."

C. His Betrayal Prophesied.

Psalm 41:9 "Yea, mine own familiar friend, in whom I trusted, which did eat of my bread, hath lifted up *his* heel against me."

This verse talked about the future betrayal of the Messiah; one of Jesus Christ's twelve disciples, Judas Iscariot did betray Jesus Christ for thirty pieces of silver. This is recorded in John, Mark and Matthew.

John 13:18-21 "I speak not of you all: I know whom I have chosen: but that the scripture may be fulfilled, He that eateth bread with me hath lifted up his heel against me. 19 Now I tell you before it come, that, when it is come to pass, ye may believe that I am *he*. 20 Verily, verily, I say unto you, He that receiveth whomsoever I send receiveth me; and he that receiveth me receiveth him that sent me. 21 When Jesus had thus said, he was troubled in spirit, and testified, and said, Verily, verily, I say unto you, that one of you shall betray me."

Mark 3:14-19 "And he ordained twelve, that they should be with him, and that he might send them forth to preach, 15 and to have power to heal sicknesses, and to cast out devils: 16 and Simon he surnamed Peter; 17 and James the *son* of Zebedee, and John the brother of James; and he surnamed them Boanerges, which is, The sons of thunder: 18 and Andrew, and Philip, and Bartholomew, and Matthew, and Thomas, and James the *son* of Alphæus, and Thaddæus, and Simon the Canaanite, 19 and Judas Iscariot, which also betrayed him: and they went into an house."

Matthew 26:14-16 "Then one of the twelve, called Judas Iscariot, went unto the chief priests, [15] and said *unto them*, What will ye give me, and I will deliver him unto you? And they covenanted with him for thirty pieces of silver. [16] And from that time he sought opportunity to betray him."

Matthew 26:20-25 "Now when the even was come, he sat down with the twelve. [21] And as they did eat, he said, Verily I say unto you, that one of you shall betray me. [22] And they were exceeding sorrowful, and began every one of them to say unto him, Lord, is it I? [23] And he answered and said, He that dippeth *his* hand with me in the dish, the same shall betray me. [24] The Son of man goeth as it is written of him: but woe unto that man by whom the Son of man is betrayed! it had been good for that man if he had not been born. [25] Then Judas, which betrayed him, answered and said, Master, is it I? He said unto him, Thou hast said."

D. Messiah To Be Sold For 30 Pieces of Silver.

Zechariah 11:12-13 "And I said unto them, If ye think good, give *me* my price; and if not, forbear. So they weighed for my price thirty *pieces* of silver. [13] And the Lord said unto me, Cast it unto the potter: a goodly price that I was prised at of them. And I took the thirty *pieces* of silver, and cast them to the potter in the house of the Lord."

Zechariah, the prophet prophesied that Messiah would be sold for 30 pieces of silver.

Judas Iscariot fulfilled it in the receipt of 30 pieces of silver from the chief priests as recorded in Matthew as follows:

Matthew 26:14-15 "Then one of the twelve, called Judas Iscariot, went unto the chief priests, [15] and said *unto them*, What will ye give me, and I will deliver him unto you? And they covenanted with him for thirty pieces of silver."

Matthew 27:3-10 "Then Judas, which had betrayed him, when he saw that he was condemned, repented himself, and brought again the thirty pieces of silver to the chief priests and elders, [4] saying, I have sinned in that I have betrayed the innocent blood. And they said, What *is that* to us? see thou *to that*. [5] And he cast down the pieces of silver in the temple, and departed, and went and hanged himself. [6] And the chief priests took the silver pieces, and said, It is not lawful for to put them into the treasury, because it is the price of blood.
[7] And they took counsel, and bought with them the potter's field, to bury strangers in. [8] Wherefore that field was called, The field of blood, unto this day. [9] Then was fulfilled that which was spoken by Jeremy the prophet, saying, And they took the thirty pieces of silver, the price of him that was valued, whom they of the children of Israel did value; [10] and gave them for the potter's field, as the Lord appointed me."

E. Messiah To Be The Rejected Stone

Psalm 118:22-23 "The stone *which* the builders refused is become the head *stone* of the corner. 23 This is the Lord's doing; it *is* marvellous in our eyes."

Isaiah 28:16 "Therefore thus saith the Lord God, Behold, I lay in Zion for a foundation a stone, a tried stone, a precious corner *stone*, a sure foundation: he that believeth shall not make haste."

The psalmist and the prophet, Isaiah foretold that Messiah would be the stone that the builders rejected, which would become the head cornerstone. These prophecies were referred to by Jesus Christ in the cause of His teaching as found in Matthew. After His ascension the apostle Peter referred to the prophecy in an address recorded in the Acts, included it in his first epistle; and the apostle Paul also referred to it with regard to the Foundation of the Church in the epistle to the Ephesians.

Matthew 21:42-43 "Jesus saith unto them, Did ye never read in the scriptures, The stone which the builders rejected, the same is become the head of the corner: this is the Lord's doing, and it is marvellous in our eyes? 43 Therefore say I unto you, The kingdom of God shall be taken from you, and given to a nation bringing forth the fruits thereof.

Acts 4:10-11 "Be it known unto you all, and to all the people of Israel, that by the name of Jesus Christ of Nazareth, whom ye crucified, whom God raised from the dead, *even* by him doth this man stand here before you whole. 11 This is the stone which was set at nought of you builders, which is become the head of the corner.

1 Peter 2:4-8 "To whom coming, *as unto* a living stone, disallowed indeed of men, but chosen of God, *and* precious, 5 ye also, as lively stones, are built up a spiritual house, an holy priesthood, to offer up spiritual sacrifices, acceptable to God by Jesus Christ. 6 Wherefore also it is contained in the scripture, Behold, I lay in Sion a chief corner stone, elect, precious: and he that believeth on him shall not be confounded. 7 Unto you therefore which believe *he is* precious: but unto them which be disobedient, the stone which the builders disallowed, the same is made the head of the corner, 8 and a stone of stumbling, and a rock of offence, *even to them* which stumble at the word, being disobedient: whereunto also they were appointed."

Ephesians 2:19-20 "Now therefore ye are no more strangers and foreigners, but fellowcitizens with the saints, and of the household of God; 20 And are built upon the foundation of the apostles and prophets, Jesus Christ himself being the chief corner *stone;*"

F. Messiah To Be Rejected.

Isaiah 53:1-3 "Who hath believed our report? and to whom is the arm of the Lord revealed? 2 For he shall grow up before him as a tender plant, and as a root out of a dry ground: he hath no form nor comeliness; and when we shall see him, *there is* no beauty that we should desire him. ³ He is despised and rejected of men; a man of sorrows, and acquainted with grief: and we hid as it were *our* faces from him; he was despised, and we esteemed him not."

This is another prophecy of the rejection of the Messiah by His people – they would hear but not believe Him. The fulfillment is found in Matthew, Mark, Luke and John.

Matthew 27:20-25 "But the chief priests and elders persuaded the multitude that they should ask Barabbas, and destroy Jesus. ²¹ The governor answered and said unto them, Whether of the twain will ye that I release unto you? They said, Barabbas. ²² Pilate saith unto them, What shall I do then with Jesus which is called Christ? They all say unto him, Let him be crucified.
²³ And the governor said, Why, what evil hath he done? But they cried out the more, saying, Let him be crucified. ²⁴ When Pilate saw that he could prevail nothing, but that rather a tumult was made, he took water, and washed his hands before the multitude, saying, I am innocent of the blood of this just person: see ye to it. ²⁵ Then answered all the people, and said, His blood be on us, and on our children."

Mark 15:8-14 "And the multitude crying aloud began to desire him to do as he had ever done unto them. ⁹ But Pilate answered them, saying, Will ye that I release unto you the King of the Jews? ¹⁰ For he knew that the chief priests had delivered him for envy. ¹¹ But the chief priests moved the people, that he should rather release Barabbas unto them.
¹² And Pilate answered and said again unto them, What will ye then that I shall do unto him whom ye call the King of the Jews? ¹³ And they cried out again, Crucify him.
¹⁴ Then Pilate said unto them, Why, what evil hath he done? And they cried out the more exceedingly, Crucify him."

Luke 23:18-23 "And they cried out all at once, saying, Away with this man, and release unto us Barabbas: ¹⁹ (Who for a certain sedition made in the city, and for murder, was cast into prison.) ²⁰ Pilate therefore, willing to release Jesus, spake again to them. ²¹ But they cried, saying, Crucify him, crucify him.
²² And he said unto them the third time, Why, what evil hath he done? I have found no cause of death in him: I will therefore chastise him, and let him go. ²³ And they were instant with loud voices, requiring that he might be crucified. And the voices of them and of the chief priests prevailed."

John 12:31-41 "Now is the judgment of this world: now shall the prince of this world be cast out. ³² And I, if I be lifted up from the earth, will draw all men unto me.
³³ This he said, signifying what death he should die. ³⁴ The people answered him, We have heard out of the law that Christ abideth for ever: and how sayest thou, The Son of man must be lifted up? who is this Son of man?
³⁵ Then Jesus said unto them, Yet a little while is the light with you. Walk while ye have the light, lest darkness come upon you: for he that walketh in darkness knoweth not

whither he goeth. [36] While ye have light, believe in the light, that ye may be the children of light. These things spake Jesus, and departed, and did hide himself from them. [37] But though he had done so many miracles before them, yet they believed not on him: [38] That the saying of Esaias the prophet might be fulfilled, which he spake, Lord, who hath believed our report? and to whom hath the arm of the Lord been revealed?
[39] Therefore they could not believe, because that Esaias said again, [40] He hath blinded their eyes, and hardened their heart; that they should not see with their eyes, nor understand with their heart, and be converted, and I should heal them. [41] These things said Esaias, when he saw his glory, and spake of him."

G. Messiah To Be Thirsty On The Cross.

Psalm 22:15 "My strength is dried up like a potsherd; and my tongue cleaveth to my jaws; and thou hast brought me into the dust of death."

The psalmist also foretold that Messiah would be thirsty on the cross. On the cross of Calvary Jesus complained of thirst as recorded in John:

John 19:28 "After this, Jesus knowing that all things were now accomplished, that the scripture might be fulfilled, saith, I thirst."

H. His Hands And Feet Would Be Pierced.

Psalm 22:16 "For dogs have compassed me: the assembly of the wicked have inclosed me: they pierced my hands and my feet."

The prophecy here talks about the Messiah to be crucifixion between criminals and that His feet and hands would be pierced. Luke and John recorded the fulfillment of the prophecy. The Luke account of the crucifixion and John's account of the display of His pierced hands and feet are reproduced as follows:

Luke 23:33 "And when they were come to the place, which is called Calvary, there they crucified him, and the malefactors, one on the right hand, and the other on the left.

Luke 24:36-39 "And as they thus spake, Jesus himself stood in the midst of them, and saith unto them, Peace be unto you. [37] But they were terrified and affrighted, and supposed that they had seen a spirit. [38] And he said unto them, Why are ye troubled? and why do thoughts arise in your hearts? [39] Behold my hands and my feet, that it is I myself: handle me, and see; for a spirit hath not flesh and bones, as ye see me have.

John 19:18 "Where they crucified him, and two other with him, on either side one, and Jesus in the midst.

John 20:19-20 "Then the same day at evening, being the first day of the week, when the doors were shut where the disciples were assembled for fear of the Jews, came Jesus and stood in the midst, and saith unto them, Peace be unto you. 20 And when he had so said, he shewed unto them his hands and his side. Then were the disciples glad, when they saw the Lord.

John 20:24-27 "But Thomas, one of the twelve, called Didymus, was not with them when Jesus came. 25 The other disciples therefore said unto him, We have seen the Lord. But he said unto them, Except I shall see in his hands the print of the nails, and put my finger into the print of the nails, and thrust my hand into his side, I will not believe.
26 And after eight days again his disciples were within, and Thomas with them: then came Jesus, the doors being shut, and stood in the midst, and said, Peace be unto you. 27 Then saith he to Thomas, Reach hither thy finger, and behold my hands; and reach hither thy hand, and thrust it into my side: and be not faithless, but believing.

I. Ownership of Messiah's Clothes To Be Determined By Lot.

Psalm 22:18 "They part my garments among them, and cast lots upon my vesture."

It was prophesied that evil men were going to cast lots to own the Messiah's clothing.

The records of the fulfillment are as follows:

Matthew 27:35 "And they crucified him, and parted his garments, casting lots: that it might be fulfilled which was spoken by the prophet, They parted my garments among them, and upon my vesture did they cast lots."

Mark 15:24 "And when they had crucified him, they parted his garments, casting lots upon them, what every man should take."

Luke 23:34 "Then said Jesus, Father, forgive them; for they know not what they do. And they parted his raiment, and cast lots."

John 19:23-24 "Then the soldiers, when they had crucified Jesus, took his garments, and made four parts, to every soldier a part; and also his coat: now the coat was without seam, woven from the top throughout. 24 They said therefore among themselves, Let us not rend it, but cast lots for it, whose it shall be: that the scripture might be fulfilled, which saith, They parted my raiment among them, and for my vesture they did cast lots. These things therefore the soldiers did."

J. His Legs Would Not Be Broken.

Psalm 34:20 "He keepeth all his bones: not one of them is broken."

It was prophesied that Messiah's legs would not be broken to facilitate dying, against the normal practice in crucifixion. We find the fulfillment recorded in John.

Fulfillment:

John 19:31-33 "The Jews therefore, because it was the preparation, that the bodies should not remain upon the cross on the sabbath day, (for that sabbath day was an high day,) besought Pilate that their legs might be broken, and that they might be taken away. 32 Then came the soldiers, and brake the legs of the first, and of the other which was crucified with him. 33 But when they came to Jesus, and saw that he was dead already, they brake not his legs: 36 For these things were done, that the scripture should be fulfilled, A bone of him shall not be broken."

K. Messiah To Be Zealous For God.

Psalm 69:9 "For the zeal of thine house hath eaten me up; and the reproaches of them that reproached thee are fallen upon me."

This prophecy says that Messiah would be zealous for the Lord:

John 2:16-17 "And said unto them that sold doves, Take these things hence; make not my Father's house an house of merchandise. 17 And his disciples remembered that it was written, The zeal of thine house hath eaten me up."

L. Messiah To Be Offered Vinegar For Water.

Psalm 69:21 "They gave me also gall for my meat; and in my thirst they gave me vinegar to drink."

Messiah would be given vinegar to drink when thirsty during His crucifixion. It occurred as was foretold.

Matthew 27:34, 48 "They gave him vinegar to drink mingled with gall: and when he had tasted thereof, he would not drink. 48 And straightway one of them ran, and took a spunge, and filled it with vinegar, and put it on a reed, and gave him to drink."

Mark 15:23 "And they gave him to drink wine mingled with myrrh: but he received it not."

John 19:29-30 "Now there was set a vessel full of vinegar: and they filled a spunge with vinegar, and put it upon hyssop, and put it to his mouth. 30 When Jesus therefore had received the vinegar, he said, It is finished: and he bowed his head, and gave up the ghost."

M. Messiah Would Be Assaulted
Isaiah 50:6 "I gave my back to the smiters, and my cheeks to them that plucked off the hair: I hid not my face from shame and spitting."

Messiah would be beaten and spat on. In the crucifixion process these happened as recorded in Matthew and Luke. The two accounts are reproduced below:

Matthew 26:67 "Then did they spit in his face, and buffeted him; and others smote him with the palms of their hands,"

Matthew 27:26-31 "Then released he Barabbas unto them: and when he had scourged Jesus, he delivered him to be crucified. 27 Then the soldiers of the governor took Jesus into the common hall, and gathered unto him the whole band of soldiers. 28 And they stripped him, and put on him a scarlet robe. 29 And when they had platted a crown of thorns, they put it upon his head, and a reed in his right hand: and they bowed the knee before him, and mocked him, saying, Hail, King of the Jews! 30 And they spit upon him, and took the reed, and smote him on the head. 31 And after that they had mocked him, they took the robe off from him, and put his own raiment on him, and led him away to crucify him."

Luke 22:63 "And the men that held Jesus mocked him, and smote him."

N. Messiah to be Silent Before His Accusers.

Isaiah 53:7 "He was oppressed, and he was afflicted, yet he opened not his mouth: he is brought as a lamb to the slaughter, and as a sheep before her shearers is dumb, so he openeth not his mouth."

The prophet Isaiah prophesied that the Messiah would be silent before His accusers, and this was fulfilled just like that during His trials as found in Matthew; Mark, Luke and John. These accounts are reproduced thus:

Matthew 26:62-63 "And the high priest arose, and said unto him, Answerest thou nothing? what is it which these witness against thee? 63 But Jesus held his peace, And the high priest answered and said unto him, I adjure thee by the living God, that thou tell us whether thou be the Christ, the Son of God."

Matthew 27:12-14 "And when he was accused of the chief priests and elders, he answered nothing. 13 Then said Pilate unto him, Hearest thou not how many things they witness against thee? 14 And he answered him to never a word; insomuch that the governor marvelled greatly."

Mark 15:3-4 "And the chief priests accused him of many things: but he answered nothing. 4 And Pilate asked him again, saying, Answerest thou nothing? behold how many things they witness against thee."

Luke 23:8-10 "And when Herod saw Jesus, he was exceeding glad: for he was desirous to see him of a long season, because he had heard many things of him; and he hoped to have seen some miracle done by him. 9 Then he questioned with him in many words; but he answered him nothing. 10 And the chief priests and scribes stood and vehemently accused him."

John 19:30 "When Jesus therefore had received the vinegar, he said, It is finished: and he bowed his head, and gave up the ghost."

O. Messiah To Be Executed.

Isaiah 53:5-8 "But he was wounded for our transgressions, he was bruised for our iniquities: the chastisement of our peace was upon him; and with his stripes we are healed. 6 All we like sheep have gone astray; we have turned every one to his own way; and the Lord hath laid on him the iniquity of us all. 7 He was oppressed, and he was afflicted, yet he opened not his mouth: he is brought as a lamb to the slaughter, and as a sheep before her shearers is dumb, so he openeth not his mouth. 8 He was taken from prison and from judgment: and who shall declare his generation? for he was cut off out of the land of the living: for the transgression of my people was he stricken."

Daniel 9:25-26 "Know therefore and understand, that from the going forth of the commandment to restore and to build Jerusalem unto the Messiah the Prince shall be seven weeks, and threescore and two weeks: the street shall be built again, and the wall, even in troublous times. 26 And after threescore and two weeks shall Messiah be cut off, but not for himself: and the people of the prince that shall come shall destroy the city and the sanctuary; and the end thereof shall be with a flood, and unto the end of the war desolations are determined."

The prophet Isaiah further foretold that the Messiah would be executed for the sake of the sin of the people. Similarly Daniel mentioned the execution (cut-off) of the Messiah.

113

Fulfillment:

Matthew 27:35-38 " And they crucified him, and parted his garments, casting lots: that it might be fulfilled which was spoken by the prophet, They parted my garments among them, and upon my vesture did they cast lots.

> [36] And sitting down they watched him there; [37] And set up over his head his accusation written, This Is Jesus The King Of The Jews. [38] Then were there two thieves crucified with him, one on the right hand, and another on the left."

Mark 15:24-28 "And when they had crucified him, they parted his garments, casting lots upon them, what every man should take. [25] And it was the third hour, and they crucified him. [26] And the superscription of his accusation was written over, The King Of The Jews. [27] And with him they crucify two thieves; the one on his right hand, and the other on his left. [28] And the scripture was fulfilled, which saith, And he was numbered with the transgressors."

Luke 23:32-34 "And there were also two other, malefactors, led with him to be put to death. [33] And when they were come to the place, which is called Calvary, there they crucified him, and the malefactors, one on the right hand, and the other on the left. [34] Then said Jesus, Father, forgive them; for they know not what they do. And they parted his raiment, and cast lots."

John 19:18, 32 "Where they crucified him, and two other with him, on either side one, and Jesus in the midst. [32] Then came the soldiers, and brake the legs of the first, and of the other which was crucified with him."

P. Messiah To Be Crucified Between Criminals.

Isaiah 53:12 "Therefore will I divide him a portion with the great, and he shall divide the spoil with the strong; because he hath poured out his soul unto death: and he was numbered with the transgressors; and he bare the sin of many, and made intercession for the transgressors."

It was prophesied that Messiah would be crucified in between criminals just as it happened that He was crucified between two thieves.

Fulfillment:

Matthew 27:38 "Then were there two thieves crucified with him, one on the right hand, and another on the left.

Mark 15:27 "And with him they crucify two thieves; the one on his right hand, and the other on his left.

114

Luke 23:32-33 "And there were also two other, malefactors, led with him to be put to death. 33 And when they were come to the place, which is called Calvary, there they crucified him, and the malefactors, one on the right hand, and the other on the left."

Q. Messiah's Disciples to be in Disarray.

Zechariah 13:7 "Awake, O sword, against my shepherd, and against the man that is my fellow, saith the Lord of hosts: smite the shepherd, and the sheep shall be scattered: and I will turn mine hand upon the little ones."

This prophecy implied that the disciples would be scattered when the Messiah was struck, and so it happened.

Matthew 26:31, 56 "Then saith Jesus unto them, All ye shall be offended because of me this night: for it is written, I will smite the shepherd, and the sheep of the flock shall be scattered abroad. 56 But all this was done, that the scriptures of the prophets might be fulfilled. Then all the disciples forsook him, and fled."

JESUS CHRIST ALSO PREDICTED HIS DEATH.

In addition to the Old Testament prophecies of the execution of the Messiah, Jesus Christ also predicted His death to the Jews who had demanded His authority for cleansing the temple. His reply is in John 2:19. But the whole story including the prediction is as follows:

John 2:12-22 " After this he went down to Capernaum, he, and his mother, and his brethren, and his disciples: and they continued there not many days. 13 And the Jews' passover was at hand, and Jesus went up to Jerusalem. 14 And found in the temple those that sold oxen and sheep and doves, and the changers of money sitting:
15 And when he had made a scourge of small cords, he drove them all out of the temple, and the sheep, and the oxen; and poured out the changers' money, and overthrew the tables; 16 And said unto them that sold doves, Take these things hence; make not my Father's house an house of merchandise.
17 And his disciples remembered that it was written, The zeal of thine house hath eaten me up.
18 Then answered the Jews and said unto him, What sign shewest thou unto us, seeing that thou doest these things? 19 Jesus answered and said unto them, Destroy this temple, and in three days I will raise it up. 20 Then said the Jews, Forty and six years was this temple in building, and wilt thou rear it up in three days? 21 But he spake of the temple of his body.

115

²² When therefore he was risen from the dead, his disciples remembered that he had said this unto them; and they believed the scripture, and the word which Jesus had said." (Emphasis added).

Then He predicted His death by crucifixion to Nicodemus:

John 3:12-15 " If I have told you earthly things, and ye believe not, how shall ye believe, if I tell you of heavenly things? ¹³ And no man hath ascended up to heaven, but he that came down from heaven, even the Son of man which is in heaven. ¹⁴ And as Moses lifted up the serpent in the wilderness, even so must the Son of man be lifted up: ¹⁵ That whosoever believeth in him should not perish, but have eternal life." (Emphasis added).

Other instances of Jesus Christ's prediction of His death are as follows.

Matthew 16:21-23 "From that time forth began Jesus to shew unto his disciples, how that he must go unto Jerusalem, and suffer many things of the elders and chief priests and scribes, and be killed, and be raised again the third day. ²² Then Peter took him, and began to rebuke him, saying, Be it far from thee, Lord: this shall not be unto thee. ²³ But he turned, and said unto Peter, Get thee behind me, Satan: thou art an offence unto me: for thou savourest not the things that be of God, but those that be of men."

Mark 8:31-33 "And he began to teach them, that the Son of man must suffer many things, and be rejected of the elders, and of the chief priests, and scribes, and be killed, and after three days rise again. ³² And he spake that saying openly. And Peter took him, and began to rebuke him. ³³ But when he had turned about and looked on his disciples, he rebuked Peter, saying, Get thee behind me, Satan: for thou savourest not the things that be of God, but the things that be of men."

Luke 9:21-22 "And he straitly charged them, and commanded them to tell no man that thing; ²² Saying, The Son of man must suffer many things, and be rejected of the elders and chief priests and scribes, and be slain, and be raised the third day."

Matthew 17:22-23 "And while they abode in Galilee, Jesus said unto them, The Son of man shall be betrayed into the hands of men: ²³ And they shall kill him, and the third day he shall be raised again. And they were exceeding sorry.

Mark 9:30-32 "And they departed thence, and passed through Galilee; and he would not that any man should know it. ³¹ For he taught his disciples, and said unto them, The Son of man is delivered into the hands of men, and they shall kill him; and after that he is killed, he shall rise the third day. ³² But they understood not that saying, and were afraid to ask him."

Luke 9:43-45 "And they were all amazed at the mighty power of God. But while they wondered every one at all things which Jesus did, he said unto his disciples, 44 Let these sayings sink down into your ears: for the Son of man shall be delivered into the hands of men. 45 But they understood not this saying, and it was hid from them, that they perceived it not: and they feared to ask him of that saying."

Matthew 20:17-19 "And Jesus going up to Jerusalem took the twelve disciples apart in the way, and said unto them, 18 Behold, we go up to Jerusalem; and the Son of man shall be betrayed unto the chief priests and unto the scribes, and they shall condemn him to death, 19 And shall deliver him to the Gentiles to mock, and to scourge, and to crucify him: and the third day he shall rise again."

Mark 10:32-34 "And they were in the way going up to Jerusalem; and Jesus went before them: and they were amazed; and as they followed, they were afraid. And he took again the twelve, and began to tell them what things should happen unto him, 33 Saying, Behold, we go up to Jerusalem; and the Son of man shall be delivered unto the chief priests, and unto the scribes; and they shall condemn him to death, and shall deliver him to the Gentiles: 34 And they shall mock him, and shall scourge him, and shall spit upon him, and shall kill him: and the third day he shall rise again."

Luke 18:31-34 "Then he took unto him the twelve, and said unto them, Behold, we go up to Jerusalem, and all things that are written by the prophets concerning the Son of man shall be accomplished. 32 For he shall be delivered unto the Gentiles, and shall be mocked, and spitefully entreated, and spitted on: 33 And they shall scourge him, and put him to death: and the third day he shall rise again.
34 And they understood none of these things: and this saying was hid from them, neither knew they the things which were spoken.

John 8:27-30 "They understood not that he spake to them of the Father.
28 Then said Jesus unto them, When ye have lifted up the Son of man, then shall ye know that I am he, and that I do nothing of myself; but as my Father hath taught me, I speak these things. 29 And he that sent me is with me: the Father hath not left me alone; for I do always those things that please him. 30 As he spake these words, many believed on him.

John 12:7-8 "Then said Jesus, Let her alone: against the day of my burying hath she kept this. 8 For the poor always ye have with you; but me ye have not always.

John 12:23"And Jesus answered them, saying, The hour is come, that the Son of man should be glorified.

John 14:25-31 "These things have I spoken unto you, being yet present with you. 26 But the Comforter, which is the Holy Ghost, whom the Father will send in my name, he shall teach you all things, and bring all things to your remembrance, whatsoever I have said unto you.

27 Peace I leave with you, my peace I give unto you: not as the world giveth, give I unto you. Let not your heart be troubled, neither let it be afraid. 28 Ye have heard how I said unto you, I go away, and come again unto you. If ye loved me, ye would rejoice, because I said, I go unto the Father: for my Father is greater than I. 29 And now I have told you before it come to pass, that, when it is come to pass, ye might believe.
30 Hereafter I will not talk much with you: for the prince of this world cometh, and hath nothing in me. 31 But that the world may know that I love the Father; and as the Father gave me commandment, even so I do. Arise, let us go hence.

R. The Death of the Messiah

Isaiah 53:9a "And he made his grave with the wicked, and with the rich in his death;"

Daniel 9:26a "And after threescore and two weeks shall Messiah be cut off, but not for himself: "

These among others were prophecies regarding the death of the Messiah and that He would be buried in the grave of the wealthy. This happened after Jesus was crucified, and He died in between two robbers.

Matthew 27:50 "Jesus, when he had cried again with a loud voice, yielded up the ghost.

Mark 15:37-39 "And Jesus cried with a loud voice, and gave up the ghost. 38 And the veil of the temple was rent in twain from the top to the bottom. 39 And when the centurion, which stood over against him, saw that he so cried out, and gave up the ghost, he said, Truly this man was the Son of God.

Luke 23:46 "And when Jesus had cried with a loud voice, he said, Father, into thy hands I commend my spirit: and having said thus, he gave up the ghost.

John 19:30 "When Jesus therefore had received the vinegar, he said, It is finished: and he bowed his head, and gave up the ghost.

S. Messiah's Burial.

Isaiah 53:9 "And he made his grave with the wicked, and with the rich in his death; because he had done no violence, neither was any deceit in his mouth."

Fulfillment

Matthew 27:59-60 "And when Joseph had taken the body, he wrapped it in a clean linen cloth, 60 And laid it in his own new tomb, which he had hewn out in the rock: and he rolled a great stone to the door of the sepulchre, and departed."

Mark 15:46 "And he bought fine linen, and took him down, and wrapped him in the linen, and laid him in a sepulchre which was hewn out of a rock, and rolled a stone unto the door of the sepulchre."

Luke 23:52-53 "This man went unto Pilate, and begged the body of Jesus.
53 And he took it down, and wrapped it in linen, and laid it in a sepulchre that was hewn in stone, wherein never man before was laid."

John 19:38-42 "And after this Joseph of Arimathaea, being a disciple of Jesus, but secretly for fear of the Jews, besought Pilate that he might take away the body of Jesus: and Pilate gave him leave. He came therefore, and took the body of Jesus. 39 And there came also Nicodemus, which at the first came to Jesus by night, and brought a mixture of myrrh and aloes, about an hundred pound weight. 40 Then took they the body of Jesus, and wound it in linen clothes with the spices, as the manner of the Jews is to bury.
41 Now in the place where he was crucified there was a garden; and in the garden a new sepulchre, wherein was never man yet laid. 42 There laid they Jesus therefore because of the Jews' preparation day; for the sepulchre was nigh at hand."

CHAPTER 6
MESSIAH'S RESURRECTION, PHYSICAL APPEARANCES AND ASCENSION.

The psalmist prophesied that the Messiah would be raised from the dead rather than be abandoned in the grave.

Messiah's Resurrection.

Psalm 16:8-11 "I have set the Lord always before me: because he is at my right hand, I shall not be moved. 9 Therefore my heart is glad, and my glory rejoiceth: my flesh also shall rest in hope. 10 For thou wilt not leave my soul in hell; neither wilt thou suffer thine Holy One to see corruption. 11 Thou wilt shew me the path of life: in thy presence is fulness of joy; at thy right hand there are pleasures for evermore."

The fulfillment:

Matthew 28:1-10 "In the end of the sabbath, as it began to dawn toward the first day of the week, came Mary Magdalene and the other Mary to see the sepulchre. 2 And, behold, there was a great earthquake: for the angel of the Lord descended from heaven, and came and rolled back the stone from the door, and sat upon it. 3 His countenance was like lightning, and his raiment white as snow: 4 And for fear of him the keepers did shake, and became as dead men. 5 And the angel answered and said unto the women, Fear not ye: for I know that ye seek Jesus, which was crucified.
6 He is not here: for he is risen, as he said. Come, see the place where the Lord lay. 7 And go quickly, and tell his disciples that he is risen from the dead; and, behold, he goeth before you into Galilee; there shall ye see him: lo, I have told you.
8 And they departed quickly from the sepulchre with fear and great joy; and did run to bring his disciples word.
9 And as they went to tell his disciples, behold, Jesus met them, saying, All hail. And they came and held him by the feet, and worshipped him. 10 Then said Jesus unto them, Be not afraid: go tell my brethren that they go into Galilee, and there shall they see me.

Mark 16:6 " And he saith unto them, Be not affrighted: Ye seek Jesus of Nazareth, which was crucified: he is risen; he is not here: behold the place where they laid him."

Luke 24:4-7 "And it came to pass, as they were much perplexed thereabout, behold, two men stood by them in shining garments: 5 And as they were afraid, and bowed down their faces to the earth, they said unto them, Why seek ye the living among the dead? 6 He is not here, but is risen: remember how he spake unto you when he was yet in Galilee, 7 Saying, The Son of man must be delivered into the hands of sinful men, and be crucified, and the third day rise again."

Acts 2:22-32 "Ye men of Israel, hear these words; Jesus of Nazareth, a man approved of God among you by miracles and wonders and signs, which God did by him in the midst of you, as ye yourselves also know: 23 Him, being delivered by the determinate counsel and foreknowledge of God, ye have taken, and by wicked hands have crucified and slain: 24 Whom God hath raised up, having loosed the pains of death: because it was not possible that he should be holden of it.
25 For David speaketh concerning him, I foresaw the Lord always before my face, for he is on my right hand, that I should not be moved: 26 Therefore did my heart rejoice, and my tongue was glad; moreover also my flesh shall rest in hope: 27 Because thou wilt not leave my soul in hell, neither wilt thou suffer thine Holy One to see corruption. 28 Thou hast made known to me the ways of life; thou shalt make me full of joy with thy countenance.
29 Men and brethren, let me freely speak unto you of the patriarch David, that he is both dead and buried, and his sepulchre is with us unto this day. 30 Therefore being a prophet, and knowing that God had sworn with an oath to him, that of the fruit of his loins, according to the flesh, he would raise up Christ to sit on his throne; 31 He seeing this before spake of the resurrection of Christ, that his soul was not left in hell, neither his flesh did see corruption. 32 This Jesus hath God raised up, whereof we all are witnesses."

Post-Resurrection Physical Appearances.

In addition to the empty tomb[17] of Jesus Christ, the physical appearances that He made to different people at different locations constituted another evidence of His resurrection. During the cause of forty days of His resurrection, starting from the day it occurred (the first day of the week), Jesus Christ physically appeared to His disciples, allowing them to see His pierced side, and His nail-pierced hands and feet; He ate with them and suggested to them that they could feel His body to ascertain that He was not a ghost.

The apostle Paul has one comprehensive summary account of these physical appearances thus:

1 Corinthians 15:3-9 "For I delivered unto you first of all that which I also received, how that Christ died for our sins according to the scriptures; 4 And

---

[17] The tomb in which Jesus Christ was laid when He died became empty when He arose, leaving behind only the burial cloths with which His body was shrouded.

that he was buried, and that he rose again the third day according to the scriptures: 5 And that he was seen of Cephas, then of the twelve: 6 After that, he was seen of above five hundred brethren at once; of whom the greater part remain unto this present, but some are fallen asleep.

7 After that, he was seen of James; then of all the apostles. 8 And last of all he was seen of me also, as of one born out of due time. 9 For I am the least of the apostles, that am not meet to be called an apostle, because I persecuted the church of God."

Other records of the post-resurrection appearances of Jesus Christ in the Gospels are as follows:

Matthew 28:8-10 "And they departed quickly from the sepulchre with fear and great joy; and did run to bring his disciples word. 9 And as they went to tell his disciples, behold, Jesus met them, saying, All hail. And they came and held him by the feet, and worshipped him. 10 Then said Jesus unto them, Be not afraid: go tell my brethren that they go into Galilee, and there shall they see me."

Matthew 28:16-20 "Then the eleven disciples went away into Galilee, into a mountain where Jesus had appointed them. 17 And when they saw him, they worshipped him: but some doubted. 18 And Jesus came and spake unto them, saying, All power is given unto me in heaven and in earth.

19 Go ye therefore, and teach all nations, baptizing them in the name of the Father, and of the Son, and of the Holy Ghost: 20 Teaching them to observe all things whatsoever I have commanded you: and, lo, I am with you always, even unto the end of the world. Amen.

Mark 16:9-20 "Now when Jesus was risen early the first day of the week, he appeared first to Mary Magdalene, out of whom he had cast seven devils. 10 And she went and told them that had been with him, as they mourned and wept. 11 And they, when they had heard that he was alive, and had been seen of her, believed not.

12 After that he appeared in another form unto two of them, as they walked, and went into the country. 13 And they went and told it unto the residue: neither believed they them. 14 Afterward he appeared unto the eleven as they sat at meat, and upbraided them with their unbelief and hardness of heart, because they believed not them which had seen him after he was risen.

15 And he said unto them, Go ye into all the world, and preach the gospel to every creature. 16 He that believeth and is baptized shall be saved; but he that believeth not shall be damned. 17 And these signs shall follow them that believe; In my name shall they cast out devils; they shall speak with new tongues; 18 They shall take up serpents; and if they drink any deadly thing, it shall not hurt them; they shall lay hands on the sick, and they shall recover.

19 So then after the Lord had spoken unto them, he was received up into heaven, and sat on the right hand of God. 20 And they went forth, and preached

every where, the Lord working with them, and confirming the word with signs following. Amen.

Luke 24:13-53
Jesus Christ and Disciples on the Road to Emmaus.

13 "And, behold, two of them went that same day to a village called Emmaus, which was from Jerusalem about threescore furlongs. **14** And they talked together of all these things which had happened. **15** And it came to pass, that, while they communed together and reasoned, Jesus himself drew near, and went with them. **16** But their eyes were holden that they should not know him. **17** And he said unto them, What manner of communications are these that ye have one to another, as ye walk, and are sad? **18** And the one of them, whose name was Cleopas, answering said unto him, Art thou only a stranger in Jerusalem, and hast not known the things which are come to pass there in these days? **19** And he said unto them, What things? And they said unto him, Concerning Jesus of Nazareth, which was a prophet mighty in deed and word before God and all the people: **20** And how the chief priests and our rulers delivered him to be condemned to death, and have crucified him.

21 But we trusted that it had been he which should have redeemed Israel: and beside all this, to day is the third day since these things were done. **22** Yea, and certain women also of our company made us astonished, which were early at the sepulchre; **23** And when they found not his body, they came, saying, that they had also seen a vision of angels, which said that he was alive. **24** And certain of them which were with us went to the sepulchre, and found it even so as the women had said: but him they saw not.

25 Then he said unto them, O fools, and slow of heart to believe all that the prophets have spoken: **26** Ought not Christ to have suffered these things, and to enter into his glory? **27** And beginning at Moses and all the prophets, he expounded unto them in all the scriptures the things concerning himself. **28** And they drew nigh unto the village, whither they went: and he made as though he would have gone further.

29 But they constrained him, saying, Abide with us: for it is toward evening, and the day is far spent. And he went in to tarry with them. **30** And it came to pass, as he sat at meat with them, he took bread, and blessed it, and brake, and gave to them. **31** And their eyes were opened, and they knew him; and he vanished out of their sight.

32 And they said one to another, Did not our heart burn within us, while he talked with us by the way, and while he opened to us the scriptures? **33** And they rose up the same hour, and returned to Jerusalem, and found the eleven gathered together, and them that were with them, **34** Saying, The Lord is risen indeed, and hath appeared to Simon. **35** And they told what things were done in the way, and how he was known of them in breaking of bread.

Jesus Christ Appeared to His Disciples.

36 And as they thus spake, Jesus himself stood in the midst of them, and saith unto them, Peace be unto you. **37** But they were terrified and affrighted, and supposed that they had seen a spirit. **38** And he said unto them, Why are ye troubled? and why do thoughts arise in your hearts?

39 Behold my hands and my feet, that it is I myself: handle me, and see; for a spirit hath not flesh and bones, as ye see me have. **40** And when he had thus spoken, he shewed them his hands and his feet. **41** And while they yet believed not for joy, and wondered, he said unto them, Have ye here any meat? **42** And they gave him a piece of a broiled fish, and of an honeycomb. **43** And he took it, and did eat before them.

44 And he said unto them, These are the words which I spake unto you, while I was yet with you, that all things must be fulfilled, which were written in the law of Moses, and in the prophets, and in the psalms, concerning me.

45 Then opened he their understanding, that they might understand the scriptures,

46 And said unto them, Thus it is written, and thus it behooved Christ to suffer, and to rise from the dead the third day: **47** And that repentance and remission of sins should be preached in his name among all nations, beginning at Jerusalem. **48** And ye are witnesses of these things. **49** And, behold, I send the promise of my Father upon you: but tarry ye in the city of Jerusalem, until ye be endued with power from on high.

Jesus Christ Ascended.

50 And he led them out as far as to Bethany, and he lifted up his hands, and blessed them. **51** And it came to pass, while he blessed them, he was parted from them, and carried up into heaven. **52** And they worshipped him, and returned to Jerusalem with great joy: **53** And were continually in the temple, praising and blessing God. Amen.

John 20:1-31
Jesus Christ was Resurrected.

"The first day of the week cometh Mary Magdalene early, when it was yet dark, unto the sepulchre, and seeth the stone taken away from the sepulchre. 2 Then she runneth, and cometh to Simon Peter, and to the other disciple, whom Jesus loved, and saith unto them, They have taken away the Lord out of the sepulchre, and we know not where they have laid him. 3 Peter therefore went forth, and that other disciple, and came to the sepulchre. 4 So they ran both together: and the other disciple did outrun Peter, and came first to the sepulchre.

5 And he stooping down, and looking in, saw the linen clothes lying; yet went he not in. 6 Then cometh Simon Peter following him, and went into the sepulchre, and seeth the linen clothes lie, 7 And the napkin, that was about his head, not lying with the linen clothes, but wrapped together in a place by itself. 8 Then went in also that other disciple, which came first to the sepulchre, and he saw, and believed. 9 For as yet they knew not the scripture, that he must rise

again from the dead. [10] Then the disciples went away again unto their own home.

Jesus Christ Appeared to Mary Magdalene.

[11] But Mary stood without at the sepulchre weeping: and as she wept, she stooped down, and looked into the sepulchre, [12] And seeth two angels in white sitting, the one at the head, and the other at the feet, where the body of Jesus had lain. [13] And they say unto her, Woman, why weepest thou? She saith unto them, Because they have taken away my Lord, and I know not where they have laid him. [14] And when she had thus said, she turned herself back, and saw Jesus standing, and knew not that it was Jesus.

[15] Jesus saith unto her, Woman, why weepest thou? whom seekest thou? She, supposing him to be the gardener, saith unto him, Sir, if thou have borne him hence, tell me where thou hast laid him, and I will take him away. [16] Jesus saith unto her, Mary. She turned herself, and saith unto him, Rabboni; which is to say, Master.

[17] Jesus saith unto her, Touch me not; for I am not yet ascended to my Father: but go to my brethren, and say unto them, I ascend unto my Father, and your Father; and to my God, and your God. [18] Mary Magdalene came and told the disciples that she had seen the Lord, and that he had spoken these things unto her.

Jesus Christ Appeared to His Disciples in the Absence of Thomas.

[19] Then the same day at evening, being the first day of the week, when the doors were shut where the disciples were assembled for fear of the Jews, came Jesus and stood in the midst, and saith unto them, Peace be unto you. [20] And when he had so said, he shewed unto them his hands and his side. Then were the disciples glad, when they saw the Lord.

[21] Then said Jesus to them again, Peace be unto you: as my Father hath sent me, even so send I you. [22] And when he had said this, he breathed on them, and saith unto them, Receive ye the Holy Ghost: [23] Whose soever sins ye remit, they are remitted unto them; and whose soever sins ye retain, they are retained.

[24] But Thomas, one of the twelve, called Didymus, was not with them when Jesus came. [25] The other disciples therefore said unto him, We have seen the Lord. But he said unto them, Except I shall see in his hands the print of the nails, and put my finger into the print of the nails, and thrust my hand into his side, I will not believe.

[26] And after eight days again his disciples were within, and Thomas with them: then came Jesus, the doors being shut, and stood in the midst, and said, Peace be unto you.

[27] Then saith he to Thomas, Reach hither thy finger, and behold my hands; and reach hither thy hand, and thrust it into my side: and be not faithless, but believing. [28] And Thomas answered and said unto him, My Lord and my God. [29] Jesus saith unto him, Thomas, because thou hast seen me, thou hast believed: blessed are they that have not seen, and yet have believed.

30 And many other signs truly did Jesus in the presence of his disciples, which are not written in this book: **31** But these are written, that ye might believe that Jesus is the Christ, the Son of God; and that believing ye might have life through his name.

John 21:1-25

Jesus Christ Appeared to Seven Disciples.

"After these things Jesus shewed himself again to the disciples at the sea of Tiberias; and on this wise shewed he himself. **2** There were together Simon Peter, and Thomas called Didymus, and Nathanael of Cana in Galilee, and the sons of Zebedee, and two other of his disciples. **3** Simon Peter saith unto them, I go a fishing. They say unto him, We also go with thee. They went forth, and entered into a ship immediately; and that night they caught nothing.

4 But when the morning was now come, Jesus stood on the shore: but the disciples knew not that it was Jesus. **5** Then Jesus saith unto them, Children, have ye any meat? They answered him, No. **6** And he said unto them, Cast the net on the right side of the ship, and ye shall find. They cast therefore, and now they were not able to draw it for the multitude of fishes.

7 Therefore that disciple whom Jesus loved saith unto Peter, It is the Lord. Now when Simon Peter heard that it was the Lord, he girt his fisher's coat unto him, (for he was naked,) and did cast himself into the sea.

8 And the other disciples came in a little ship; (for they were not far from land, but as it were two hundred cubits,) dragging the net with fishes. **9** As soon then as they were come to land, they saw a fire of coals there, and fish laid thereon, and bread. **10** Jesus saith unto them, Bring of the fish which ye have now caught. **11** Simon Peter went up, and drew the net to land full of great fishes, an hundred and fifty and three: and for all there were so many, yet was not the net broken. **12** Jesus saith unto them, Come and dine. And none of the disciples durst ask him, Who art thou? knowing that it was the Lord. **13** Jesus then cometh, and taketh bread, and giveth them, and fish likewise. **14** This is now the third time that Jesus shewed himself to his disciples, after that he was risen from the dead.

Jesus Christ Addressed Simon Peter.

15 So when they had dined, Jesus saith to Simon Peter, Simon, son of Jonas, lovest thou me more than these? He saith unto him, Yea, Lord; thou knowest that I love thee. He saith unto him, Feed my lambs. **16** He saith to him again the second time, Simon, son of Jonas, lovest thou me? He saith unto him, Yea, Lord; thou knowest that I love thee. He saith unto him, Feed my sheep.

17 He saith unto him the third time, Simon, son of Jonas, lovest thou me? Peter was grieved because he said unto him the third time, Lovest thou me? And he said unto him, Lord, thou knowest all things; thou knowest that I love thee. Jesus saith unto him, Feed my sheep. **18** Verily, verily, I say unto thee, When thou wast young, thou girdest thyself, and walkedst whither thou wouldest: but when thou shalt be old, thou shalt stretch forth thy hands, and another shall gird thee, and carry thee whither thou wouldest not. **19** This spake he, signifying by what death he should glorify God. And when he had spoken this, he saith unto him, Follow me.

20 Then Peter, turning about, seeth the disciple whom Jesus loved following; which also leaned on his breast at supper, and said, Lord, which is he that betrayeth thee? 21 Peter seeing him saith to Jesus, Lord, and what shall this man do? 22 Jesus saith unto him, If I will that he tarry till I come, what is that to thee? follow thou me.
23 Then went this saying abroad among the brethren, that that disciple should not die: yet Jesus said not unto him, He shall not die; but, If I will that he tarry till I come, what is that to thee?

Evidence of John's Authorship and His Purpose.
24 This is the disciple which testifieth of these things, and wrote these things: and we know that his testimony is true. 25 And there are also many other things which Jesus did, the which, if they should be written every one, I suppose that even the world itself could not contain the books that should be written. Amen.

Knowledge of, and belief in, the death, burial resurrection and physical appearances of Jesus Christ are very important to Christendom. They are the major factors that distinguish Christianity from the various religions. The founders of all the religions died and remain dead and buried till the forthcoming general resurrection. But Jesus Christ died, was buried, arose as He said He would, and remains alive forever.

Ascension of the Messiah.

The psalmist (King David), who lived about one thousand years before Jesus Christ was born, foretold the ascension of Jesus Christ into heaven when he wrote:

Psalm 24:7-10 "Lift up your heads, O ye gates; and be ye lift up, ye everlasting doors; and the King of glory shall come in. 8 Who is this King of glory? The Lord strong and mighty, the Lord mighty in battle. 9 Lift up your heads, O ye gates; even lift them up, ye everlasting doors; and the King of glory shall come in. 10 Who is this King of glory? The Lord of hosts, he is the King of glory.

Psalm 68:18 "Thou hast ascended on high, thou hast led captivity captive: thou hast received gifts for men; yea, for the rebellious also, that the Lord God might dwell among them.

While carrying out His ministry Jesus Christ also predicted His ascension into heaven as found in the following passages:

John 6:62 "What and if ye shall see the Son of man ascend up where he was before?"

John 7:33-34 "Then said Jesus unto them, Yet a little while am I with you, and then I go unto him that sent me. 34 Ye shall seek me, and shall not find me: and where I am, thither ye cannot come."

John 16:5 "But now I go my way to him that sent me; and none of you asketh me, Whither goest thou?"

John 14:2 "In my Father's house are many mansions: if it were not so, I would have told you. I go to prepare a place for you."

John 14:12 "Verily, verily, I say unto you, He that believeth on me, the works that I do shall he do also; and greater works than these shall he do; because I go unto my Father."

John 14:28 "Ye have heard how I said unto you, I go away, and come again unto you. If ye loved me, ye would rejoice, because I said, I go unto the Father: for my Father is greater than I."

John 16:28 "I came forth from the Father, and am come into the world: again, I leave the world, and go to the Father.

Somebody may argue that the location or place of the Father to Whom Jesus said He was returning is not known. This would not be right. When Jesus Christ earlier taught His disciples how to pray, the prayer format began thus: "... *Our Father, Which art in heaven, ..."* (Matthew 6:9).

The gospels and the Acts of the Apostles say that after commissioning His disciples to go and make disciples of all nations, Jesus Christ bodily and physically ascended into heaven while the disciples were watching and continued to gaze into the sky.

Further more, as regards His return to earth He said, "*And then shall appear the sign of the Son of man in heaven: and then shall all the tribes of the earth mourn, and they shall see the Son of man coming in the clouds of heaven with power and great glory*" (Matthew 24:30). That implies that He will come down from above. God lives in heaven ABOVE!

Mark 16:15-20 "And he said unto them, Go ye into all the world, and preach the gospel to every creature. 16 He that believeth and is baptized shall be saved; but he that believeth not shall be damned. 17 And these signs shall follow them that believe; In my name shall they cast out devils; they shall speak with new tongues; 18 They shall take up serpents; and if they drink any deadly thing, it shall not hurt them; they shall lay hands on the sick, and they shall recover. 19 So then after the Lord had spoken unto them, he was received up into heaven, and sat on the right hand of God. 20 And they went forth, and preached every where, the Lord working with them, and confirming the word with signs following. Amen.

Luke 24:50-53 "And he led them out as far as to Bethany, and he lifted up his hands, and blessed them. 51 And it came to pass, while he blessed them, he was parted from them, and carried up into heaven. 52 And they worshipped him, and returned to Jerusalem with great joy: 53 And were continually in the temple, praising and blessing God. Amen.

Acts 1:6-11 "When they therefore were come together, they asked of him, saying, Lord, wilt thou at this time restore again the kingdom to Israel? 7 And he said unto them, It is not for you to know the times or the seasons, which the Father hath put in his own power. 8 But ye shall receive power, after that the Holy Ghost is come upon you: and ye shall be witnesses unto me both in Jerusalem, and in all Judaea, and in Samaria, and unto the uttermost part of the earth.
9 And when he had spoken these things, while they beheld, he was taken up; and a cloud received him out of their sight. 10 And while they looked stedfastly toward heaven as he went up, behold, two men stood by them in white apparel; 11 Which also said, Ye men of Galilee, why stand ye gazing up into heaven? this same Jesus, which is taken up from you into heaven, shall so come in like manner as ye have seen him go into heaven.

The apostle Paul beautifully summarized the incarnation of Christ, His holiness, ministry and departure from earth in his letter to Timothy as follows:

1 Timothy 3:16 "And without controversy great is the mystery of godliness: God was manifest in the flesh, justified in the Spirit, seen of angels, preached unto the Gentiles, believed on in the world, received up into glory.

CHAPTER 7

THE COMING OF THE HOLY SPIRIT.

The Holy Spirit is the third Person of the Holy Trinity – God the Father, God the Son and God the Holy Spirit. The Holy Spirit is invisible and intangible. However, over the ages He is symbolized in Scriptures by such elements as water, oil, wind, dove, etc. He has all the attributes of God because He is God, inseparable from the other Persons of the Triune God.

In the Old Testament it is recorded that Prophet Isaiah prophesied that the character/personality of the Messiah would include having the Spirit of God on Him and delighting in the fear and righteousness of the Lord. The prophecy is as follows:

Isaiah 11:2-5 "And the spirit of the Lord shall rest upon him, the spirit of wisdom and understanding, the spirit of counsel and might, the spirit of knowledge and of the fear of the Lord; 3 And shall make him of quick understanding in the fear of the Lord: and he shall not judge after the sight of his eyes, neither reprove after the hearing of his ears: 4 But with righteousness shall he judge the poor, and reprove with equity for the meek of the earth: and he shall smite the earth: with the rod of his mouth, and with the breath of his lips shall he slay the wicked. 5 And righteousness shall be the girdle of his loins, and faithfulness the girdle of his reins.

Isaiah 61:1-2 "The Spirit of the Lord God is upon me; because the Lord hath anointed me to preach good tidings unto the meek; he hath sent me to bind up the brokenhearted, to proclaim liberty to the captives, and the opening of the prison to them that are bound; 2 To proclaim the acceptable year of the Lord, and the day of vengeance of our God; to comfort all that mourn.

The fulfillment:

Luke 4:18-21 "The Spirit of the Lord is upon me, because he hath anointed me to preach the gospel to the poor; he hath sent me to heal the brokenhearted, to preach deliverance to the captives, and recovering of sight to the blind, to set at liberty them that are bruised, 19 To preach the acceptable year of the Lord. 20 And he closed the book, and he gave it again to the minister, and sat down. And the eyes of all them that were in the synagogue were fastened on him. 21 And he began to say unto them, This day is this scripture fulfilled in your ears.

From the inception of the First Advent of Jesus Christ, the Holy Spirit had all along been involved – from the Immaculate Conception through the earthly ministry of

Jesus to the end of all the events of this Church Age.[18] Briefly we shall take a look below into some of the roles of the Holy Spirit in making the advents of the Messiah a reality in fulfillment of the prophecies.

I. At the Immaculate Conception of Christ.

Jesus Christ has been described as the only sinless man that has walked this earth. This is largely accounted for by the fact that though He was born of a virgin woman, Mary yet His conception was not by the will and or contribution/intervention of any sinful man. Before the pregnancy the angel Gabriel from God visited Mary and announced to her that the Holy Spirit would overshadow her, which would result in the pregnancy of the Son of God that would save His people. The relevant narrative is in Luke's gospel.

Jesus Christ's Birth Announced to Mary.

Luke 1:26-38 "And in the sixth month the angel Gabriel was sent from God unto a city of Galilee, named Nazareth, 27 To a virgin espoused to a man whose name was Joseph, of the house of David; and the virgin's name was Mary. 28 And the angel came in unto her, and said, Hail, thou that art highly favoured, the Lord is with thee: blessed art thou among women.
29 And when she saw him, she was troubled at his saying, and cast in her mind what manner of salutation this should be. 30 And the angel said unto her, Fear not, Mary: for thou hast found favour with God. 31 And, behold, thou shalt conceive in thy womb, and bring forth a son, and shalt call his name Jesus. 32 He shall be great, and shall be called the Son of the Highest: and the Lord God shall give unto him the throne of his father David: 33 And he shall reign over the house of Jacob for ever; and of his kingdom there shall be no end.
34 Then said Mary unto the angel, How shall this be, seeing I know not a man? 35 And the angel answered and said unto her, The Holy Ghost shall come upon thee, and the power of the Highest shall overshadow thee: therefore also that holy thing which shall be born of thee shall be called the Son of God.
36 And, behold, thy cousin Elisabeth, she hath also conceived a son in her old age: and this is the sixth month with her, who was called barren. 37 For with God nothing shall be impossible. 38 And Mary said, Behold the handmaid of the Lord; be it unto me according to thy word. And the angel departed from her.

---

[18] The Church Age: The period from the founding of the Church on the Day of Pentecost (as many theologians believe) until the day of the Rapture of the Church when the Church shall be joined to her Bridegroom – the Lord Jesus Christ.

Similarly, the same angel appeared to Joseph, to whom Mary was betrothed. He explained to Joseph that Mary's pregnancy was by the Holy Spirit, hence he should no longer consider putting her away (as a fornicator). This is in Matthew's account:

<u>Jesus Christ to Be Born of Mary – Announced To Joseph.</u>

Matthew 1:18-25 "Now the birth of Jesus Christ was on this wise: When as his mother Mary was espoused to Joseph, before they came together, she was found with child of the Holy Ghost. [19] Then Joseph her husband, being a just man, and not willing to make her a public example, was minded to put her away privily. [20] But while he thought on these things, behold, the angel of the Lord appeared unto him in a dream, saying, Joseph, thou son of David, fear not to take unto thee Mary thy wife: for that which is conceived in her is of the Holy Ghost. [21] And she shall bring forth a son, and thou shalt call his name Jesus: for he shall save his people from their sins.
[22] Now all this was done, that it might be fulfilled which was spoken of the Lord by the prophet, saying, [23] Behold, a virgin shall be with child, and shall bring forth a son, and they shall call his name Emmanuel, which being interpreted is, God with us. [24] Then Joseph being raised from sleep did as the angel of the Lord had bidden him, and took unto him his wife: [25] And knew her not till she had brought forth her firstborn son: and he called his name Jesus.

II. <u>At The Baptism And Temptation Of Jesus Christ.</u>

John the Baptist was baptizing people in the River Jordan and Jesus Christ also approached him to be baptized. Of course, while John was performing baptism of repentance, Jesus Christ had no sin to repent of. So, His was just "to fulfill all righteousness" and a way to identify with the people He came to save. The Holy Spirit descended as a dove on Jesus, anointing Him as He came out of the water.

Matthew 3:8-17 "Bring forth therefore fruits meet for repentance: [9] And think not to say within yourselves, We have Abraham to our father: for I say unto you, that God is able of these stones to raise up children unto Abraham. [10] And now also the axe is laid unto the root of the trees: therefore every tree which bringeth not forth good fruit is hewn down, and cast into the fire. [11] I indeed baptize you with water unto repentance. but he that cometh after me is mightier than I, whose shoes I am not worthy to bear: he shall baptize you with the Holy Ghost, and with fire: [12] Whose fan is in his hand, and he will throughly purge his floor, and gather his wheat into the garner; but he will burn up the chaff with unquenchable fire. [13] Then cometh Jesus from Galilee to Jordan unto John, to be baptized of him. [14] But John forbad him, saying, I have need to be baptized of thee, and comest thou to me?
[15] And Jesus answering said unto him, Suffer it to be so now: for thus it becometh us to fulfil all righteousness. Then he suffered him. [16] And Jesus, when he was baptized, went up straightway out of the water: and, lo, the heavens were opened unto him, and

he saw the Spirit of God descending like a dove, and lighting upon him: 17 And lo a voice from heaven, saying, This is my beloved Son, in whom I am well pleased.

After the baptism, the Spirit led Jesus Christ into the wilderness where He was tempted by the devil with Jesus coming out victorious. The Bible in the Epistle to the Hebrews says:

"For we have not an high priest which cannot be touched with the feeling of our infirmities; but was in all points tempted like as we are, yet without sin. (Hebrews 4:15)

III. Empowering The Disciples of Christ.

Prior to the crucifixion of Jesus Christ, He promised His disciples to send them the Holy Spirit for various purposes including to comfort them and remind them of all He had taught them.

John 14:16-18 "And I will pray the Father, and he shall give you another Comforter, that he may abide with you for ever; 17 Even the Spirit of truth; whom the world cannot receive, because it seeth him not, neither knoweth him: but ye know him; for he dwelleth with you, and shall be in you. 18 I will not leave you comfortless: I will come to you.

John 16:13-14 "Howbeit when he, the Spirit of truth, is come, he will guide you into all truth: for he shall not speak of himself; but whatsoever he shall hear, that shall he speak: and he will shew you things to come. 14 He shall glorify me: for he shall receive of mine, and shall shew it unto you.

Sequel to His resurrection, He further promised to send the disciples the Holy Spirit for their empowerment thus:

Acts 1:4-5, 8 "And, being assembled together with them, commanded them that they should not depart from Jerusalem, but wait for the promise of the Father, which, saith he, ye have heard of me. 5 For John truly baptized with water; but ye shall be baptized with the Holy Ghost not many days hence.
8 But ye shall receive power, after that the Holy Ghost is come upon you: and ye shall be witnesses unto me both in Jerusalem, and in all Judaea, and in Samaria, and unto the uttermost part of the earth."

Luke 24:49 "And, behold, I send the promise of my Father upon you: but tarry ye in the city of Jerusalem, until ye be endued with power from on high."

Jesus Christ made good the promises. On the Day of Pentecost the Holy Spirit came down upon the disciples in the Upper Room, where the 120 of them were prayerfully awaiting "the promise of the Father" (Luke 24:49), and He filled them all such that they all spoke in other tongues.

Coming of the Holy Spirit.

Acts 2:1-13 "And when the day of Pentecost was fully come, they were all with one accord in one place. 2 And suddenly there came a sound from heaven as of a rushing mighty wind, and it filled all the house where they were sitting. 3 And there appeared unto them cloven tongues like as of fire, and it sat upon each of them. 4 And they were all filled with the Holy Ghost, and began to speak with other tongues, as the Spirit gave them utterance. 5 And there were dwelling at Jerusalem Jews, devout men, out of every nation under heaven.
6 Now when this was noised abroad, the multitude came together, and were confounded, because that every man heard them speak in his own language. 7 And they were all amazed and marvelled, saying one to another, Behold, are not all these which speak Galilaeans? 8 And how hear we every man in our own tongue, wherein we were born? 9 Parthians, and Medes, and Elamites, and the dwellers in Mesopotamia, and in Judaea, and Cappadocia, in Pontus, and Asia, 10 Phrygia, and Pamphylia, in Egypt, and in the parts of Libya about Cyrene, and strangers of Rome, Jews and proselytes, 11 Cretes and Arabians, we do hear them speak in our tongues the wonderful works of God. 12 And they were all amazed, and were in doubt, saying one to another, What meaneth this?

Consequently the disciples, who had previously gone into hiding sequel to the crucifixion of their Lord became emboldened by the power of the Holy Spirit, to the extent that the apostle Peter preached his first challenging kerygma to which three thousand persons responded and were added in one day to the Church.

Acts 2:14-41 "But Peter, standing up with the eleven, lifted up his voice, and said unto them, Ye men of Judaea, and all ye that dwell at Jerusalem, be this known unto you, and hearken to my words: 15 For these are not drunken, as ye suppose, seeing it is but the third hour of the day.
16 But this is that which was spoken by the prophet Joel; 17 And it shall come to pass in the last days, saith God, I will pour out of my Spirit upon all flesh: and your sons and your daughters shall prophesy, and your young men shall see visions, and your old men shall dream dreams: 18 And on my servants and on my handmaidens I will pour out in those days of my Spirit; and they shall prophesy: 19 And I will shew wonders in heaven above, and signs in the earth beneath; blood, and fire, and vapour of smoke: 20 The sun shall be turned into darkness, and the moon into blood, before the great and notable day of the Lord come: 21 And it shall come to pass, that whosoever shall call on the name of the Lord shall be saved.
22 Ye men of Israel, hear these words; Jesus of Nazareth, a man approved of God among you by miracles and wonders and signs, which God did by him in the midst of you, as

ye yourselves also know: ²³ Him, being delivered by the determinate counsel and foreknowledge of God, ye have taken, and by wicked hands have crucified and slain: ²⁴ Whom God hath raised up, having loosed the pains of death: because it was not possible that he should be holden of it.

²⁵ For David speaketh concerning him, I foresaw the Lord always before my face, for he is on my right hand, that I should not be moved: ²⁶ Therefore did my heart rejoice, and my tongue was glad; moreover also my flesh shall rest in hope: ²⁷ Because thou wilt not leave my soul in hell, neither wilt thou suffer thine Holy One to see corruption. ²⁸ Thou hast made known to me the ways of life; thou shalt make me full of joy with thy countenance.

²⁹ Men and brethren, let me freely speak unto you of the patriarch David, that he is both dead and buried, and his sepulchre is with us unto this day. ³⁰ Therefore being a prophet, and knowing that God had sworn with an oath to him, that of the fruit of his loins, according to the flesh, he would raise up Christ to sit on his throne; ³¹ He seeing this before spake of the resurrection of Christ, that his soul was not left in hell, neither his flesh did see corruption. ³² This Jesus hath God raised up, whereof we all are witnesses.

³³ Therefore being by the right hand of God exalted, and having received of the Father the promise of the Holy Ghost, he hath shed forth this, which ye now see and hear. ³⁴ For David is not ascended into the heavens: but he saith himself, The Lord said unto my Lord, Sit thou on my right hand, ³⁵ Until I make thy foes thy footstool.

³⁶ Therefore let all the house of Israel know assuredly, that God hath made the same Jesus, whom ye have crucified, both Lord and Christ.

³⁷ Now when they heard this, they were pricked in their heart, and said unto Peter and to the rest of the apostles, Men and brethren, what shall we do? ³⁸ Then Peter said unto them, Repent, and be baptized every one of you in the name of Jesus Christ for the remission of sins, and ye shall receive the gift of the Holy Ghost. ³⁹ For the promise is unto you, and to your children, and to all that are afar off, even as many as the Lord our God shall call. ⁴⁰ And with many other words did he testify and exhort, saying, Save yourselves from this untoward generation. ⁴¹ Then they that gladly received his word were baptized: and the same day there were added unto them about three thousand souls.

Subsequently by the power of the Holy Spirit and in the name of Jesus Christ the apostles performed many miracles (*"And fear came upon every soul: and many wonders and signs were done by the apostles"* (Acts 2:43). For instance Peter and John in the name of Jesus Christ healed the cripple at the gate known as 'Beautiful,' a miracle that astonished the people around, causing Peter to peach his second kerygma:

Acts 3:12-26 "And when Peter saw it, he answered unto the people, Ye men of Israel, why marvel ye at this? or why look ye so earnestly on us, as though by our own power or holiness we had made this man to walk? ¹³ The God of Abraham, and of Isaac, and of Jacob, the God of our fathers, hath glorified his Son Jesus; whom ye delivered up, and denied him in the presence of Pilate, when he was determined to let him go. 14 But ye denied the Holy One and the Just, and desired a murderer to be granted unto you; 15 And killed the Prince of life, whom God hath raised from the dead; whereof we are witnesses. 16 And his name through faith in his name hath made this man strong, whom ye see and know: yea, the faith which is by him hath given him this perfect soundness in the presence of you all.

17 And now, brethren, I wot that through ignorance ye did it, as did also your rulers. 18 But those things, which God before had shewed by the mouth of all his prophets, that Christ should suffer, he hath so fulfilled. 19 Repent ye therefore, and be converted, that your sins may be blotted out, when the times of refreshing shall come from the presence of the Lord. 20 And he shall send Jesus Christ, which before was preached unto you: 21 Whom the heaven must receive until the times of restitution of all things, which God hath spoken by the mouth of all his holy prophets since the world began. 22 For Moses truly said unto the fathers, A prophet shall the Lord your God raise up unto you of your brethren, like unto me; him shall ye hear in all things whatsoever he shall say unto you. 23 And it shall come to pass, that every soul, which will not hear that prophet, shall be destroyed from among the people.

24 Yea, and all the prophets from Samuel and those that follow after, as many as have spoken, have likewise foretold of these days. 25 Ye are the children of the prophets, and of the covenant which God made with our fathers, saying unto Abraham, And in thy seed shall all the kindreds of the earth be blessed. 26 Unto you first God, having raised up his Son Jesus, sent him to bless you, in turning away every one of you from his iniquities.

This resulted in the arrest of Peter and John who were brought before the Sanhedrin the following day. Acts 4:8-20 really shows the boldness of the disciples due to their empowerment by the Holy Spirit, whom the Lord sent to them.

Acts 4:8-20 "Then Peter, filled with the Holy Ghost, said unto them, Ye rulers of the people, and elders of Israel, 9 If we this day be examined of the good deed done to the impotent man, by what means he is made whole; 10 Be it known unto you all, and to all the people of Israel, that by the name of Jesus Christ of Nazareth, whom ye crucified, whom God raised from the dead, even by him doth this man stand here before you whole.

11 This is the stone which was set at nought of you builders, which is become the head of the corner. 12 Neither is there salvation in any other: for there is none other name under heaven given among men, whereby we must be saved.

13 Now when they saw the boldness of Peter and John, and perceived that they were unlearned and ignorant men, they marvelled; and they took knowledge of them, that they had been with Jesus. 14 And beholding the man which was healed standing with them, they could say nothing against it. 15 But when they had commanded them to go aside out of the council, they conferred among themselves, 16 Saying, What shall we do to these men? for that indeed a notable miracle hath been done by them is manifest

to all them that dwell in Jerusalem; and we cannot deny it. [17] But that it spread no further among the people, let us straitly threaten them, that they speak henceforth to no man in this name.

[18] And they called them, and commanded them not to speak at all nor teach in the name of Jesus. [19] But Peter and John answered and said unto them, Whether it be right in the sight of God to hearken unto you more than unto God, judge ye. [20] For we cannot but speak the things which we have seen and heard.

This same Holy Spirit indwells everyone that believes in Jesus Christ as Lord and Savior. Many Bible passages say this. Some of such passages are:

Romans 8:9-11 "But ye are not in the flesh, but in the Spirit, if so be that the Spirit of God dwell in you. Now if any man have not the Spirit of Christ, he is none of his. [10] And if Christ be in you, the body is dead because of sin; but the Spirit is life because of righteousness. [11] But if the Spirit of him that raised up Jesus from the dead dwell in you, he that raised up Christ from the dead shall also quicken your mortal bodies by his Spirit that dwelleth in you.

1 Corinthians 3:16 "Know ye not that ye are the temple of God, and that the Spirit of God dwelleth in you?

1 Corinthians 6:19 "What? know ye not that your body is the temple of the Holy Ghost which is in you, which ye have of God, and ye are not your own?

Galatians 4:5-6 "To redeem them that were under the law, that we might receive the adoption of sons. [6] And because ye are sons, God hath sent forth the Spirit of his Son into your hearts, crying, Abba, Father.

Revelation 3:20 " Behold, I stand at the door, and knock: if any man hear my voice, and open the door, I will come in to him, and will sup with him, and he with me.

The Holy Spirit also gives gifts to individual believers in Christ for the purpose of edifying the Church of Christ. Some of such gifts are listed in Romans, 1 Corinthians and Ephesians.

Romans 12:6-8 "Having then gifts differing according to the grace that is given to us, whether prophecy, let us prophesy according to the proportion of faith; [7] Or ministry, let us wait on our ministering: or he that teacheth, on teaching; [8] Or he that exhorteth, on exhortation: he that giveth, let him do it with simplicity; he that ruleth, with diligence; he that sheweth mercy, with cheerfulness.

1 Corinthians 12:1-12 "Now concerning spiritual gifts, brethren, I would not have you ignorant. [2] Ye know that ye were Gentiles, carried away unto these dumb idols, even as ye were led. ³ Wherefore I give you to understand, that no man speaking by the Spirit of God calleth Jesus accursed: and that no man can say that Jesus is the Lord, but by the Holy Ghost. ⁴ Now there are diversities of gifts, but the same Spirit. ⁵ And there are differences of administrations, but the same Lord. ⁶ And there are diversities of operations, but it is the same God which worketh all in all.

⁷ But the manifestation of the Spirit is given to every man to profit withal. ⁸ For to one is given by the Spirit the word of wisdom; to another the word of knowledge by the same Spirit; ⁹ To another faith by the same Spirit; to another the gifts of healing by the same Spirit; ¹⁰ To another the working of miracles; to another prophecy; to another discerning of spirits; to another divers kinds of tongues; to another the interpretation of tongues: ¹¹ But all these worketh that one and the selfsame Spirit, dividing to every man severally as he will. ¹² For as the body is one, and hath many members, and all the members of that one body, being many, are one body: so also is Christ.

Ephesians 4:4-13 ⁴There is one body, and one Spirit, even as ye are called in one hope of your calling; ⁵ One Lord, one faith, one baptism, ⁶ One God and Father of all, who is above all, and through all, and in you all. ⁷ But unto every one of us is given grace according to the measure of the gift of Christ.

⁸ Wherefore he saith, When he ascended up on high, he led captivity captive, and gave gifts unto men. ⁹ (Now that he ascended, what is it but that he also descended first into the lower parts of the earth? ¹⁰ He that descended is the same also that ascended up far above all heavens, that he might fill all things.) ¹¹ And he gave some, apostles; and some, prophets; and some, evangelists; and some, pastors and teachers; ¹² For the perfecting of the saints, for the work of the ministry, for the edifying of the body of Christ: ¹³ Till we all come in the unity of the faith, and of the knowledge of the Son of God, unto a perfect man, unto the measure of the stature of the fulness of Christ:

CHAPTER 8

PROPHECIES IN THE OLD TESTAMENT AND NEW TESTAMENT ABOUT THE FUTURE RETURN AND MINISTRY OF THE MESSIAH

The only messianic prophecies that are yet to be fulfilled are those of the end times, including mainly the second coming of Jesus Christ to reign as King of kings and Lord of lords in His millennial kingdom. These prophecies are stated below in two parts – Old Testament prophecies and New Testament prophecies.

OLD TESTAMENT PROPHECIES OF MESSIAH'S FUTURE RETURN.

The Triumph and Kingdom of the Messiah
Psalm 2:1-12 "Why do the heathen rage, and the people imagine a vain thing? 2 The kings of the earth set themselves, and the rulers take counsel together, against the Lord, and against his anointed, saying, 3 Let us break their bands asunder, and cast away their cords from us. 4 He that sitteth in the heavens shall laugh: the Lord shall have them in derision.
5 Then shall he speak unto them in his wrath, and vex them in his sore displeasure.
6 Yet have I set my king upon my holy hill of Zion. 7 I will declare the decree: the Lord hath said unto me, Thou art my Son; this day have I begotten thee. 8 Ask of me, and I shall give thee the heathen for thine inheritance, and the uttermost parts of the earth for thy possession. 9 Thou shalt break them with a rod of iron; thou shalt dash them in pieces like a potter's vessel.
10 Be wise now therefore, O ye kings: be instructed, ye judges of the earth. 11 Serve the Lord with fear, and rejoice with trembling. 12 Kiss the Son, lest he be angry, and ye perish from the way, when his wrath is kindled but a little. Blessed are all they that put their trust in him.

The Coming of the Righteous Judge.
Psalm 50:2-6 "Out of Zion, the perfection of beauty, God hath shined. 3 Our God shall come, and shall not keep silence: a fire shall devour before him, and it shall be very tempestuous round about him. 4 He shall call to the heavens from above, and to the earth, that he may judge his people. 5 Gather my saints together unto me; those that have made a covenant with me by 139,. 6 And the heavens shall declare his righteousness: for God is judge himself.

Messiah Will Return to Judge.
Psalm 96:13 "Before the Lord: for he cometh, for he cometh to judge the earth: he shall judge the world with righteousness, and the people with his truth.

Psalm 110:1 "The Lord said unto my Lord, Sit thou at my right hand, until I make thine enemies thy footstool."

The judgment of God is going to be carried out by Jesus Christ, to whom God the

Father has delegated it. Jesus Christ and His apostles confirmed this claim in the New Testament. Read the following NT passages:

John 5:22 "For the Father judgeth no man, but hath committed all judgment unto the Son:"

Acts 17:30-31 "And the times of this ignorance God winked at; but now commandeth all men every where to repent: [31] Because he hath appointed a day, in the which he will judge the world in righteousness by that man whom he hath ordained; whereof he hath given assurance unto all men, in that he hath raised him from the dead."

Romans 2:16 "In the day when God shall judge the secrets of men by Jesus Christ according to my gospel."

Revelation 19:11 "And I saw heaven opened, and behold a white horse; and he that sat upon him was called Faithful and True, and in righteousness he doth judge and make war."

<u>Messiah Will Run an Endless, Great and Peaceful Government.</u>

Isaiah 9:6–7 "For unto us a child is born, unto us a son is given: and the government shall be upon his shoulder: and his name shall be called Wonderful, Counsellor, The mighty God, The everlasting Father, The Prince of Peace. [7] Of the increase of his government and peace there shall be no end, upon the throne of David, and upon his kingdom, to order it, and to establish it with judgment and with justice from henceforth even for ever. The zeal of the Lord of hosts will perform this."

<u>Messiah Shall Gather All Nations to Worship</u>

Isaiah 66:18-23 "For I know their works and their thoughts: it shall come, that I will gather all nations and tongues; and they shall come, and see my glory. [19] And I will set a sign among them, and I will send those that escape of them unto the nations, to Tarshish, Pul, and Lud, that draw the bow, to Tubal, and Javan, to the isles afar off, that have not heard my fame, neither have seen my glory; and they shall declare my glory among the Gentiles.
[20] And they shall bring all your brethren for an offering unto the Lord out of all nations upon horses, and in chariots, and in litters, and upon mules, and upon swift beasts, to my holy mountain Jerusalem, saith the Lord, as the children of Israel bring an offering in a clean vessel into the house of the Lord. [21] And I will also take of them for priests and for Levites, saith the Lord. [22] For as the new heavens and the new earth, which I will make, shall remain before me, saith the Lord, so shall your seed and your name remain. [23] And it shall come to pass, that from one new moon to another, and from one sabbath to another, shall all flesh come to worship before me, saith the Lord.

Messiah Will Reign Forever on David's Throne.

Ezekiel 37:24-28 "And David my servant shall be king over them; and they all shall have one shepherd: they shall also walk in my judgments, and observe my statutes, and do them. 25 And they shall dwell in the land that I have given unto Jacob my servant, wherein your fathers have dwelt; and they shall dwell therein, even they, and their children, and their children's children for ever: and my servant David shall be their prince for ever. 26 Moreover I will make a covenant of peace with them; it shall be an everlasting covenant with them: and I will place them, and multiply them, and will set my sanctuary in the midst of them for evermore. 27 My tabernacle also shall be with them: yea, I will be their God, and they shall be my people.28 And the heathen shall know that I the Lord do sanctify Israel, when my sanctuary shall be in the midst of them for evermore."

The Messiah Will Come Back With Power.

Daniel 7:13-14 "I saw in the night visions, and, behold, one like the Son of man came with the clouds of heaven, and came to the Ancient of days, and they brought him near before him.14 And there was given him dominion, and glory, and a kingdom, that all people, nations, and languages, should serve him: his dominion is an everlasting dominion, which shall not pass away, and his kingdom that which shall not be destroyed."

Messiah Will Return, Conquer and Reign

Zechariah 14:1-9 "Behold, the day of the Lord cometh, and thy spoil shall be divided in the midst of thee. 2 For I will gather all nations against Jerusalem to battle; and the city shall be taken, and the houses rifled, and the women ravished; and half of the city shall go forth into captivity, and the residue of the people shall not be cut off from the city. 3 Then shall the Lord go forth, and fight against those nations, as when he fought in the day of battle.
4 And his feet shall stand in that day upon the mount of Olives, which is before Jerusalem on the east, and the mount of Olives shall cleave in the midst thereof toward the east and toward the west, and there shall be a very great valley; and half of the mountain shall remove toward the north, and half of it toward the south. 5 And ye shall flee to the valley of the mountains; for the valley of the mountains shall reach unto Azal: yea, ye shall flee, like as ye fled from before the earthquake in the days of Uzziah king of Judah: and the Lord my God shall come, and all the saints with thee. 6 And it shall come to pass in that day, that the light shall not be clear, nor dark: 7 But it shall be one day which shall be known to the Lord, not day, nor night: but it shall come to pass, that at evening time it shall be light. 8 And it shall be in that day, that living waters shall go out from Jerusalem; half of them toward the former sea, and half of them toward the hinder sea: in summer and in winter shall it be. 9 And the Lord shall be king over all the earth: in that day shall there be one Lord, and his name one."

NEW TESTAMENT PROPHECIES OF MESSIAH'S FUTURE RETURN.

In the New Testament Jesus Christ Himself prophesied His future return in the gospels. Some prophecies by Jesus Christ are in the form of parables or in answer to questions. His apostles also mentioned it in their epistles. The records of these prophecies are as follows:

Prophecies Of Messiah's Future Return By Jesus In The Gospels.

Matthew 16:27-28 "For the Son of man shall come in the glory of his Father with his angels; and then he shall reward every man according to his works. 28 Verily I say unto you, There be some standing here, which shall not taste of death, till they see the Son of man coming in his kingdom.

Matthew 19:28-30 "And Jesus said unto them, Verily I say unto you, That ye which have followed me, in the regeneration when the Son of man shall sit in the throne of his glory, ye also shall sit upon twelve thrones, judging the twelve tribes of Israel.
29 And every one that hath forsaken houses, or brethren, or sisters, or father, or mother, or wife, or children, or lands, for my name's sake, shall receive an hundredfold, and shall inherit everlasting life. 30 But many that are first shall be last; and the last shall be first.

Mark 10:29-30 "And Jesus answered and said, Verily I say unto you, There is no man that hath left house, or brethren, or sisters, or father, or mother, or wife, or children, or lands, for my sake, and the gospel's, 30 But he shall receive an hundredfold now in this time, houses, and brethren, and sisters, and mothers, and children, and lands, with persecutions; and in the world to come eternal life.

Matthew 23:39 "For I say unto you, Ye shall not see me henceforth, till ye shall say, Blessed is he that cometh in the name of the Lord.

Matthew 24:3-51
The Signs of the Times and the End of the Age
"And as he sat upon the mount of Olives, the disciples came unto him privately, saying, Tell us, when shall these things be? and what shall be the sign of thy coming, and of the end of the world?
4 And Jesus answered and said unto them, Take heed that no man deceive you. 5 For many shall come in my name, saying, I am Christ; and shall deceive many. 6 And ye shall hear of wars and rumours of wars: see that ye be not troubled: for all these things must come to pass, but the end is not yet. 7 For nation shall rise against nation, and kingdom against kingdom: and there shall be famines, and pestilences, and earthquakes, in divers places. 8 All these are the beginning of sorrows.
9 Then shall they deliver you up to be afflicted, and shall kill you: and ye shall be hated of all nations for my name's sake. 10 And then shall many be offended, and shall betray one another, and shall hate one another. 11 And many false prophets shall rise, and shall deceive many. 12 And because iniquity shall abound, the love of many shall wax cold. 13 But he that shall endure unto the end, the same shall be saved. 14 And this

gospel of the kingdom shall be preached in all the world for a witness unto all nations; and then shall the end come.

The Great Tribulation

15 When ye therefore shall see the abomination of desolation, spoken of by Daniel the prophet, stand in the holy place, (whoso readeth, let him understand:) 16 Then let them which be in Judaea flee into the mountains: 17 Let him which is on the housetop not come down to take any thing out of his house: 18 Neither let him which is in the field return back to take his clothes. 19 And woe unto them that are with child, and to them that give suck in those days! 20 But pray ye that your flight be not in the winter, neither on the sabbath day: 21 For then shall be great tribulation, such as was not since the beginning of the world to this time, no, nor ever shall be. 22 And except those days should be shortened, there should no flesh be saved: but for the elect's sake those days shall be shortened.

23 Then if any man shall say unto you, Lo, here is Christ, or there; believe it not. 24 For there shall arise false Christs, and false prophets, and shall shew great signs and wonders; insomuch that, if it were possible, they shall deceive the very elect. 25 Behold, I have told you before. 26 Wherefore if they shall say unto you, Behold, he is in the desert; go not forth: behold, he is in the secret chambers; believe it not.

27 For as the lightning cometh out of the east, and shineth even unto the west; so shall also the coming of the Son of man be. 28 For wheresoever the carcase is, there will the eagles be gathered together.

The Appearing of the Son of Man

29 Immediately after the tribulation of those days shall the sun be darkened, and the moon shall not give her light, and the stars shall fall from heaven, and the powers of the heavens shall be shaken:

30 And then shall appear the sign of the Son of man in heaven: and then shall all the tribes of the earth mourn, and they shall see the Son of man coming in the clouds of heaven with power and great glory. 31 And he shall send his angels with a great sound of a trumpet, and they shall gather together his elect from the four winds, from one end of heaven to the other.

Parable of the Fig Tree

32 Now learn a parable of the fig tree; When his branch is yet tender, and putteth forth leaves, ye know that summer is nigh: 33 So likewise ye, when ye shall see all these things, know that it is near, even at the doors. 34 Verily I say unto you, This generation shall not pass, till all these things be fulfilled. 35 Heaven and earth shall pass away, but my words shall not pass away.

No One Knows the Day or Hour

36 But of that day and hour knoweth no man, no, not the angels of heaven, but my Father only. 37 But as the days of Noah were, so shall also the coming of the Son of man be. 38 For as in the days that were before the flood they were eating and drinking, marrying and giving in marriage, until the day that Noe entered into the ark, 39 And

knew not until the flood came, and took them all away; so shall also the coming of the Son of man be.

⁴⁰ Then shall two be in the field; the one shall be taken, and the other left. ⁴¹ Two women shall be grinding at the mill; the one shall be taken, and the other left. ⁴² Watch therefore: for ye know not what hour your Lord doth come. ⁴³ But know this, that if the goodman of the house had known in what watch the thief would come, he would have watched, and would not have suffered his house to be broken up. ⁴⁴ Therefore be ye also ready: for in such an hour as ye think not the Son of man cometh.

Parable of the Faithful Servant and the Evil Servant

⁴⁵ Who then is a faithful and wise servant, whom his lord hath made ruler over his household, to give them meat in due season? ⁴⁶ Blessed is that servant, whom his lord when he cometh shall find so doing. ⁴⁷ Verily I say unto you, That he shall make him ruler over all his goods. ⁴⁸ But and if that evil servant shall say in his heart, My lord delayeth his coming; ⁴⁹ And shall begin to smite his fellowservants, and to eat and drink with the drunken; ⁵⁰ The lord of that servant shall come in a day when he looketh not for him, and in an hour that he is not aware of, ⁵¹ And shall cut him asunder, and appoint him his portion with the hypocrites: there shall be weeping and gnashing of teeth.

Matthew 25:1-46

Parable of the Wise and Foolish Virgins

"Then shall the kingdom of heaven be likened unto ten virgins, which took their lamps, and went forth to meet the bridegroom. ² And five of them were wise, and five were foolish. ³ They that were foolish took their lamps, and took no oil with them: ⁴ But the wise took oil in their vessels with their lamps. ⁵ While the bridegroom tarried, they all slumbered and slept. ⁶ And at midnight there was a cry made, Behold, the bridegroom cometh; go ye out to meet him. ⁷ Then all those virgins arose, and trimmed their lamps. ⁸ And the foolish said unto the wise, Give us of your oil; for our lamps are gone out. ⁹ But the wise answered, saying, Not so; lest there be not enough for us and you: but go ye rather to them that sell, and buy for yourselves.

¹⁰ And while they went to buy, the bridegroom came; and they that were ready went in with him to the marriage: and the door was shut. ¹¹ Afterward came also the other virgins, saying, Lord, Lord, open to us. ¹² But he answered and said, Verily I say unto you, I know you not. ¹³ Watch therefore, for ye know neither the day nor the hour wherein the Son of man cometh.

Parable of the Talents

¹⁴ For the kingdom of heaven is as a man travelling into a far country, who called his own servants, and delivered unto them his goods. ¹⁵ And unto one he gave five talents, to another two, and to another one; to every man according to his several ability; and straightway took his journey. ¹⁶ Then he that had received the five talents went and traded with the same, and made them other five talents. ¹⁷ And likewise he that had received two, he also gained other two. ¹⁸ But he that had received one went and digged in the earth, and hid his lord's money.

¹⁹ After a long time the lord of those servants cometh, and reckoneth with them. ²⁰ And so he that had received five talents came and brought other five talents, saying, Lord, thou deliveredst unto me five talents: behold, I have gained beside them five talents more. ²¹ His lord said unto him, Well done, thou good and faithful servant: thou hast been faithful over a few things, I will make thee ruler over many things: enter thou into the joy of thy lord.

²² He also that had received two talents came and said, Lord, thou deliveredst unto me two talents: behold, I have gained two other talents beside them. ²³ His lord said unto him, Well done, good and faithful servant; thou hast been faithful over a few things, I will make thee ruler over many things: enter thou into the joy of thy lord. ²⁴ Then he which had received the one talent came and said, Lord, I knew thee that thou art an hard man, reaping where thou hast not sown, and gathering where thou hast not strawed: ²⁵ And I was afraid, and went and hid thy talent in the earth: lo, there thou hast that is thine. ²⁶ His lord answered and said unto him, Thou wicked and slothful servant, thou knewest that I reap where I sowed not, and gather where I have not strawed: ²⁷ Thou oughtest therefore to have put my money to the exchangers, and then at my coming I should have received mine own with usury.

²⁸ Take therefore the talent from him, and give it unto him which hath ten talents.

²⁹ For unto every one that hath shall be given, and he shall have abundance: but from him that hath not shall be taken away even that which he hath. ³⁰ And cast ye the unprofitable servant into outer darkness: there shall be weeping and gnashing of teeth.

The Son of Man to Judge the Nations

³¹ When the Son of man shall come in his glory, and all the holy angels with him, then shall he sit upon the throne of his glory: ³² And before him shall be gathered all nations: and he shall separate them one from another, as a shepherd divideth his sheep from the goats: ³³ And he shall set the sheep on his right hand, but the goats on the left.

³⁴ Then shall the King say unto them on his right hand, Come, ye blessed of my Father, inherit the kingdom prepared for you from the foundation of the world: ³⁵ For I was an hungred, and ye gave me meat: I was thirsty, and ye gave me drink: I was a stranger, and ye took me in: ³⁶ Naked, and ye clothed me: I was sick, and ye visited me: I was in prison, and ye came unto me.

³⁷ Then shall the righteous answer him, saying, Lord, when saw we thee an hungred, and fed thee? or thirsty, and gave thee drink? ³⁸ When saw we thee a stranger, and took thee in? or naked, and clothed thee? ³⁹ Or when saw we thee sick, or in prison, and came unto thee? ⁴⁰ And the King shall answer and say unto them, Verily I say unto you, Inasmuch as ye have done it unto one of the least of these my brethren, ye have done it unto me.

⁴¹ Then shall he say also unto them on the left hand, Depart from me, ye cursed, into everlasting fire, prepared for the devil and his angels: ⁴² For I was an hungred, and ye gave me no meat: I was thirsty, and ye gave me no drink: ⁴³ I was a stranger, and ye took me not in: naked, and ye clothed me not: sick, and in prison, and ye visited me not. ⁴⁴ Then shall they also answer him, saying, Lord, when saw we thee an hungred, or athirst, or a stranger, or naked, or sick, or in prison, and did not minister unto thee?

⁴⁵ Then shall he answer them, saying, Verily I say unto you, Inasmuch as ye did it not to one of the least of these, ye did it not to me. ⁴⁶ And these shall go away into everlasting punishment: but the righteous into life eternal."

Matthew 26:64 "Jesus saith unto him, Thou hast said: nevertheless I say unto you, Hereafter shall ye see the Son of man sitting on the right hand of power, and coming in the clouds of heaven."

Mark 9:1 "And he said unto them, Verily I say unto you, That there be some of them that stand here, which shall not taste of death, till they have seen the kingdom of God come with power."

Jesus Shall Come Again in His Greatness

Mark 13:24-37 "But in those days, after that tribulation, the sun shall be darkened, and the moon shall not give her light, ²⁵ And the stars of heaven shall fall, and the powers that are in heaven shall be shaken. ²⁶ And then shall they see the Son of man coming in the clouds with great power and glory. ²⁷ And then shall he send his angels, and shall gather together his elect from the four winds, from the uttermost part of the earth to the uttermost part of heaven.
²⁸ Now learn a parable of the fig tree; When her branch is yet tender, and putteth forth leaves, ye know that summer is near: ²⁹ So ye in like manner, when ye shall see these things come to pass, know that it is nigh, even at the doors. ³⁰ Verily I say unto you, that this generation shall not pass, till all these things be done. ³¹ Heaven and earth shall pass away: but my words shall not pass away. ³² But of that day and that hour knoweth no man, no, not the angels which are in heaven, neither the Son, but the Father.
³³ Take ye heed, watch and pray: for ye know not when the time is. ³⁴ For the Son of Man is as a man taking a far journey, who left his house, and gave authority to his servants, and to every man his work, and commanded the porter to watch. ³⁵ Watch ye therefore: for ye know not when the master of the house cometh, at even, or at midnight, or at the cockcrowing, or in the morning: ³⁶ Lest coming suddenly he find you sleeping. ³⁷ And what I say unto you I say unto all, Watch."

Luke 9:26 "For whosoever shall be ashamed of me and of my words, of him shall the Son of man be ashamed, when he shall come in his own glory, and in his Father's, and of the holy angels."

Jesus Says to Be Ready.
Luke 12:35-48 "Let your loins be girded about, and your lights burning; ³⁶ And ye yourselves like unto men that wait for their lord, when he will return from the wedding; that when he cometh and knocketh, they may open unto him immediately. ³⁷ Blessed are those servants, whom the lord when he cometh shall find watching: verily I say unto you, that he shall gird himself, and make them to sit down to meat, and will come forth and serve them. ³⁸ And if he shall come in the second watch, or come in the third watch, and find them so, blessed are those servants. ³⁹ And this

know, that if the goodman of the house had known what hour the thief would come, he would have watched, and not have suffered his house to be broken through. ⁴⁰ Be ye therefore ready also: for the Son of man cometh at an hour when ye think not.

⁴¹ Then Peter said unto him, Lord, speakest thou this parable unto us, or even to all?

⁴² And the Lord said, Who then is that faithful and wise steward, whom his lord shall make ruler over his household, to give them their portion of meat in due season? ⁴³ Blessed is that servant, whom his lord when he cometh shall find so doing. ⁴⁴ Of a truth I say unto you, that he will make him ruler over all that he hath. ⁴⁵ But and if that servant say in his heart, My lord delayeth his coming; and shall begin to beat the menservants and maidens, and to eat and drink, and to be drunken; ⁴⁶ The lord of that servant will come in a day when he looketh not for him, and at an hour when he is not aware, and will cut him in sunder, and will appoint him his portion with the unbelievers.

⁴⁷ And that servant, which knew his lord's will, and prepared not himself, neither did according to his will, shall be beaten with many stripes. ⁴⁸ But he that knew not, and did commit things worthy of stripes, shall be beaten with few stripes. For unto whomsoever much is given, of him shall be much required: and to whom men have committed much, of him they will ask the more."

Jesus Tells of His Second Coming

Luke 17:22-37 "And he said unto the disciples, The days will come, when ye shall desire to see one of the days of the Son of man, and ye shall not see it. ²³ And they shall say to you, See here; or, see there: go not after them, nor follow them.

²⁴ For as the lightning, that lighteneth out of the one part under heaven, shineth unto the other part under heaven; so shall also the Son of man be in his day. ²⁵ But first must he suffer many things, and be rejected of this generation. ²⁶ And as it was in the days of Noe, so shall it be also in the days of the Son of man. ²⁷ They did eat, they drank, they married wives, they were given in marriage, until the day that Noah entered into the ark, and the flood came, and destroyed them all. ²⁸ Likewise also as it was in the days of Lot; they did eat, they drank, they bought, they sold, they planted, they builded;

²⁹ But the same day that Lot went out of Sodom it rained fire and brimstone from heaven, and destroyed them all. ³⁰ Even thus shall it be in the day when the Son of man is revealed. ³¹ In that day, he which shall be upon the housetop, and his stuff in the house, let him not come down to take it away: and he that is in the field, let him likewise not return back.

³² Remember Lot's wife. ³³ Whosoever shall seek to save his life shall lose it; and whosoever shall lose his life shall preserve it. ³⁴ I tell you, in that night there shall be two men in one bed; the one shall be taken, and the other shall be left. ³⁵ Two women shall be grinding together; the one shall be taken, and the other left. ³⁶ Two men shall be in the field; the one shall be taken, and the other left. ³⁷ And they answered and said unto him, Where, Lord? And he said unto them, Wheresoever the body is, thither will the eagles be gathered together."

Luke 18:8 "I tell you that he will avenge them speedily. Nevertheless when the Son of man cometh, shall he find faith on the earth?"

Luke 19:15 "And it came to pass, that when he was returned, having received the kingdom, then he commanded these servants to be called unto him, to whom he had given the money, that he might know how much every man had gained by trading."

Luke 21:25-28 "And there shall be signs in the sun, and in the moon, and in the stars; and upon the earth distress of nations, with perplexity; the sea and the waves roaring; 26 Men's hearts failing them for fear, and for looking after those things which are coming on the earth: for the powers of heaven shall be shaken. 27 And then shall they see the Son of man coming in a cloud with power and great glory. 28 And when these things begin to come to pass, then look up, and lift up your heads; for your redemption draweth nigh.

John 14:1-3 "Let not your heart be troubled: ye believe in God, believe also in me. 2 In my Father's house are many mansions: if it were not so, I would have told you. I go to prepare a place for you. 3 And if I go and prepare a place for you, I will come again, and receive you unto myself; that where I am, there ye may be also."

John 14:18-20 "I will not leave you comfortless: I will come to you. 19 Yet a little while, and the world seeth me no more; but ye see me: because I live, ye shall live also. 20 At that day ye shall know that I am in my Father, and ye in me, and I in you."

Prophecies Of Messiah's Future Return According to Paul In His Epistles.

1 Corinthians 1:4-8 "I thank my God always on your behalf, for the grace of God which is given you by Jesus Christ; 5 That in every thing ye are enriched by him, in all utterance, and in all knowledge; 6 Even as the testimony of Christ was confirmed in you: 7 So that ye come behind in no gift; waiting for the coming of our Lord Jesus Christ: 8 Who shall also confirm you unto the end, that ye may be blameless in the day of our Lord Jesus Christ."

1 Corinthians 5:4-5 "In the name of our Lord Jesus Christ, when ye are gathered together, and my spirit, with the power of our Lord Jesus Christ, 5 To deliver such an one unto Satan for the destruction of the flesh, that the spirit may be saved in the day of the Lord Jesus."

1 Corinthians 11:26 "For as often as ye eat this bread, and drink this cup, ye do shew the Lord's death till he come."

1 Corinthians 15:21-25 "For since by man came death, by man came also the resurrection of the dead. 22 For as in Adam all die, even so in Christ shall all be made alive. 23 But every man in his own order: Christ the firstfruits; afterward they that are Christ's at his coming. 24 Then cometh the end, when he shall have delivered up the kingdom to God, even the Father; when he shall have put down all rule and all authority and power. 25 For he must reign, till he hath put all enemies under his feet."

2 Corinthians 5:9-10 "Wherefore we labour, that, whether present or absent, we may be accepted of him. [10] For we must all appear before the judgment seat of Christ; that every one may receive the things done in his body, according to that he hath done, whether it be good or bad."

Philippians 3:20-21 "For our conversation is in heaven; from whence also we look for the Saviour, the Lord Jesus Christ: [21] Who shall change our vile body, that it may be fashioned like unto his glorious body, according to the working whereby he is able even to subdue all things unto himself.

Colossians 3:4 "When Christ, who is our life, shall appear, then shall ye also appear with him in glory."

1 Thessalonians 3:13 "To the end he may stablish your hearts unblameable in holiness before God, even our Father, at the coming of our Lord Jesus Christ with all his saints."

1 Thessalonians 5:1-2 "But of the times and the seasons, brethren, ye have no need that I write unto you. [2] For yourselves know perfectly that the day of the Lord so cometh as a thief in the night."

1 Thessalonians 5:23 "And the very God of peace sanctify you wholly; and I pray God your whole spirit and soul and body be preserved blameless unto the coming of our Lord Jesus Christ."

2 Thessalonians 1:7-10 "And to you who are troubled rest with us, when the Lord Jesus shall be revealed from heaven with his mighty angels, [8] In flaming fire taking vengeance on them that know not God, and that obey not the gospel of our Lord Jesus Christ: [9] Who shall be punished with everlasting destruction from the presence of the Lord, and from the glory of his power; [10] When he shall come to be glorified in his saints, and to be admired in all them that believe (because our testimony among you was believed) in that day."

2 Thessalonians 2:1-6 "Now we beseech you, brethren, by the coming of our Lord Jesus Christ, and by our gathering together unto him, [2] That ye be not soon shaken in mind, or be troubled, neither by spirit, nor by word, nor by letter as from us, as that the day of Christ is at hand. [3] Let no man deceive you by any means: for that day shall not come, except there come a falling away first, and that man of sin be revealed, the son of perdition;
[4] Who opposeth and exalteth himself above all that is called God, or that is worshipped; so that he as God sitteth in the temple of God, shewing himself that he is God. [5] Remember ye not, that, when I was yet with you, I told you these things? [6] And now ye know what withholdeth that he might be revealed in his time.

1 Timothy 6:13-14 "I give thee charge in the sight of God, who quickeneth all things, and before Christ Jesus, who before Pontius Pilate witnessed a good confession; 14 That thou keep this commandment without spot, unrebukable, until the appearing of our Lord Jesus Christ."

2 Timothy 4:1, 8 "I charge thee therefore before God, and the Lord Jesus Christ, who shall judge the quick and the dead at his appearing and his kingdom; 8 Henceforth there is laid up for me a crown of righteousness, which the Lord, the righteous judge, shall give me at that day: and not to me only, but unto all them also that love his appearing."

Titus 2:12-13 "Teaching us that, denying ungodliness and worldly lusts, we should live soberly, righteously, and godly, in this present world; 13 Looking for that blessed hope, and the glorious appearing of the great God and our Saviour Jesus Christ."

Prophecies Of Messiah's Future Return By Peter In His Epistles

2 Peter 3:1-13 "This second epistle, beloved, I now write unto you; in both which I stir up your pure minds by way of remembrance: 2 That ye may be mindful of the words which were spoken before by the holy prophets, and of the commandment of us the apostles of the Lord and Saviour: 3 Knowing this first, that there shall come in the last days scoffers, walking after their own lusts, 4 And saying, Where is the promise of his coming? for since the fathers fell asleep, all things continue as they were from the beginning of the creation.
5 For this they willingly are ignorant of, that by the word of God the heavens were of old, and the earth standing out of the water and in the water: 6 Whereby the world that then was, being overflowed with water, perished: 7 But the heavens and the earth, which are now, by the same word are kept in store, reserved unto fire against the day of judgment and perdition of ungodly men. 8 But, beloved, be not ignorant of this one thing, that one day is with the Lord as a thousand years, and a thousand years as one day.
9 The Lord is not slack concerning his promise, as some men count slackness; but is longsuffering to us-ward, not willing that any should perish, but that all should come to repentance. 10 But the day of the Lord will come as a thief in the night; in the which the heavens shall pass away with a great noise, and the elements shall melt with fervent heat, the earth also and the works that are therein shall be burned up.
11 Seeing then that all these things shall be dissolved, what manner of persons ought ye to be in all holy conversation and godliness,
12 Looking for and hasting unto the coming of the day of God, wherein the heavens being on fire shall be dissolved, and the elements shall melt with fervent heat?
13 Nevertheless we, according to his promise, look for new heavens and a new earth, wherein dwelleth righteousness.

Prophecies of Messiah's Future Return By the Apostle James

Acts 15:13-18 "And after they had held their peace, James answered, saying, Men and brethren, hearken unto me: [14] Simeon hath declared how God at the first did visit the Gentiles, to take out of them a people for his name. [15] And to this agree the words of the prophets; as it is written, [16] After this I will return, and will build again the tabernacle of David, which is fallen down; and I will build again the ruins thereof, and I will set it up: [17] That the residue of men might seek after the Lord, and all the Gentiles, upon whom my name is called, saith the Lord, who doeth all these things. [18] Known unto God are all his works from the beginning of the world."

James 5:7-8 "Be patient therefore, brethren, unto the coming of the Lord. Behold, the husbandman waiteth for the precious fruit of the earth, and hath long patience for it, until he receive the early and latter rain. [8] Be ye also patient; stablish your hearts: for the coming of the Lord draweth nigh."

Prophecies of Messiah's Future Return By John In His Epistles and Revelation

1 John 2:28 "And now, little children, abide in him; that, when he shall appear, we may have confidence, and not be ashamed before him at his coming."

1 John 3:2-3 "Beloved, now are we the sons of God, and it doth not yet appear what we shall be: but we know that, when he shall appear, we shall be like him; for we shall see him as he is. [3] And every man that hath this hope in him purifieth himself, even as he is pure."

Revelation 1:7-8 " Behold, he cometh with clouds; and every eye shall see him, and they also which pierced him: and all kindreds of the earth shall wail because of him. Even so, Amen. [8] I am Alpha and Omega, the beginning and the ending, saith the Lord, which is, and which was, and which is to come, the Almighty.

Revelation 16:15 "Behold, I come as a thief. Blessed is he that watcheth, and keepeth his garments, lest he walk naked, and they see his shame."

Revelation 22:12 "And, behold, I come quickly; and my reward is with me, to give every man according as his work shall be."

Revelation 22:20 "He which testifieth these things saith, Surely I come quickly. Amen. Even so, come, Lord Jesus."

Prophecies of Messiah's Future Return By Jude In His Epistle

Jude 14-15 "And Enoch also, the seventh from Adam, prophesied of these, saying, Behold, the Lord cometh with ten thousands of his saints, [15] To execute judgment upon all, and to convince all that are ungodly among them of all their ungodly deeds which they have ungodly committed, and of all their hard speeches which ungodly sinners have spoken against him."

Prophecies of Messiah's Future Return By The Author of Hebrews

Hebrews 9:28 "So Christ was once offered to bear the sins of many; and unto them that look for him shall he appear the second time without sin unto salvation."

In this section of the prophecies regarding the future return of the Messiah is included the specific mention of His future ministry as King of kings, Lord of lords and Righteous Judge. During His First Advent, Jesus Christ was meant to establish His Kingdom, but His people that were to constitute the nucleus of the kingdom (the Jews) rejected Him and His rule over them, for which reason the kingdom 'was postponed.' Although it is evident that Jesus was born a King according to Matthew and John, His kingdom was not of this world (John). Though Governor Pilate was, as it appears, sarcastically calling Jesus a king, he was unwittingly saying a fact. The rejection of Jesus Christ's kingship by the Jews did not cause Him to cease to be King. He died "King of the Jews" as John recorded.

Matthew 2:1-2 Now when Jesus was born in Bethlehem of Judaea in the days of Herod the king, behold, there came wise men from the east to Jerusalem, 2 Saying, Where is he that is born King of the Jews? for we have seen his star in the east, and are come to worship him."

John 18:36-39 "Jesus answered, My kingdom is not of this world: if my kingdom were of this world, then would my servants fight, that I should not be delivered to the Jews: but now is my kingdom not from hence. 37 Pilate therefore said unto him, Art thou a king then? Jesus answered, Thou sayest that I am a king. To this end was I born, and for this cause came I into the world, that I should bear witness unto the truth. Every one that is of the truth heareth my voice.
38 Pilate saith unto him, What is truth? And when he had said this, he went out again unto the Jews, and saith unto them, I find in him no fault at all. 39 But ye have a custom, that I should release unto you one at the passover: will ye therefore that I release unto you the King of the Jew."

John 19:19-22 "And Pilate wrote a title, and put it on the cross. And the writing was Jesus Of Nazareth The King Of The Jews. 20 This title then read many of the Jews: for the place where Jesus was crucified was nigh to the city: and it was written in Hebrew, and Greek, and Latin. 21 Then said the chief priests of the Jews to Pilate, Write not, The King of the Jews; but that he said, I am King of the Jews."

Pilate refused to change what he had written for he said, "What I have written I have written" (John 19:22). Actually Jesus Christ never said He was King of the Jews. But that was one of the false accusations framed and leveled against Him by the Jewish leaders in order to make His purported offense treasonable enough to warrant execution.

Following are some prophecies in the Old Testament and New Testament which were about Jesus Christ's future ministry as a King:

Psalm 110:2-3 "The Lord shall send the rod of thy strength out of Zion: rule thou in the midst of thine enemies. ³ Thy people shall be willing in the day of thy power, in the beauties of holiness from the womb of the morning: thou hast the dew of thy youth."

Isaiah 9:6 "For unto us a child is born, unto us a son is given: and the government shall be upon his shoulder: and his name shall be called Wonderful, Counsellor, The mighty God, The everlasting Father, The Prince of Peace."

Luke 1:30-33 "And the angel said unto her, Fear not, Mary: for thou hast found favour with God. ³¹ And, behold, thou shalt conceive in thy womb, and bring forth a son, and shalt call his name Jesus. ³² He shall be great, and shall be called the Son of the Highest: and the Lord God shall give unto him the throne of his father David: ³³ And he shall reign over the house of Jacob for ever; and of his kingdom there shall be no end."

John 12:12-13 "On the next day much people that were come to the feast, when they heard that Jesus was coming to Jerusalem, 13 Took branches of palm trees, and went forth to meet him, and cried, Hosanna: Blessed is the King of Israel that cometh in the name of the Lord."

Revelation 19:15 "And out of his mouth goeth a sharp sword, that with it he should smite the nations: and he shall rule them with a rod of iron: and he treadeth the winepress of the fierceness and wrath of Almighty God."

Jesus also predicted that He will come with pomp and pageantry (in His/His Father's glory) to reign as King of kings):

Matthew 16:27 "For the Son of man shall come in the glory of his Father with his angels; and then he shall reward every man according to his works."

Matthew 25:31 "When the Son of man shall come in his glory, and all the holy angels with him, then shall he sit upon the throne of his glory."

As King one of His duties shall be execution of judgment. Righteous judgment has eluded this world over the ages, because no earthly judge has any righteousness in

153

him or her. And "no one gives what he does not have," according to a Latin adage.[19] But when Jesus Christ comes He will judge all believers in Him for the purpose of rewarding us for, and according to, our works for Him on earth. And He will judge unbelievers to sentence them for rejecting Him.

Matthew 16:27 "For the Son of man shall come in the glory of his Father with his angels; and then he shall reward every man according to his works."

2 Corinthians 5:10 "For we must all appear before the judgment seat of Christ; that every one may receive the things done in his body, according to that he hath done, whether it be good or bad."

Ephesians 6:7-8 "With good will doing service, as to the Lord, and not to men: 8 Knowing that whatsoever good thing any man doeth, the same shall he receive of the Lord, whether he be bond or free.

Jesus Christ as King will also judge all unbelievers to properly condemn them to their eternal punishment

Matthew 25:31-33 "When the Son of man shall come in his glory, and all the holy angels with him, then shall he sit upon the throne of his glory: 32 And before him shall be gathered all nations: and he shall separate them one from another, as a shepherd divideth his sheep from the goats: 33 And he shall set the sheep on his right hand, but the goats on the left."

Matthew 25:41 "Then shall he say also unto them on the left hand, Depart from me, ye cursed, into everlasting fire, prepared for the devil and his angels:"

Matthew 25:46 "And these shall go away into everlasting punishment: but the righteous into life eternal."

2 Thessalonians 1:6-10 "Seeing it is a righteous thing with God to recompense tribulation to them that trouble you; 7 And to you who are troubled rest with us, when the Lord Jesus shall be revealed from heaven with his mighty angels, 8 In flaming fire taking vengeance on them that know not God, and that obey not the gospel of our Lord Jesus Christ: 9 Who shall be punished with everlasting destruction from the presence of the Lord, and from the glory of his power; 10 When he shall come to be glorified in his saints, and to be admired in all them that believe (because our testimony among you was believed) in that day."

---

[19] Latin: *Nemo dat quod non habet.*

PART 3

SUMMARIES, CONCLUSIONS AND RECOMMENDATIONS

In this part we shall look into the bases for drawing our conclusions in this book, to be able to make recommendations accordingly. The part shall consist of six chapters as follows:

Chapter 9 Jesus Christ was Supernatural

Chapter 10 He Was A Prophet, High Priest And King

Chapter 11 He Died, Arose and Ascended

Chapter 12 Jesus Did God's Will

Chapter 13 Conclusions

Chapter 14 Recommendations

CHAPTER 9

JESUS CHRIST WAS SUPERNATURAL

"And they feared exceedingly, and said one to another, What manner of man is this, that even the wind and the sea obey him?" (Mark 4:41; Matthew 8:27; Luke 8:25).

That was an expression of surprise after Jesus Christ miraculously stilled the sea storm by words of mouth.

While He was physically here on earth, Jesus Christ had the divine attributes of God notwithstanding that He was in human flesh. Although He referred to Himself as the "Son of Man," the Bible tells us that Jesus was "[God's] only begotten Son" – the Son of God.

John 3:16 "For God so loved the world, that he gave his only begotten Son, that whosoever believeth in him should not perish, but have everlasting life."

Naturally, anyone (and indeed anything) begotten has the attributes of the 'begetter.'

The psalmist prophesied that the Messiah would be God's Son:

Psalm 2:7-8 "I will declare the decree: the Lord hath said unto me, Thou art my Son; this day have I begotten thee. 8 Ask of me, and I shall give thee the heathen for thine inheritance, and the uttermost parts of the earth for thy possession."

God the Father personally confirmed Jesus Christ's Sonship twice in the New Testament – firstly at His baptism by John the Baptist, and secondly at the transfiguration, which Peter, James and John did witness.

Baptism of Jesus Christ

Matthew 3:16-17 "And Jesus, when he was baptized, went up straightway out of the water: and, lo, the heavens were opened unto him, and he saw the Spirit of God descending like a dove, and lighting upon him: 17 And lo a voice from heaven, saying, This is my beloved Son, in whom I am well pleased."

Luke 3:21-22 "Now when all the people were baptized, it came to pass, that Jesus also being baptized, and praying, the heaven was opened, 22 And the Holy Ghost descended in a bodily shape like a dove upon him, and a voice came from heaven, which said, Thou art my beloved Son; in thee I am well pleased."

Transfiguration of Jesus Christ

Matthew 17:1-5 "And after six days Jesus taketh Peter, James, and John his brother, and bringeth them up into an high mountain apart, [2] And was transfigured before them: and his face did shine as the sun, and his raiment was white as the light. [3] And, behold, there appeared unto them Moses and Elias talking with him. [4] Then answered Peter, and said unto Jesus, Lord, it is good for us to be here: if thou wilt, let us make here three tabernacles; one for thee, and one for Moses, and one for Elias. [5] While he yet spake, behold, a bright cloud overshadowed them: and behold a voice out of the cloud, which said, This is my beloved Son, in whom I am well pleased; hear ye him. (Emphasis added).

Mark 9:2-8 "And after six days Jesus taketh with him Peter, and James, and John, and leadeth them up into an high mountain apart by themselves: and he was transfigured before them. [3] And his raiment became shining, exceeding white as snow; so as no fuller on earth can white them. [4] And there appeared unto them Elias with Moses: and they were talking with Jesus.
[5] And Peter answered and said to Jesus, Master, it is good for us to be here: and let us make three tabernacles; one for thee, and one for Moses, and one for Elias. [6] For he wist not what to say; for they were sore afraid. [7] And there was a cloud that overshadowed them: and a voice came out of the cloud, saying, This is my beloved Son: hear him. [8] And suddenly, when they had looked round about, they saw no man any more, save Jesus only with themselves."

Luke 9:28-36 "And it came to pass about an eight days after these sayings, he took Peter and John and James, and went up into a mountain to pray. [29] And as he prayed, the fashion of his countenance was altered, and his raiment was white and glistering. [30] And, behold, there talked with him two men, which were Moses and Elias: [31] Who appeared in glory, and spake of his decease which he should accomplish at Jerusalem. [32] But Peter and they that were with him were heavy with sleep: and when they were awake, they saw his glory, and the two men that stood with him. [33] And it came to pass, as they departed from him, Peter said unto Jesus, Master, it is good for us to be here: and let us make three tabernacles; one for thee, and one for Moses, and one for Elias: not knowing what he said.
[34] While he thus spake, there came a cloud, and overshadowed them: and they feared as they entered into the cloud. [35] And there came a voice out of the cloud, saying, This is my beloved Son: hear him. [36] And when the voice was past, Jesus was found alone. And they kept it close, and told no man in those days any of those things which they had seen."

Let us consider the factors based on which it is right to consider Jesus Christ supernatural and the Son of God: -

1 **He is Eternal**.

Jesus Christ was and is eternal. The things He knew, which were strange to His listeners constitute an evidence to this. For example, He taught the Pharisees that asked Him whether it was lawful for a man to put away his wife for every cause (Matt. 19:3):

Matthew 19:4-6 " . . . Have ye not read, that he which made them at the beginning made them male and female, 5 And said, For this cause shall a man leave father and mother, and shall cleave to his wife: and they twain shall be one flesh? 6 Wherefore they are no more twain, but one flesh. What therefore God hath joined together, let not man put asunder."

On another occasion it sounded incredible to the Jews that their patriarch, Abraham, who died many centuries earlier, rejoiced to see the day of this young Jesus Christ that was not even fifty years old. And surprisingly Jesus told the Jews that He had been in existence even before Abraham:

John 8:56-58 " Your father Abraham rejoiced to see my day: and he saw it, and was glad. 57 Then said the Jews unto him, Thou art not yet fifty years old, and hast thou seen Abraham? 58 Jesus said unto them, Verily, verily, I say unto you, Before Abraham was, I am."

Conscious of His personality Jesus did not say, "Before Abraham I was." Rather He said, "Before Abraham was I AM," which when interpreted signifies that (as God) I was, I am and I will be.

Also without a prior contact with the woman of Samaria that He met at Jacob's well, He told her of her past, which shocked her:"

John 4:16-19 ""Jesus saith unto her, Go, call thy husband, and come hither. 17 The woman answered and said, I have no husband. Jesus said unto her, Thou hast well said, I have no husband: 18 For thou hast had five husbands; and he whom thou now hast is not thy husband: in that saidst thou truly. 19 The woman saith unto him, Sir, I perceive that thou art a prophet."

Several authorities believe that most of OT theophanies were Jesus Christ in His pre-incarnate times. For example, Willmington describes a theophany as a pre-Bethlehem appearance of Jesus Christ and adds, "Most Bible theologians hold that the recurring angel of the Lord episode in the Old Testament is to be identified with Christ Himself."[20] Further more, Thiessen says, "Although the second person of the Trinity

---

[20] H. L. Willmington. *Willmington's Guide To The Bible* (Wheaton: Tyndale House Publishers, INC., 1981), 610.

often appears in the Old Testament, He is never referred to as Christ. Instead we have the names "Son," "Jehovah," and "the Angel of Jehovah." [21] Charles Ryrie also commented as follows:

"Clearly the Angel of Yahweh is a self-manifestation of Yahweh, for He speaks as God, identifies Himself with God, and claims to exercise the prerogatives of God . . . .. That He is a member of the Trinity is indicated by the fact that the appearances of the Angel of Yahweh ceased after the incarnation. This is confirmed by the Old Testament statement that the Angel of God accompanied Israel when they left Egypt (Ex. 14:19; cf. 23:20) and the New Testament statement that the Rock who followed Israel was Christ (1 Cor. 10:4)." [22]

Other Bible passages that point to the eternality of Jesus Christ, including the theophanies in the OT are as follows:

Genesis 16:7-14 "And the angel of the Lord found her by a fountain of water in the wilderness, by the fountain in the way to Shur. ⁸ And he said, Hagar, Sarai's maid, whence camest thou? and whither wilt thou go? And she said, I flee from the face of my mistress Sarai. ⁹ And the angel of the Lord said unto her, Return to thy mistress, and submit thyself under her hands.

¹⁰ And the angel of the Lord said unto her, I will multiply thy seed exceedingly, that it shall not be numbered for multitude. ¹¹ And the angel of the Lord said unto her, Behold, thou art with child and shalt bear a son, and shalt call his name Ishmael; because the Lord hath heard thy affliction. ¹² And he will be a wild man; his hand will be against every man, and every man's hand against him; and he shall dwell in the presence of all his brethren. ¹³ And she called the name of the Lord that spake unto her, Thou God seest me: for she said, Have I also here looked after him that seeth me? ¹⁴ Wherefore the well was called Beerlahairoi; behold, it is between Kadesh and Bered

Genesis 22:11-18 "And the angel of the Lord called unto him out of heaven, and said, Abraham, Abraham: and he said, Here am I. ¹² And he said, Lay not thine hand upon the lad, neither do thou any thing unto him: for now I know that thou fearest God, seeing thou hast not withheld thy son, thine only son from me. ¹³ And Abraham lifted up his eyes, and looked, and behold behind him a ram caught in a thicket by his horns: and Abraham went and took the ram, and offered him up for a burnt offering in the stead of his son.

¹⁴ And Abraham called the name of that place Jehovahjireh: as it is said to this day, In the mount of the Lord it shall be seen. ¹⁵ And the angel of the Lord called unto Abraham out of heaven the second time, ¹⁶ And said, By myself have I sworn, saith the Lord, for because thou hast done this thing, and hast not withheld thy son, thine only son: ¹⁷ That in blessing I will bless thee, and in multiplying I will multiply thy seed as the stars of the heaven, and as the sand which is upon the sea shore; and thy

---

[21] Henry Clarence Thiessen. *Introductory Lectures In Systematic Theology* (Grand Rapids: WM. B. Eerdmans Publishing Company, 1949), 287.

[22] Charles C. Ryrie. *Basic Theology* (USA, Canada, England: Victor Books, 1981), 239.

seed shall possess the gate of his enemies; [18] And in thy seed shall all the nations of the earth be blessed; because thou hast obeyed my voice."

Genesis 31:11-13 "And the angel of God spake unto me in a dream, saying, Jacob: And I said, Here am I. [12] And he said, Lift up now thine eyes, and see, all the rams which leap upon the cattle are ringstraked, speckled, and grisled: for I have seen all that Laban doeth unto thee. [13] I am the God of Bethel, where thou anointedst the pillar, and where thou vowedst a vow unto me: now arise, get thee out from this land, and return unto the land of thy kindred."

Genesis 32:22-30 "And he rose up that night, and took his two wives, and his two womenservants, and his eleven sons, and passed over the ford Jabbok. [23] And he took them, and sent them over the brook, and sent over that he had. [24] And Jacob was left alone; and there wrestled a man with him until the breaking of the day.
[25] And when he saw that he prevailed not against him, he touched the hollow of his thigh; and the hollow of Jacob's thigh was out of joint, as he wrestled with him. [26] And he said, Let me go, for the day breaketh. And he said, I will not let thee go, except thou bless me.
[27] And he said unto him, What is thy name? And he said, Jacob. [28] And he said, Thy name shall be called no more Jacob, but Israel: for as a prince hast thou power with God and with men, and hast prevailed. [29] And Jacob asked him, and said, Tell me, I pray thee, thy name. And he said, Wherefore is it that thou dost ask after my name? And he blessed him there. [30] And Jacob called the name of the place Peniel: for I have seen God face to face, and my life is preserved."

Genesis 48:16 "The Angel which redeemed me from all evil, bless the lads; and let my name be named on them, and the name of my fathers Abraham and Isaac; and let them grow into a multitude in the midst of the earth."

Exodus 3:2-5 "And the angel of the Lord appeared unto him in a flame of fire out of the midst of a bush: and he looked, and, behold, the bush burned with fire, and the bush was not consumed. [3] And Moses said, I will now turn aside, and see this great sight, why the bush is not burnt.
[4] And when the Lord saw that he turned aside to see, God called unto him out of the midst of the bush, and said, Moses, Moses. And he said, Here am I. [5] And he said, Draw not nigh hither: put off thy shoes from off thy feet, for the place whereon thou standest is holy ground.

Exodus 14:19 (cf. 1 Cor. 10:4) "And the angel of God, which went before the camp of Israel, removed and went behind them; and the pillar of the cloud went from before their face, and stood behind them."

Exodus 23:20 "Behold, I send an Angel before thee, to keep thee in the way, and to bring thee into the place which I have prepared."

Joshua 5:13-15 "And it came to pass, when Joshua was by Jericho, that he lifted up his eyes and looked, and, behold, there stood a man over against him with his sword drawn in his hand: and Joshua went unto him, and said unto him, Art thou for us, or for our adversaries? 14 And he said, Nay; but as captain of the host of the Lord am I now come. And Joshua fell on his face to the earth, and did worship, and said unto him, What saith my Lord unto his servant? 15 And the captain of the Lord's host said unto Joshua, Loose thy shoe from off thy foot; for the place whereon thou standest is holy. And Joshua did so."

Judges 6:11-24 "And there came an angel of the Lord, and sat under an oak which was in Ophrah, that pertained unto Joash the Abiezrite: and his son Gideon threshed wheat by the winepress, to hide it from the Midianites. 12 And the angel of the Lord appeared unto him, and said unto him, The Lord is with thee, thou mighty man of valour.
13 And Gideon said unto him, Oh my Lord, if the Lord be with us, why then is all this befallen us? and where be all his miracles which our fathers told us of, saying, Did not the Lord bring us up from Egypt? but now the Lord hath forsaken us, and delivered us into the hands of the Midianites. 14 And the Lord looked upon him, and said, Go in this thy might, and thou shalt save Israel from the hand of the Midianites: have not I sent thee? 15 And he said unto him, Oh my Lord, wherewith shall I save Israel? behold, my family is poor in Manasseh, and I am the least in my father's house. 16 And the Lord said unto him, Surely I will be with thee, and thou shalt smite the Midianites as one man. 17 And he said unto him, If now I have found grace in thy sight, then shew me a sign that thou talkest with me.
18 Depart not hence, I pray thee, until I come unto thee, and bring forth my present, and set it before thee. And he said, I will tarry until thou come again. 19 And Gideon went in, and made ready a kid, and unleavened cakes of an ephah of flour: the flesh he put in a basket, and he put the broth in a pot, and brought it out unto him under the oak, and presented it.
20 And the angel of God said unto him, Take the flesh and the unleavened cakes, and lay them upon this rock, and pour out the broth. And he did so. 21 Then the angel of the Lord put forth the end of the staff that was in his hand, and touched the flesh and the unleavened cakes; and there rose up fire out of the rock, and consumed the flesh and the unleavened cakes. Then the angel of the Lord departed out of his sight. 22 And when Gideon perceived that he was an angel of the Lord, Gideon said, Alas, O LordGod! for because I have seen an angel of the Lord face to face. 23 And the Lord said unto him, Peace be unto thee; fear not: thou shalt not die. 24 Then Gideon built an altar there unto the Lord, and called it Jehovahshalom: unto this day it is yet in Ophrah of the Abiezrites."

Judges 13:18 "And the angel of the Lord said unto him, Why askest thou thus after my name, seeing it is secret?"

Isaiah 9:6 "For unto us a child is born, unto us a son is given: and the government shall be upon his shoulder: and his name shall be called Wonderful, Counsellor, The mighty God, The everlasting Father, The Prince of Peace."

Daniel 3:25 "He answered and said, Lo, I see four men loose, walking in the midst of the fire, and they have no hurt; and the form of the fourth is like the Son of God."

Daniel 6:22 "My God hath sent his angel, and hath shut the lions' mouths, that they have not hurt me: forasmuch as before him innocency was found in me; and also before thee, O king, have I done no hurt."

Daniel 7:9-14 "I beheld till the thrones were cast down, and the Ancient of days did sit, whose garment was white as snow, and the hair of his head like the pure wool: his throne was like the fiery flame, and his wheels as burning fire. 10 A fiery stream issued and came forth from before him: thousand thousands ministered unto him, and ten thousand times ten thousand stood before him: the judgment was set, and the books were opened. 11 I beheld then because of the voice of the great words which the horn spake: I beheld even till the beast was slain, and his body destroyed, and given to the burning flame.
12 As concerning the rest of the beasts, they had their dominion taken away: yet their lives were prolonged for a season and time. 13 I saw in the night visions, and, behold, one like the Son of man came with the clouds of heaven, and came to the Ancient of days, and they brought him near before him. 14 And there was given him dominion, and glory, and a kingdom, that all people, nations, and languages, should serve him: his dominion is an everlasting dominion, which shall not pass away, and his kingdom that which shall not be destroyed."

Micah 5:2 "But thou, Bethlehem Ephratah, though thou be little among the thousands of Judah, yet out of thee shall he come forth unto me that is to be ruler in Israel; whose goings forth have been from of old, from everlasting."

John 1:1-3 "In the beginning was the Word, and the Word was with God, and the Word was God. 2 The same was in the beginning with God. 3 All things were made by him; and without him was not any thing made that was made."

John 1:15 "John bare witness of him, and cried, saying, This was he of whom I spake, He that cometh after me is preferred before me: for he was before me."

The birth narratives concerning John the Baptist and Jesus Christ say that John was born before Jesus Christ. But here John in his witness of Christ said that Christ was before him in view of His eternality.

John 1:26-27 "John answered them, saying, I baptize with water: but there standeth one among you, whom ye know not; 27 He it is, who coming after me is preferred before me, whose shoe's latchet I am not worthy to unloose."

John 1:29-30 "The next day John seeth Jesus coming unto him, and saith, Behold the Lamb of God, which taketh away the sin of the world. 30 This is he of whom I said, After me cometh a man which is preferred before me: for he was before me."

John 6:38-40 "For I came down from heaven, not to do mine own will, but the will of him that sent me. 39 And this is the Father's will which hath sent me, that of all which he hath given me I should lose nothing, but should raise it up again at the last day. 40 And this is the will of him that sent me, that every one which seeth the Son, and believeth on him, may have everlasting life: and I will raise him up at the last day."

John 6:46-51 "Not that any man hath seen the Father, save he which is of God, he hath seen the Father. 47 Verily, verily, I say unto you, He that believeth on me hath everlasting life. 48 I am that bread of life. 49 Your fathers did eat manna in the wilderness, and are dead. 50 This is the bread which cometh down from heaven, that a man may eat thereof, and not die. 51 I am the living bread which came down from heaven: if any man eat of this bread, he shall live for ever: and the bread that I will give is my flesh, which I will give for the life of the world."

John 6:61-62 "When Jesus knew in himself that his disciples murmured at it, he said unto them, Doth this offend you? 62 What and if ye shall see the Son of man ascend up where he was before?"

John 17:5 "And now, O Father, glorify thou me with thine own self with the glory which I had with thee before the world was."

1 Corinthians 10:1-4 "Moreover, brethren, I would not that ye should be ignorant, how that all our fathers were under the cloud, and all passed through the sea; 2 And were all baptized unto Moses in the cloud and in the sea; 3 And did all eat the same spiritual meat; 4 And did all drink the same spiritual drink: for they drank of that spiritual Rock that followed them: and that Rock was Christ."

Philippians 2:5-8 "Let this mind be in you, which was also in Christ Jesus: 6 Who, being in the form of God, thought it not robbery to be equal with God: 7 But made himself of no reputation, and took upon him the form of a servant, and was made in the likeness of men: 8 And being found in fashion as a man, he humbled himself, and became obedient unto death, even the death of the cross.

Colossians 1:15-17 "Who is the image of the invisible God, the firstborn of every creature: 16 For by him were all things created, that are in heaven, and that are in earth, visible and invisible, whether they be thrones, or dominions, or principalities, or powers: all things were created by him, and for him: [17] And he is before all things, and by him all things consist.

Hebrews 1:1-2 "God, who at sundry times and in divers manners spake in time past unto the fathers by the prophets, [2] Hath in these last days spoken unto us by his Son, whom he hath appointed heir of all things, by whom also he made the worlds;"

Hebrews 1:8 "But unto the Son he saith, Thy throne, O God, is for ever and ever: a sceptre of righteousness is the sceptre of thy kingdom.

Hebrews 7:1-3 "For this Melchisedec, king of Salem, priest of the most high God, who met Abraham returning from the slaughter of the kings, and blessed him; [2] To whom also Abraham gave a tenth part of all; first being by interpretation King of righteousness, and after that also King of Salem, which is, King of peace; [3] Without father, without mother, without descent, having neither beginning of days, nor end of life; but made like unto the Son of God; abideth a priest continually."

Hebrews 13:8 "Jesus Christ the same yesterday, and to day, and for ever."

Hebrews 7:17 "For he testifieth, Thou art a priest for ever after the order of Melchisedec."

Hebrews 7:24 "But this man, because he continueth ever, hath an unchangeable priesthood."

1 Peter 1:19-20 "But with the precious blood of Christ, as of a lamb without blemish and without spot: [20] Who verily was foreordained before the foundation of the world, but was manifest in these last times for you,"

1 John 1:1 "That which was from the beginning, which we have heard, which we have seen with our eyes, which we have looked upon, and our hands have handled, of the Word of life;"

Jude 25 "To the only wise God our Saviour, be glory and majesty, dominion and power, both now and ever. Amen"

Revelation 1:8 "I am Alpha and Omega, the beginning and the ending, saith the Lord, which is, and which was, and which is to come, the Almighty."

2 **His Virgin Birth.**

Jesus had a supernatural (virgin) birth – a kind that no one before Him ever had, neither will there be any other after Him. As seen earlier, Prophet Isaiah foretold His birth about seven hundred years before He was born and Prophet Micah also foretold the place of birth. These and all related prophecies were fulfilled.

Isaiah 7:14 Therefore the Lord himself shall give you a sign; Behold, a virgin shall conceive, and bear a son, and shall call his name Immanuel."

Micah 5:2 "But thou, Bethlehem Ephratah, though thou be little among the thousands of Judah, yet out of thee shall he come forth unto me that is to be ruler in Israel; whose goings forth have been from of old, from everlasting."

-        His mother, Mary was a virgin, betrothed to Joseph, who never had carnal knowledge of her until after she had given birth to Jesus.

Matthew 1:24-25 "Then Joseph being raised from sleep did as the angel of the Lord had bidden him, and took unto him his wife: 25 And knew her not till she had brought forth her firstborn son: and he called his name JESUS."
-        Jesus was conceived of the Holy Spirit rather than by the will and (sexual) act of man.

Matthew 1:20 "But while he thought on these things, behold, the angel of the LORD appeared unto him in a dream, saying, Joseph, thou son of David, fear not to take unto thee Mary thy wife: for that which is conceived in her is of the Holy Ghost."

-        Angels announced His birth to humble shepherds that were watching their flocks by night and heavenly hosts sang and praised God.

Luke 2:7-16 "And she brought forth her firstborn son, and wrapped him in swaddling clothes, and laid him in a manger; because there was no room for them in the inn. 8 And there were in the same country shepherds abiding in the field, keeping watch over their flock by night. 9 And, lo, the angel of the Lord came upon them, and the glory of the Lord shone round about them: and they were sore afraid.

10 And the angel said unto them, Fear not: for, behold, I bring you good tidings of great joy, which shall be to all people. 11 For unto you is born this day in the city of David a Saviour, which is Christ the Lord. 12 And this shall be a sign unto you; Ye shall find the babe wrapped in swaddling clothes, lying in a manger. 13 And suddenly there was with the angel a multitude of the heavenly host praising God, and saying, 14 Glory to God in the highest, and on earth peace, good will toward men.

15 And it came to pass, as the angels were gone away from them into heaven, the shepherds said one to another, Let us now go even unto Bethlehem, and see this thing which is come to pass, which the Lord hath made known unto us. 16 And they came with haste, and found Mary, and Joseph, and the babe lying in a manger."

-       Wise men (Magi), led by a star went from the East, and worshipped Him as King of the Jews, even though a Baby.

Matthew 2:1-2, 11 "Now when Jesus was born in Bethlehem of Judaea in the days of Herod the king, behold, there came wise men from the east to Jerusalem, ² Saying, Where is he that is born King of the Jews? for we have seen his star in the east, and are come to worship him.

¹¹ And when they were come into the house, they saw the young child with Mary his mother, and fell down, and worshipped him: and when they had opened their treasures, they presented unto him gifts; gold, and frankincense and myrrh."

-       Although it is not certain the exact year or day Jesus Christ was born, it is important to note that dating changed from B.C. (Before Christ) to A.D. (Anno Domini – In the year of the Lord) after Jesus Christ's birth. Some authorities suggest that He was born about 6 B.C. or 4 B.C., implying that there were still a few years after His birth to the winding down of years BC. However there was no year 0 (Zero) B.C. or year 0 (Zero) A.D.

3 Omnipotence.

Omnipotence is one of the divine attributes of God. Omnipotence is the ability of God to do anything in accordance with His holy, just and perfect nature as God. He is all-powerful!

Even though Jesus Christ was in the flesh, as God He performed many miracles and made several comments that portrayed Him as supernatural and omnipotent. He taught with authority – "not as the Scribes and the Pharisees taught" (Matt. 7:28-29; Mark 1:22). His miracles showed that He had power over all manners of sickness and disease by healing the sick; He had power over death portrayed by, apart from His own death and resurrection, raising dead people; power over demons as He cast them out of some possessed people, and He had power over the elements of nature exemplified in stilling raging sea storm by words of mouth, walking on the sea, feeding Five thousand men with **Five loaves and Two fishes, as well as** Four thousand men with Seven loaves and a few little fishes. Also some of His apostles made comments that showed the omnipotence of Jesus Christ. But first of all, read the prophecies of Isaiah that show this attribute of God in Jesus Christ:

Isaiah 9:6 "For unto us a child is born, unto us a son is given: and the government shall be upon his shoulder: and his name shall be called Wonderful, Counsellor, The mighty God, The everlasting Father, The Prince of Peace."

Isaiah 63:1 "Who is this that cometh from Edom, with dyed garments from Bozrah? this that is glorious in his apparel, travelling in the greatness of his strength? I that speak in righteousness, mighty to save."

The New Testament references for the omnipotence of Jesus Christ are as follows:

Matthew 7:28-29 "And it came to pass, when Jesus had ended these sayings, the people were astonished at his doctrine: 29 For he taught them as one having authority, and not as the scribes."

Mark 1:22 "And they were astonished at his doctrine: for he taught them as one that had authority, and not as the scribes."

Matthew 8:3 "And Jesus put forth his hand, and touched him, saying, I will; be thou clean. And immediately his leprosy was cleansed."

Matthew 8:16 "When the even was come, they brought unto him many that were possessed with devils: and he cast out the spirits with his word, and healed all that were sick:"

Matthew 8:27 "But the men marvelled, saying, What manner of man is this, that even the winds and the sea obey him!"

Matthew 9:6-7 "But that ye may know that the Son of man hath power on earth to forgive sins, (then saith he to the sick of the palsy,) Arise, take up thy bed, and go unto thine house. 7 And he arose, and departed to his house."

Matthew 10:1 "And when he had called unto him his twelve disciples, he gave them power against unclean spirits, to cast them out, and to heal all manner of sickness and all manner of disease."

Mark 6:7 "And he called unto him the twelve, and began to send them forth by two and two; and gave them power over unclean spirits;"

Luke 9:1 "Then he called his twelve disciples together, and gave them power and authority over all devils, and to cure diseases."

Matthew 12:11-13 "And he said unto them, What man shall there be among you, that shall have one sheep, and if it fall into a pit on the sabbath day, will he not lay hold on it, and lift it out? 12 How much then is a man better than a sheep? Wherefore it is lawful to do well on the sabbath days. 13 Then saith he to the man, Stretch forth thine hand. And he stretched it forth; and it was restored whole, like as the other."

Matthew 12:27-29 "And if I by Beelzebub cast out devils, by whom do your children cast them out? therefore they shall be your judges. 28 But if I cast out devils by the Spirit of God, then the kingdom of God is come unto you. 29 Or else how can one enter into a strong man's house, and spoil his goods, except he first bind the strong man? and then he will spoil his house."

Mark 3:27 " No man can enter into a strong man's house, and spoil his goods, except he will first bind the strong man; and then he will spoil his house."

Matthew 28:18 " And Jesus came and spake unto them, saying, All power is given unto me in heaven and in earth"

Luke 5:17 "And it came to pass on a certain day, as he was teaching, that there were Pharisees and doctors of the law sitting by, which were come out of every town of Galilee, and Judaea, and Jerusalem: and the power of the Lord was present to heal them."

Luke 11:20-22 " But if I with the finger of God cast out devils, no doubt the kingdom of God is come upon you. 21 When a strong man armed keepeth his palace, his goods are in peace: 22 But when a stronger than he shall come upon him, and overcome him, he taketh from him all his armour wherein he trusted, and divideth his spoils.

John 2:19 " Jesus answered and said unto them, Destroy this temple, and in three days I will raise it up."

John 5:21 " For as the Father raiseth up the dead, and quickeneth them; even so the Son quickeneth whom he will."

John 5:28-29 " Marvel not at this: for the hour is coming, in the which all that are in the graves shall hear his voice, 29 And shall come forth; they that have done good, unto the resurrection of life; and they that have done evil, unto the resurrection of damnation."

John 6:19 " So when they had rowed about five and twenty or thirty furlongs, they see Jesus walking on the sea, and drawing nigh unto the ship: and they were afraid."

John 10:17-18 "Therefore doth my Father love me, because I lay down my life, that I might take it again. [18] No man taketh it from me, but I lay it down of myself. I have power to lay it down, and I have power to take it again. This commandment have I received of my Father."

John 10:27-28 " My sheep hear my voice, and I know them, and they follow me: [28] And I give unto them eternal life; and they shall never perish, neither shall any man pluck them out of my hand."

John 17:1-2 "These words spake Jesus, and lifted up his eyes to heaven, and said, Father, the hour is come; glorify thy Son, that thy Son also may glorify thee: [2] As thou hast given him power over all flesh, that he should give eternal life to as many as thou hast given him."

John 17:5 "And now, O Father, glorify thou me with thine own self with the glory which I had with thee before the world was."

Philippians 3:20-21 "For our conversation is in heaven; from whence also we look for the Saviour, the Lord Jesus Christ: [21] Who shall change our vile body, that it may be fashioned like unto his glorious body, according to the working whereby he is able even to subdue all things unto himself."

Colossians 1:15-17 "Who is the image of the invisible God, the firstborn of every creature: [16] For by him were all things created, that are in heaven, and that are in earth, visible and invisible, whether they be thrones, or dominions, or principalities, or powers: all things were created by him, and for him: [17] And he is before all things, and by him all things consist."

2 Thessalonians 1:7-9 "And to you who are troubled rest with us, when the Lord Jesus shall be revealed from heaven with his mighty angels, [8] In flaming fire taking vengeance on them that know not God, and that obey not the gospel of our Lord Jesus Christ: [9] Who shall be punished with everlasting destruction from the presence of the Lord, and from the glory of his power;"

1 Timothy 6:13-16 "I give thee charge in the sight of God, who quickeneth all things, and before Christ Jesus, who before Pontius Pilate witnessed a good confession; [14] That thou keep this commandment without spot, unrebukable, until the appearing of our Lord Jesus Christ: [15] Which in his times he shall shew, who is the blessed and only Potentate, the King of kings, and Lord of lords; [16] Who only hath immortality, dwelling in the light which no man can approach unto; whom no man hath seen, nor can see: to whom be honour and power everlasting. Amen."

Hebrews 1:3 "Who being the brightness of his glory, and the express image of his person, and upholding all things by the word of his power, when he had by himself purged our sins, sat down on the right hand of the Majesty on high:"

Hebrews 7:24-25 " But this man, because he continueth ever, hath an unchangeable priesthood. 25 Wherefore he is able also to save them to the uttermost that come unto God by him, seeing he ever liveth to make intercession for them."

2 Peter 1:16 "For we have not followed cunningly devised fables, when we made known unto you the power and coming of our Lord Jesus Christ, but were eyewitnesses of his majesty.'

Revelation 1:8 "I am Alpha and Omega, the beginning and the ending, saith the Lord, which is, and which was, and which is to come, the Almighty.'

Revelation 3:7 "And to the angel of the church in Philadelphia write; These things saith he that is holy, he that is true, he that hath the key of David, he that openeth, and no man shutteth; and shutteth, and no man openeth;"

Revelation 5:12 "Saying with a loud voice, Worthy is the Lamb that was slain to receive power, and riches, and wisdom, and strength, and honour, and glory, and blessing."

Forgiving, And Power To Forgive Sins On Earth

It was generally known and believed that only God could forgive sins. True. But because Jesus Christ was God in the flesh He did pronounce extension of forgiveness for which He was criticized and even condemned as blasphemous by the Jewish leaders including Pharisees and the Scribes. Of Himself Jesus said,

John 5:22-23 "For the Father judgeth no man, but hath committed all judgment unto the Son: 23 That all men should honour the Son, even as they honour the Father. He that honoureth not the Son honoureth not the Father which hath sent him."

He asked the Father to forgive His crucifiers. He practiced what He preached. He was not a "Do what I say, but not what I do" preacher that would teach others to do something but would not do it.

Luke 23:33-34 "And when they were come to the place, which is called Calvary, there they crucified him, and the malefactors, one on the right hand, and the other on the left. 34 Then said Jesus, Father, forgive them; for they know not what they do."

Matthew 8:1-3 "When he was come down from the mountain, great multitudes followed him. ² And, behold, there came a leper and worshipped him, saying, Lord, if thou wilt, thou canst make me clean. ³ And Jesus put forth his hand, and touched him, saying, I will; be thou clean. And immediately his leprosy was cleansed.

Matthew 9:1-8 "And he entered into a ship, and passed over, and came into his own city. ² And, behold, they brought to him a man sick of the palsy, lying on a bed: and Jesus seeing their faith said unto the sick of the palsy; Son, be of good cheer; thy sins be forgiven thee. ³ And, behold, certain of the scribes said within themselves, This man blasphemeth.
⁴ And Jesus knowing their thoughts said, Wherefore think ye evil in your hearts? ⁵ For whether is easier, to say, Thy sins be forgiven thee; or to say, Arise, and walk?
⁶ But that ye may know that the Son of man hath power on earth to forgive sins, (then saith he to the sick of the palsy,) Arise, take up thy bed, and go unto thine house. ⁷ And he arose, and departed to his house. ⁸ But when the multitudes saw it, they marvelled, and glorified God, which had given such power unto men.

Jesus Christ Accepted Worship

Jesus Christ accepted worship from man with no objection, which was considered contrary to the first two of the Ten Commandments (stated below) that forbid worship of anyone else and anything else but God. The Jewish leaders also saw this as blasphemy because they saw Him as any other Jew.

Exodus 20:3-5 "Thou shalt have no other gods before me.
⁴ Thou shalt not make unto thee any graven image, or any likeness of any thing that is in heaven above, or that is in the earth beneath, or that is in the water under the earth. ⁵ Thou shalt not bow down thyself to them, nor serve them: for I the Lord thy God am a jealous God, visiting the iniquity of the fathers upon the children unto the third and fourth generation of them that hate me;"

Matthew 14:28-33 "And Peter answered him and said, Lord, if it be thou, bid me come unto thee on the water. ²⁹ And he said, Come. And when Peter was come down out of the ship, he walked on the water, to go to Jesus. ³⁰ But when he saw the wind boisterous, he was afraid; and beginning to sink, he cried, saying, Lord, save me.
³¹ And immediately Jesus stretched forth his hand, and caught him, and said unto him, O thou of little faith, wherefore didst thou doubt? ³² And when they were come into the ship, the wind ceased. ³³ Then they that were in the ship came and worshipped him, saying, Of a truth thou art the Son of God."

Matthew 15:23-25 "But he answered her not a word. And his disciples came and besought him, saying, Send her away; for she crieth after us. ²⁴ But he answered and said, I am not sent but unto the lost sheep of the house of Israel. ²⁵ Then came she and worshipped him, saying, Lord, help me."

Matthew 28:9 "And as they went to tell his disciples, behold, Jesus met them, saying, All hail. And they came and held him by the feet, and worshipped him. [17] And when they saw him, they worshipped him: but some doubted."

Mark 1:40-44 "And there came a leper to him, beseeching him, and kneeling down to him, and saying unto him, If thou wilt, thou canst make me clean. [41] And Jesus, moved with compassion, put forth his hand, and touched him, and saith unto him, I will; be thou clean. [42] And as soon as he had spoken, immediately the leprosy departed from him, and he was cleansed. [43] And he straitly charged him, and forthwith sent him away; [44] And saith unto him, See thou say nothing to any man: but go thy way, shew thyself to the priest, and offer for thy cleansing those things which Moses commanded, for a testimony unto them."

Mark 2:1-12 "And again he entered into Capernaum after some days; and it was noised that he was in the house. [2] And straightway many were gathered together, insomuch that there was no room to receive them, no, not so much as about the door: and he preached the word unto them. [3] And they come unto him, bringing one sick of the palsy, which was borne of four. [4] And when they could not come nigh unto him for the press, they uncovered the roof where he was: and when they had broken it up, they let down the bed wherein the sick of the palsy lay.
[5] When Jesus saw their faith, he said unto the sick of the palsy, Son, thy sins be forgiven thee. [6] But there was certain of the scribes sitting there, and reasoning in their hearts, [7] Why doth this man thus speak blasphemies? who can forgive sins but God only?
[8] And immediately when Jesus perceived in his spirit that they so reasoned within themselves, he said unto them, Why reason ye these things in your hearts? [9] Whether is it easier to say to the sick of the palsy, Thy sins be forgiven thee; or to say, Arise, and take up thy bed, and walk?
[10] But that ye may know that the Son of man hath power on earth to forgive sins, (he saith to the sick of the palsy,) [11] I say unto thee, Arise, and take up thy bed, and go thy way into thine house. [12] And immediately he arose, took up the bed, and went forth before them all; insomuch that they were all amazed, and glorified God, saying, We never saw it on this fashion."

Luke 5:17-26 "And it came to pass on a certain day, as he was teaching, that there were Pharisees and doctors of the law sitting by, which were come out of every town of Galilee, and Judaea, and Jerusalem: and the power of the Lord was present to heal them. [18] And, behold, men brought in a bed a man which was taken with a palsy: and they sought means to bring him in, and to lay him before him. [19] And when they could not find by what way they might bring him in because of the multitude, they went upon the housetop, and let him down through the tiling with his couch into the midst before Jesus. [20] And when he saw their faith, he said unto him, Man, thy sins are forgiven thee.
[21] And the scribes and the Pharisees began to reason, saying, Who is this which speaketh blasphemies? Who can forgive sins, but God alone? [22] But when Jesus perceived their thoughts, he answering said unto them, What reason ye in your

hearts? 23 Whether is easier, to say, Thy sins be forgiven thee; or to say, Rise up and walk? 24 But that ye may know that the Son of man hath power upon earth to forgive sins, (he said unto the sick of the palsy,) I say unto thee, Arise, and take up thy couch, and go into thine house. 25 And immediately he rose up before them, and took up that whereon he lay, and departed to his own house, glorifying God. 26 And they were all amazed, and they glorified God, and were filled with fear, saying, We have seen strange things to day."

Luke 7:40-49 "And Jesus answering said unto him, Simon, I have somewhat to say unto thee. And he saith, Master, say on. 41 There was a certain creditor which had two debtors: the one owed five hundred pence, and the other fifty. 42 And when they had nothing to pay, he frankly forgave them both. Tell me therefore, which of them will love him most?
43 Simon answered and said, I suppose that he, to whom he forgave most. And he said unto him, Thou hast rightly judged. 44 And he turned to the woman, and said unto Simon, Seest thou this woman? I entered into thine house, thou gavest me no water for my feet: but she hath washed my feet with tears, and wiped them with the hairs of her head. 45 Thou gavest me no kiss: but this woman since the time I came in hath not ceased to kiss my feet. 46 My head with oil thou didst not anoint: but this woman hath anointed my feet with ointment.
47 Wherefore I say unto thee, Her sins, which are many, are forgiven; for she loved much: but to whom little is forgiven, the same loveth little. 48 And he said unto her, Thy sins are forgiven. 49 And they that sat at meat with him began to say within themselves, Who is this that forgiveth sins also?"

Luke 24:50-52 "And he led them out as far as to Bethany, and he lifted up his hands, and blessed them. 51 And it came to pass, while he blessed them, he was parted from them, and carried up into heaven. 52 And they worshipped him, and returned to Jerusalem with great joy:"

John 9:29-38 "We know that God spake unto Moses: as for this fellow, we know not from whence he is. 30 The man answered and said unto them, Why herein is a marvellous thing, that ye know not from whence he is, and yet he hath opened mine eyes. 31 Now we know that God heareth not sinners: but if any man be a worshipper of God, and doeth his will, him he heareth. 32 Since the world began was it not heard that any man opened the eyes of one that was born blind. 33 If this man were not of God, he could do nothing. 34 They answered and said unto him, Thou wast altogether born in sins, and dost thou teach us? And they cast him out.
35 Jesus heard that they had cast him out; and when he had found him, he said unto him, Dost thou believe on the Son of God? 36 He answered and said, Who is he, Lord, that I might believe on him? 37 And Jesus said unto him, Thou hast both seen him, and it is he that talketh with thee. 38 And he said, Lord, I believe. And he worshipped him.

John 20:26-28 "And after eight days again his disciples were within, and Thomas with them: then came Jesus, the doors being shut, and stood in the midst, and said, Peace be unto you. 27 Then saith he to Thomas, Reach hither thy finger, and behold my hands; and reach hither thy hand, and thrust it into my side: and be not faithless, but believing. [28] And Thomas answered and said unto him, My Lord and my God."

John 10:29-30 "My Father, which gave them me, is greater than all; and no man is able to pluck them out of my Father's hand. [30] I and my Father are one."

4 OMNISCIENCE.

Omniscience is another attribute of God. It means that "He knows Himself and all other things, whether they be actual or merely possible, whether they be past, present or future, and . . . from eternity."[23] Jesus Christ was also omniscient – all-knowing. We have already talked about His eternality, indicating that He knew things in eternity past. Many times during His earthly ministry and walk, He did and said many things that revealed His omniscience.

At age 12 for example, Jesus was in the midst of learned Jewish men in the temple at Jerusalem asking them questions and answering theirs. That was more than just high I.Q. (Intelligence Quotient). And on many occasions He followed up some of His actions with questions or explanations in line with the people's thought, because He knew their thought. Some of such instances are indicated below.

Matthew 9:2-5 "And, behold, they brought to him a man sick of the palsy, lying on a bed: and Jesus seeing their faith said unto the sick of the palsy; Son, be of good cheer; thy sins be forgiven thee. [3] And, behold, certain of the scribes said within themselves, This man blasphemeth. [4] And Jesus knowing their thoughts said, Wherefore think ye evil in your hearts? [5] For whether is easier, to say, Thy sins be forgiven thee; or to say, Arise, and walk?"

Luke 5:20-23 "And when he saw their faith, he said unto him, Man, thy sins are forgiven thee. [21] And the scribes and the Pharisees began to reason, saying, Who is this which speaketh blasphemies? Who can forgive sins, but God alone? [22] But when Jesus perceived their thoughts, he answering said unto them, What reason ye in your hearts? [23] Whether is easier, to say, Thy sins be forgiven thee; or to say, Rise up and walk?"

---

[23] Henry Clarence Thiessen. *Introductory Lectures in Systematic Theology.* (Grand Rapids: WM. B. Eerdmans Publishing Company, 1949),124.

Matthew 11:27 "All things are delivered unto me of my Father: and no man knoweth the Son, but the Father; neither knoweth any man the Father, save the Son, and he to whomsoever the Son will reveal him."

Matthew 12:14-15 "Then the Pharisees went out, and held a council against him, how they might destroy him. 15 But when Jesus knew it, he withdrew himself from thence: and great multitudes followed him, and he healed them all;"

Matthew 12:24-25 "But when the Pharisees heard it, they said, This fellow doth not cast out devils, but by Beelzebub the prince of the devils. 25 And Jesus knew their thoughts, and said unto them, Every kingdom divided against itself is brought to desolation; and every city or house divided against itself shall not stand:"

Matthew 16:6-8 "Then Jesus said unto them, Take heed and beware of the leaven of the Pharisees and of the Sadducees. 7 And they reasoned among themselves, saying, It is because we have taken no bread. 8 Which when Jesus perceived, he said unto them, O ye of little faith, why reason ye among yourselves, because ye have brought no bread?"

Matthew 22:16-21 "And they sent out unto him their disciples with the Herodians, saying, Master, we know that thou art true, and teachest the way of God in truth, neither carest thou for any man: for thou regardest not the person of men. 17 Tell us therefore, What thinkest thou? Is it lawful to give tribute unto Caesar, or not? 18 But Jesus perceived their wickedness, and said, Why tempt ye me, ye hypocrites? 19 Shew me the tribute money. And they brought unto him a penny. 20 And he saith unto them, Whose is this image and superscription? 21 They say unto him, Caesar's. Then saith he unto them, Render therefore unto Caesar the things which are Caesar's; and unto God the things that are God's."

Mark 12:13-17 "And they send unto him certain of the Pharisees and of the Herodians, to catch him in his words. 14 And when they were come, they say unto him, Master, we know that thou art true, and carest for no man: for thou regardest not the person of men, but teachest the way of God in truth: Is it lawful to give tribute to Caesar, or not? 15 Shall we give, or shall we not give? But he, knowing their hypocrisy, said unto them, Why tempt ye me? bring me a penny, that I may see it. 16 And they brought it. And he saith unto them, Whose is this image and superscription? And they said unto him, Caesar's. 17 And Jesus answering said unto them, Render to Caesar the things that are Caesar's, and to God the things that are God's. And they marvelled at him."

Luke 20:21-25 "And they asked him, saying, Master, we know that thou sayest and teachest rightly, neither acceptest thou the person of any, but teachest the way of God truly: 22 Is it lawful for us to give tribute unto Caesar, or no? 23 But he perceived their craftiness, and said unto them, Why tempt ye me? 24 Shew me a penny. Whose image and superscription hath it? They answered and said, Caesar's. 25 And he said unto them, Render therefore unto Caesar the things which be Caesar's, and unto God the things which be God's."

Mark 2:6-8 "But there was certain of the scribes sitting there, and reasoning in their hearts, 7 Why doth this man thus speak blasphemies? who can forgive sins but God only? 8 And immediately when Jesus perceived in his spirit that they so reasoned within themselves, he said unto them, Why reason ye these things in your hearts?"

Mark 8:15-17 "And he charged them, saying, Take heed, beware of the leaven of the Pharisees, and of the leaven of Herod. 16 And they reasoned among themselves, saying, It is because we have no bread. 17 And when Jesus knew it, he saith unto them, Why reason ye, because ye have no bread? perceive ye not yet, neither understand? have ye your heart yet hardened?"

Luke 7:37-46 "And, behold, a woman in the city, which was a sinner, when she knew that Jesus sat at meat in the Pharisee's house, brought an alabaster box of ointment, 38 And stood at his feet behind him weeping, and began to wash his feet with tears, and did wipe them with the hairs of her head, and kissed his feet, and anointed them with the ointment. 39 Now when the Pharisee which had bidden him saw it, he spake within himself, saying, This man, if he were a prophet, would have known who and what manner of woman this is that toucheth him: for she is a sinner.
40 And Jesus answering said unto him, Simon, I have somewhat to say unto thee. And he saith, Master, say on. 41 There was a certain creditor which had two debtors: the one owed five hundred pence, and the other fifty. 42 And when they had nothing to pay, he frankly forgave them both. Tell me therefore, which of them will love him most? 43 Simon answered and said, I suppose that he, to whom he forgave most. And he said unto him, Thou hast rightly judged.
44 And he turned to the woman, and said unto Simon, Seest thou this woman? I entered into thine house, thou gavest me no water for my feet: but she hath washed my feet with tears, and wiped them with the hairs of her head. 45 Thou gavest me no kiss: but this woman since the time I came in hath not ceased to kiss my feet. 46 My head with oil thou didst not anoint: but this woman hath anointed my feet with ointment."

Luke 6:6-9 "And it came to pass also on another sabbath, that he entered into the synagogue and taught: and there was a man whose right hand was withered. 7 And the scribes and Pharisees watched him, whether he would heal on the sabbath day; that they might find an accusation against him. 8 But he knew their thoughts, and said to the man which had the withered hand, Rise up, and stand forth in the midst. And he arose and stood forth. 9 Then said Jesus unto them, I will ask you one thing; Is it lawful on the sabbath days to do good, or to do evil? to save life, or to destroy it?"

Luke 9:43-48 "And they were all amazed at the mighty power of God. But while they wondered every one at all things which Jesus did, he said unto his disciples, 44 Let these sayings sink down into your ears: for the Son of man shall be delivered into the hands of men. 45 But they understood not this saying, and it was hid from them, that

they perceived it not: and they feared to ask him of that saying. ⁴⁶ Then there arose a reasoning among them, which of them should be greatest.
⁴⁷ And Jesus, perceiving the thought of their heart, took a child, and set him by him, ⁴⁸ And said unto them, Whosoever shall receive this child in my name receiveth me: and whosoever shall receive me receiveth him that sent me: for he that is least among you all, the same shall be great."

Luke 11:15-17 "But some of them said, He casteth out devils through Beelzebub the chief of the devils. ¹⁶ And others, tempting him, sought of him a sign from heaven. ¹⁷ But he, knowing their thoughts, said unto them, Every kingdom divided against itself is brought to desolation; and a house divided against a house falleth."

John 1:46-48 "And Nathanael said unto him, Can there any good thing come out of Nazareth? Philip saith unto him, Come and see. ⁴⁷ Jesus saw Nathanael coming to him, and saith of him, Behold an Israelite indeed, in whom is no guile! ⁴⁸ Nathanael saith unto him, Whence knowest thou me? Jesus answered and said unto him, Before that Philip called thee, when thou wast under the fig tree, I saw thee."

John 2:23-25 "Now when he was in Jerusalem at the passover, in the feast day, many believed in his name, when they saw the miracles which he did. ²⁴ But Jesus did not commit himself unto them, because he knew all men, ²⁵ And needed not that any should testify of man: for he knew what was in man."

John 4:1-3 "When therefore the Lord knew how the Pharisees had heard that Jesus made and baptized more disciples than John, ² (Though Jesus himself baptized not, but his disciples,) ³ He left Judaea, and departed again into Galilee."

John 4:26-29, 39 "Jesus saith unto her, I that speak unto thee am he.
²⁷ And upon this came his disciples, and marvelled that he talked with the woman: yet no man said, What seekest thou? or, Why talkest thou with her? ²⁸ The woman then left her waterpot, and went her way into the city, and saith to the men, ²⁹ Come, see a man, which told me all things that ever I did: is not this the Christ? ³⁹ And many of the Samaritans of that city believed on him for the saying of the woman, which testified, He told me all that ever I did."

John 5:5-6 "And a certain man was there, which had an infirmity thirty and eight years. ⁶ When Jesus saw him lie, and knew that he had been now a long time in that case, he saith unto him, Wilt thou be made whole?"

John 5:39-43 "Search the scriptures; for in them ye think ye have eternal life: and they are they which testify of me. ⁴⁰ And ye will not come to me, that ye might have life. ⁴¹ I receive not honour from men. ⁴² But I know you, that ye have not the love of God in you. ⁴³ I am come in my Father's name, and ye receive me not: if another shall come in his own name, him ye will receive."

John 6:14-15 "Then those men, when they had seen the miracle that Jesus did, said, This is of a truth that prophet that should come into the world. 15 When Jesus therefore perceived that they would come and take him by force, to make him a king, he departed again into a mountain himself alone."

John 6:59-61 "These things said he in the synagogue, as he taught in Capernaum. 60 Many therefore of his disciples, when they had heard this, said, This is an hard saying; who can hear it? 61 When Jesus knew in himself that his disciples murmured at it, he said unto them, Doth this offend you?"

John 6:63-64 " It is the spirit that quickeneth; the flesh profiteth nothing: the words that I speak unto you, they are spirit, and they are life. 64 But there are some of you that believe not. For Jesus knew from the beginning who they were that believed not, and who should betray him."

John 13:10-11 "Jesus saith to him, He that is washed needeth not save to wash his feet, but is clean every whit: and ye are clean, but not all. 11 For he knew who should betray him; therefore, said he, Ye are not all clean."

John 16:29-30 "His disciples said unto him, Lo, now speakest thou plainly, and speakest no proverb. 30 Now are we sure that thou knowest all things, and needest not that any man should ask thee: by this, we believe that thou camest forth from God."

John 21:17 "He saith unto him the third time, Simon, son of Jonas, lovest thou me? Peter was grieved because he said unto him the third time, Lovest thou me? And he said unto him, Lord, thou knowest all things; thou knowest that I love thee. Jesus saith unto him, Feed my sheep."

Revelation 2:1-2 "Unto the angel of the church of Ephesus write; These things saith he that holdeth the seven stars in his right hand, who walketh in the midst of the seven golden candlesticks; 2 I know thy works, and thy labour, and thy patience, and how thou canst not bear them which are evil: and thou hast tried them which say they are apostles, and are not, and hast found them liars:"

Revelation 2:8-9 "And unto the angel of the church in Smyrna write; These things saith the first and the last, which was dead, and is alive; 9 I know thy works, and tribulation, and poverty, (but thou art rich) and I know the blasphemy of them which say they are Jews, and are not, but are the synagogue of Satan."

Revelation 2:12-13 "And to the angel of the church in Pergamos write; These things saith he which hath the sharp sword with two edges; 13 I know thy works, and where thou dwellest, even where Satan's seat is: and thou holdest fast my name, and hast not denied my faith, even in those days wherein Antipas was my faithful martyr, who was slain among you, where Satan dwelleth."

Revelation 2:18-19 "And unto the angel of the church in Thyatira write; These things saith the Son of God, who hath his eyes like unto a flame of fire, and his feet are like fine brass; 19 I know thy works, and charity, and service, and faith, and thy patience, and thy works; and the last to be more than the first."

Revelation 3:1 "And unto the angel of the church in Sardis write; These things saith he that hath the seven Spirits of God, and the seven stars; I know thy works, that thou hast a name that thou livest, and art dead.

Revelation 3:7-8 "And to the angel of the church in Philadelphia write; These things saith he that is holy, he that is true, he that hath the key of David, he that openeth, and no man shutteth; and shutteth, and no man openeth; 8 I know thy works: behold, I have set before thee an open door, and no man can shut it: for thou hast a little strength, and hast kept my word, and hast not denied my name."

Revelation 3:14-15 "And unto the angel of the church of the Laodiceans write; These things saith the Amen, the faithful and true witness, the beginning of the creation of God; 15 I know thy works, that thou art neither cold nor hot: I would thou wert cold or hot."

5 OMNIPRESENCE.

Omnipresence is the attribute of God that means, simply put, that God is present everywhere at all times. This can be inferred from one of the psalms of King David:

Psalm 139:7-12 "Whither shall I go from thy spirit? or whither shall I flee from thy presence? 8 If I ascend up into heaven, thou art there: if I make my bed in hell, behold, thou art there. 9 If I take the wings of the morning, and dwell in the uttermost parts of the sea; 10 Even there shall thy hand lead me, and thy right hand shall hold me. 11 If I say, Surely the darkness shall cover me; even the night shall be light about me. 12 Yea, the darkness hideth not from thee; but the night shineth as the day: the darkness and the light are both alike to thee"

The omnipresence of Jesus Christ appears a bit technical to discuss because of His seeming limitation by human flesh. All the same, Jesus was (and is) omnipresent! While on earth His presence was also in heaven as He mentioned to Nicodemus, the Pharisee that went to see Him by night thus:

John 3:13 "And no man hath ascended up to heaven, but he that came down from heaven, even the Son of man which is in heaven" (emphasis added).

Although some recent Bible translations have omitted this aspect of John 3:13, while some authorities have tried to relate it to statements that Jesus made in which He talked about His next destination, yet the statement is not ambiguous. He did not use future tense. There are other claims of Jesus Christ that pass the same message, for example

John 7:34 "Ye shall seek me, and shall not find me: and <u>where I am,</u> thither ye cannot come" (emphasis mine).

John 14:9-11 "Jesus saith unto him, Have I been so long time with you, and yet hast thou not known me, Philip? he that hath seen me hath seen the Father; and how sayest thou then, Show us the Father? 10 Believest thou not that <u>I am in the Father, and the Father in me</u>? the words that I speak unto you I speak not of myself: but the Father that dwelleth in me, he doeth the works. 11 Believe me that <u>I am in the Father,</u> and the Father in me: or else believe me for the very works' sake. (Emphases added).

If Jesus Christ was in the Father that is omnipresent and the Father was in Him, it is easy to infer that Jesus was also omnipresent like the Father.

Matthew 18:20 "For where two or three are gathered together in my name, <u>there am I</u> in the midst of them." (Emphasis added).

Jesus Christ made this statement while still flesh and blood - before He went to the cross. He would have said, "there I will be" rather than "there I am in their midst" if He was referring to His future omnipresence in view.

Matthew 28:18-20 "And Jesus came and spake unto them, saying, All power is given unto me in heaven and in earth. 19 Go ye therefore, and teach all nations, baptizing them in the name of the Father, and of the Son, and of the Holy Ghost: 20 Teaching them to observe all things whatsoever I have commanded you: and, lo, <u>I am with you always, even unto the end of the world.</u> Amen." (Emphasis added).

The pre-existence of Christ has been seen and discussed earlier like in John's introductory words that "In the beginning was the Word, and the Word was with God, and the Word was God." In the above promise of Jesus Christ, we see Him in the present and being in the future. There is a relationship between omnipresence and omniscience. It has been said earlier that Jesus knew all things including things happening in distant places. For instance, when a message was sent to Jesus Christ that Lazarus His friend was sick, He knew that Lazarus was dead.

John 11:11-17 "These things said he: and after that he saith unto them, Our friend Lazarus sleepeth; but I go, that I may awake him out of sleep. 12 Then said his disciples, Lord, if he sleep, he shall do well. 13 Howbeit Jesus spake of his death: but they thought that he had spoken of taking of rest in sleep. 14 Then said Jesus unto them plainly,

Lazarus is dead. 15 And I am glad for your sakes that I was not there, to the intent ye may believe; nevertheless let us go unto him. 16 Then said Thomas, which is called Didymus, unto his fellow disciples, Let us also go, that we may die with him. 17 Then when Jesus came, he found that he had lain in the grave four days already.

The story of Lazarus and the rich man was not a parable. It was a real life situation that Jesus Christ was privy to. The story is as follows:

Luke 16:19-31 "There was a certain rich man, which was clothed in purple and fine linen, and fared sumptuously every day: 20 And there was a certain beggar named Lazarus, which was laid at his gate, full of sores, 21 And desiring to be fed with the crumbs which fell from the rich man's table: moreover the dogs came and licked his sores. 22 And it came to pass, that the beggar died, and was carried by the angels into Abraham's bosom: the rich man also died, and was buried; 23 And in hell he lift up his eyes, being in torments, and seeth Abraham afar off, and Lazarus in his bosom. 24 And he cried and said, Father Abraham, have mercy on me, and send Lazarus, that he may dip the tip of his finger in water, and cool my tongue; for I am tormented in this flame.
25 But Abraham said, Son, remember that thou in thy lifetime receivedst thy good things, and likewise Lazarus evil things: but now he is comforted, and thou art tormented. 26 And beside all this, between us and you there is a great gulf fixed: so that they which would pass from hence to you cannot; neither can they pass to us, that would come from thence. 27 Then he said, I pray thee therefore, father, that thou wouldest send him to my father's house: 28 For I have five brethren; that he may testify unto them, lest they also come into this place of torment.
29 Abraham saith unto him, They have Moses and the prophets; let them hear them. 30 And he said, Nay, father Abraham: but if one went unto them from the dead, they will repent. 31 And he said unto him, If they hear not Moses and the prophets, neither will they be persuaded, though one rose from the dead."

6. COMPASSION

Compassion may be described as an inward feeling of sympathy, pity and distress for someone suffering some sort of pain or ill. Jesus Christ was compassionate while He was physically here performing the works of His ministry. No wonder the book of Hebrews says,

Hebrews 4:15 "For we have not an high priest which cannot be touched with the feeling of our infirmities; but was in all points tempted like as we are, yet without sin."

He showed compassion and taught it. Jesus Christ had compassion on the people that crucified Him and prayed to His Father: "

Luke 23:34 "Then said Jesus, Father, forgive them; for they know not what they do."

Some of the many Bible verses that refer to the compassion of Jesus Christ are as follows:

Matthew 9:36 "But when he saw the multitudes, he was moved with compassion on them, because they fainted, and were scattered abroad, as sheep having no shepherd."

Matthew 14:14 "And Jesus went forth, and saw a great multitude, and was moved with compassion toward them, and he healed their sick."

Matthew 15:32 "Then Jesus called his disciples unto him, and said, I have compassion on the multitude, because they continue with me now three days, and have nothing to eat: and I will not send them away fasting, lest they faint in the way. Matthew 18:27 "Then the lord of that servant was moved with compassion, and loosed him, and forgave him the debt."

Matthew 20:34 "So Jesus had compassion on them, and touched their eyes: and immediately their eyes received sight, and they followed him."

Mark 1:40-41 "And there came a leper to him, beseeching him, and kneeling down to him, and saying unto him, If thou wilt, thou canst make me clean. 41 And Jesus, moved with compassion, put forth his hand, and touched him, and saith unto him, I will; be thou clean."

Mark 3:5 "And when he had looked round about on them with anger, being grieved for the hardness of their hearts, he saith unto the man, Stretch forth thine hand. And he stretched it out: and his hand was restored whole as the other."

Mark 5:1-19 "And they came over unto the other side of the sea, into the country of the Gadarenes. 2 And when he was come out of the ship, immediately there met him out of the tombs a man with an unclean spirit, 3 Who had his dwelling among the tombs; and no man could bind him, no, not with chains: 4 Because that he had been often bound with fetters and chains, and the chains had been plucked asunder by him, and the fetters broken in pieces: neither could any man tame him. 5 And always, night and day, he was in the mountains, and in the tombs, crying, and cutting himself with stones.
6 But when he saw Jesus afar off, he ran and worshipped him, 7 And cried with a loud voice, and said, What have I to do with thee, Jesus, thou Son of the most high God? I adjure thee by God, that thou torment me not. 8 For he said unto him, Come out of the man, thou unclean spirit. 9 And he asked him, What is thy name? And he answered, saying, My name is Legion: for we are many. 10 And he besought him much that he would not send them away out of the country.

¹¹ Now there was there nigh unto the mountains a great herd of swine feeding. ¹² And all the devils besought him, saying, Send us into the swine, that we may enter into them. ¹³ And forthwith Jesus gave them leave. And the unclean spirits went out, and entered into the swine: and the herd ran violently down a steep place into the sea, (they were about two thousand;) and were choked in the sea.

¹⁴ And they that fed the swine fled, and told it in the city, and in the country. And they went out to see what it was that was done. ¹⁵ And they come to Jesus, and see him that was possessed with the devil, and had the legion, sitting, and clothed, and in his right mind: and they were afraid. ¹⁶ And they that saw it told them how it befell to him that was possessed with the devil, and also concerning the swine. ¹⁷ And they began to pray him to depart out of their coasts. ¹⁸ And when he was come into the ship, he that had been possessed with the devil prayed him that he might be with him. ¹⁹ Howbeit Jesus suffered him not, but saith unto him, Go home to thy friends, and tell them how great things the Lord hath done for thee, and hath had compassion on thee."

Mark 6:34 "And Jesus, when he came out, saw much people, and was moved with compassion toward them, because they were as sheep not having a shepherd: and he began to teach them many things."

Mark 8:2-3 "I have compassion on the multitude, because they have now been with me three days, and have nothing to eat: ³ And if I send them away fasting to their own houses, they will faint by the way: for divers of them came from far."

Luke 6:38 "Give, and it shall be given unto you; good measure, pressed down, and shaken together, and running over, shall men give into your bosom. For with the same measure that ye mete withal it shall be measured to you again."

Luke 7:11-13 "And it came to pass the day after, that he went into a city called Nain; and many of his disciples went with him, and much people. ¹² Now when he came nigh to the gate of the city, behold, there was a dead man carried out, the only son of his mother, and she was a widow: and much people of the city was with her. ¹³ And when the Lord saw her, he had compassion on her, and said unto her, Weep not."

Luke 9:11 "And the people, when they knew it, followed him: and he received them, and spake unto them of the kingdom of God, and healed them that had need of healing."

Luke 10:33-36 "But a certain Samaritan, as he journeyed, came where he was: and when he saw him, he had compassion on him, ³⁴ And went to him, and bound up his wounds, pouring in oil and wine, and set him on his own beast, and brought him to an inn, and took care of him. ³⁵ And on the morrow when he departed, he took out two pence, and gave them to the host, and said unto him, Take care of him; and whatsoever thou spendest more, when I come again, I will repay thee. ³⁶ Which now of these three, thinkest thou, was neighbour unto him that fell among the thieves?"

Luke 15:11-20 "And he said, A certain man had two sons: 12 And the younger of them said to his father, Father, give me the portion of goods that falleth to me. And he divided unto them his living. 13 And not many days after the younger son gathered all together, and took his journey into a far country, and there wasted his substance with riotous living. 14 And when he had spent all, there arose a mighty famine in that land; and he began to be in want. 15 And he went and joined himself to a citizen of that country; and he sent him into his fields to feed swine. 16 And he would fain have filled his belly with the husks that the swine did eat: and no man gave unto him. 17 And when he came to himself, he said, How many hired servants of my father's have bread enough and to spare, and I perish with hunger! 18 I will arise and go to my father, and will say unto him, Father, I have sinned against heaven, and before thee, 19 And am no more worthy to be called thy son: make me as one of thy hired servants. 20 And he arose, and came to his father. But when he was yet a great way off, his father saw him, and had compassion, and ran, and fell on his neck, and kissed him."

John 7:48-49 " Have any of the rulers or of the Pharisees believed on him? 49 But this people who knoweth not the law are cursed."

John 11:33-38 "When Jesus therefore saw her weeping, and the Jews also weeping which came with her, he groaned in the spirit, and was troubled. 34 And said, Where have ye laid him? They said unto him, Lord, come and see.
35 Jesus wept.
36 Then said the Jews, Behold how he loved him! 37 And some of them said, Could not this man, which opened the eyes of the blind, have caused that even this man should not have died? 38 Jesus therefore again groaning in himself cometh to the grave. It was a cave, and a stone lay upon it."

7 JESUS IS IMMUTABLE.

One of the attributes of God is immutability – the unchangeable nature. He cannot be a better or worse God. In Malachi 3:6, the Lord said, " For I am the Lord, I change not ; . . ." Thiessen says that this is true of the plans, promises and person of Jesus Christ. [24] The Bible says,

Hebrews 13:8 "Jesus Christ the same yesterday, and to day, and for ever."

8 JESUS CHRIST WAS GOD.
All the attributes above that show Him as supernatural are actually attributes of God. Additionally, there are passages in Scriptures in which Jesus Christ ascribed to Himself divine authority. He did sometimes quote from Scriptures but other times He

---

[24] Thiessen, 140.

originated His sayings. Some of these references have, of course, been mentioned earlier under different discussions. They are as follows:

Matthew 4:5-7 (cff. Deut. 6:16) "Then the devil taketh him up into the holy city, and setteth him on a pinnacle of the temple, 6 And saith unto him, If thou be the Son of God, cast thyself down: for it is written, He shall give his angels charge concerning thee: and in their hands they shall bear thee up, lest at any time thou dash thy foot against a stone. 7 Jesus said unto him, It is written again, Thou shalt not tempt **the Lord thy God.**" (Emphasis added).

Deuteronomy 6:16 "Ye shall not tempt the Lord your God, as ye tempted him in Massah."

Matthew 5:21-22 "Ye have heard that it was said of them of old time, Thou shalt not kill; and whosoever shall kill shall be in danger of the judgment: 22 **But I say unto you,** That whosoever is angry with his brother without a cause shall be in danger of the judgment: and whosoever shall say to his brother, Raca, shall be in danger of the council: but whosoever shall say, Thou fool, shall be in danger of hell fire. (Emphasis added).

Matthew 5:27-28 "Ye have heard that it was said by them of old time, Thou shalt not commit adultery: 28 **But I say unto you,** That whosoever looketh on a woman to lust after her hath committed adultery with her already in his heart." (Emphasis added).

Matthew 5:31-32 "It hath been said, Whosoever shall put away his wife, let him give her a writing of divorcement: 32 **But I say unto you,** That whosoever shall put away his wife, saving for the cause of fornication, causeth her to commit adultery: and whosoever shall marry her that is divorced committeth adultery." (Emphasis added).

Matthew 5:33-37 "Again, ye have heard that it hath been said by them of old time, Thou shalt not forswear thyself, but shalt perform unto the Lord thine oaths: 34 **But I say unto you,** Swear not at all; neither by heaven; for it is God's throne: 35 Nor by the earth; for it is his footstool: neither by Jerusalem; for it is the city of the great King. 36 Neither shalt thou swear by thy head, because thou canst not make one hair white or black. 37 But let your communication be, Yea, yea; Nay, nay: for whatsoever is more than these cometh of evil."

Matthew 5:38-39 "Ye have heard that it hath been said, An eye for an eye, and a tooth for a tooth: 39 **But I say unto you,** That ye resist not evil: but whosoever shall smite thee on thy right cheek, turn to him the other also."

Matthew 5:43-44 "Ye have heard that it hath been said, Thou shalt love thy neighbour, and hate thine enemy. 44 **But I say unto you,** Love your enemies, bless them that curse you, do good to them that hate you, and pray for them which despitefully use you, and persecute you;"

Matthew 7:21-23 "**Not every one that saith unto me, Lord, Lord, shall enter into the kingdom of heaven**; but he that doeth the will of my Father which is in heaven. [22] Many will say to me in that day, Lord, Lord, have we not prophesied in thy name? and in thy name have cast out devils? and in thy name done many wonderful works? [23] And then will I profess unto them, I never knew you: depart from me, ye that work iniquity."

Having Power to Forgive Sins on Earth.

Matthew 9:6 "But that ye may know that the Son of man hath power on earth to forgive sins, (then saith he to the sick of the palsy,) Arise, take up thy bed, and go unto thine house."

Matthew 10:14-15 "And whosoever shall not receive you, nor hear your words, when ye depart out of that house or city, shake off the dust of your feet. [15] Verily I say unto you, It shall be more tolerable for the land of Sodom and Gomorrha in the day of judgment, than for that city."

Matthew 10:31-33 "Fear ye not therefore, ye are of more value than many sparrows. [32] Whosoever therefore shall confess me before men, him will I confess also before my Father which is in heaven. [33] But whosoever shall deny me before men, him will I also deny before my Father which is in heaven."

Matthew 11:27-28 "All things are delivered unto me of my Father: and no man knoweth the Son, but the Father; neither knoweth any man the Father, save the Son, and he to whomsoever the Son will reveal him. [28] Come unto me, all ye that labour and are heavy laden, and I will give you rest."

Matthew 12:5-6 "Or have ye not read in the law, how that on the sabbath days the priests in the temple profane the sabbath, and are blameless? [6] But I say unto you, That in this place is one greater than the temple."

Matthew 12:7-8 "But if ye had known what this meaneth, I will have mercy, and not sacrifice, ye would not have condemned the guiltless. [8] For the Son of man is Lord even of the sabbath day.

Matthew 12:41-42 "The men of Nineveh shall rise in judgment with this generation, and shall condemn it: because they repented at the preaching of Jonas; and, behold, a greater than Jonas is here. [42] The queen of the south shall rise up in the judgment with this generation, and shall condemn it: for she came from the uttermost parts of the earth to hear the wisdom of Solomon; and, behold, a greater than Solomon is here."

Matthew 13:41-43 "The Son of man shall send forth his angels, and they shall gather out of his kingdom all things that offend, and them which do iniquity;
42 And shall cast them into a furnace of fire: there shall be wailing and gnashing of teeth. 43 Then shall the righteous shine forth as the sun in the kingdom of their Father. Who hath ears to hear, let him hear."

Matthew 18:18-19 "Verily I say unto you, Whatsoever ye shall bind on earth shall be bound in heaven: and whatsoever ye shall loose on earth shall be loosed in heaven. 19 Again I say unto you, That if two of you shall agree on earth as touching any thing that they shall ask, it shall be done for them of my Father which is in heaven."

Matthew 18:35 "So likewise shall my heavenly Father do also unto you, if ye from your hearts forgive not everyone his brother their trespasses."

Matthew 19:8 "He saith unto them, Moses because of the hardness of your hearts suffered you to put away your wives: but from the beginning it was not so."

Matthew 24:35 "Heaven and earth shall pass away, but my words shall not pass away."

Matthew 25:31-32 "When the Son of man shall come in his glory, and all the holy angels with him, then shall he sit upon the throne of his glory: 32 And before him shall be gathered all nations: and he shall separate them one from another, as a shepherd divideth his sheep from the goats:"

Matthew 28:18 "And Jesus came and spake unto them, saying, All power is given unto me in heaven and in earth."

Mark 2:5 "When Jesus saw their faith, he said unto the sick of the palsy, Son, thy sins be forgiven thee. 18 And Jesus came and spake unto them, saying, All power is given unto me in heaven and in earth."

Mark 2:27-28 "And he said unto them, The sabbath was made for man, and not man for the sabbath: 28 Therefore the Son of man is Lord also of the sabbath."

Mark 5:19 "Howbeit Jesus suffered him not, but saith unto him, Go home to thy friends, and tell them how great things the Lord hath done for thee, and hath had compassion on thee."

Luke 10:19-20 "Behold, I give unto you power to tread on serpents and scorpions, and over all the power of the enemy: and nothing shall by any means hurt you. 20 Notwithstanding in this rejoice not, that the spirits are subject unto you; but rather rejoice, because your names are written in heaven."

Luke 10:22 "All things are delivered to me of my Father: and no man knoweth who the Son is, but the Father; and who the Father is, but the Son, and he to whom the Son will reveal him."

John 4:10 "Jesus answered and said unto her, If thou knewest the gift of God, and who it is that saith to thee, Give me to drink; thou wouldest have asked of him, and he would have given thee living water."

John 4:14 "But whosoever drinketh of the water that I shall give him shall never thirst; but the water that I shall give him shall be in him a well of water springing up into everlasting life."

John 4:26 "Jesus saith unto her, I that speak unto thee am he."

John 5:34-38 "But I receive not testimony from man: but these things I say, that ye might be saved. 35 He was a burning and a shining light: and ye were willing for a season to rejoice in his light. 36 But I have greater witness than that of John: for the works which the Father hath given me to finish, the same works that I do, bear witness of me, that the Father hath sent me. 37 And the Father himself, which hath sent me, hath borne witness of me. Ye have neither heard his voice at any time, nor seen his shape. 38 And ye have not his word abiding in you: for whom he hath sent, him ye believe not."

John 13:19 "Now I tell you before it come, that, when it is come to pass, ye may believe that I am he."

John 14:2 "In my Father's house are many mansions: if it were not so, I would have told you. I go to prepare a place for you."

John 14:6-9 "Jesus saith unto him, I am the way, the truth, and the life: no man cometh unto the Father, but by me. 7 If ye had known me, ye should have known my Father also: and from henceforth ye know him, and have seen him. 8 Philip saith unto him, Lord, show us the Father, and it sufficeth us. 9 Jesus saith unto him, Have I been so long time with you, and yet hast thou not known me, Philip? he that hath seen me hath seen the Father; and how sayest thou then, Show us the Father?"

John 14:12 "Verily, verily, I say unto you, He that believeth on me, the works that I do shall he do also; and greater works than these shall he do; because I go unto my Father."

John 14:20 "At that day ye shall know that I am in my Father, and ye in me, and I in you."

John 14:23-24 "Jesus answered and said unto him, If a man love me, he will keep my words: and my Father will love him, and we will come unto him, and make our abode with him. ²⁴ He that loveth me not keepeth not my sayings: and the word which ye hear is not mine, but the Father's which sent me.

CHAPTER 10

JESUS CHRIST WAS PROPHET, HIGH PRIEST AND KING

While preaching and teaching, Jesus Christ spoke forth. He rebuked the Scribes and Pharisees and, occasionally, His disciples. He taught the truths of the Kingdom of God, and heaven and hell as no one else did – in parables and in plain language. His *Sermon on the Mount (Matt. 5, 6, 7)*, teaching on the Mount of Olives, and the Upper Room discourse were prophetic. He foretold events such as His death and resurrection, that His disciples would flee at His arrest, Peter's denials of ever knowing Him, as well as the signs of the end times and His future return to earth to start His millennial kingdom. All these prophecies, with the exception of His Second Coming, have been fulfilled. These were characteristic of a prophet.

His High Priestly functions became more pronounced in the 'Upper Room' when He interceded for His disciples (present and future) recorded in John 17. Aaronic priesthood involved many sacrifices to God on behalf of themselves and the people. Jesus satisfied that function despite that He was not a Levite. He offered a once-for-all sacrifice with His own unblemished blood. But, on the other hand, Jesus Christ is described as Priest after the order of Melchizedek – a king-priest with unknown genealogy. This priesthood was superior to the Levitical priesthood because it was a royal priesthood. Also Jesus Christ entered the physical presence of the Father with His own blood rather than the blood of goats and bulls.

Jesus Christ was 'born King' as the Magi requested to be shown the whereabouts of Him that was born King of the Jews (Matthew 2:2). When the Magi found Him they worshipped Him. During the trials by Pontius Pilate the dialogue with Jesus Christ, in which Jesus confirmed His kingship, makes for interesting reading as follows:

John 18:33-37 "Then Pilate entered into the judgment hall again, and called Jesus, and said unto him, Art thou the King of the Jews? 34 Jesus answered him, Sayest thou this thing of thyself, or did others tell it thee of me? 35 Pilate answered, Am I a Jew? Thine own nation and the chief priests have delivered thee unto me: what hast thou done?

191

[36] Jesus answered, My kingdom is not of this world: if my kingdom were of this world, then would my servants fight, that I should not be delivered to the Jews: but now is my kingdom not from hence.
[37] Pilate therefore said unto him, Art thou a king then? Jesus answered, Thou sayest that I am a king. To this end was I born, and for this cause came I into the world, that I should bear witness unto the truth. Every one that is of the truth heareth my voice."

During the same trial period, people mockingly bowed down to Him and hailed Him King. Secondly, Pilate's inscription above the head of Jesus Christ on the cross described Him as King of the Jews. So Jesus Christ died a King,

Luke 23:38 "And a superscription also was written over him in letters of Greek, and Latin, and Hebrew, THIS IS THE KING OF THE JEWS."

Jesus Christ will also return in glory to earth as a King.

If Jesus Christ was acting a movie script the duration of the movie would not have spanned over a period of 3½ years, but a few hours. For over 2000 years rather than die Christianity, the "offspring" of Christ has been growing in spite of persecution. The counsel of Gamaliel, a Pharisee to the Sanhedrin has been proven right that if the "movement" was of God (and it is), man cannot stop it. The celebrated counsel is reproduced here:

Acts 5:29-39 "Then Peter and the other apostles answered and said, We ought to obey God rather than men. [30] The God of our fathers raised up Jesus, whom ye slew and hanged on a tree. [31] Him hath God exalted with his right hand to be a Prince and a Saviour, for to give repentance to Israel, and forgiveness of sins. [32] And we are his witnesses of these things; and so is also the Holy Ghost, whom God hath given to them that obey him. [33] When they heard that, they were cut to the heart, and took counsel to slay them.
[34] Then stood there up one in the council, a Pharisee, named Gamaliel, a doctor of the law, had in reputation among all the people, and commanded to put the apostles forth a little space; [35] And said unto them, Ye men of Israel, take heed to yourselves what ye intend to do as touching these men. [36] For before these days rose up Theudas, boasting himself to be somebody; to whom a number of men, about four hundred, joined themselves: who was slain; and all, as many as obeyed him, were scattered, and brought to nought.
[37] After this man rose up Judas of Galilee in the days of the taxing, and drew away much people after him: he also perished; and all, even as many as obeyed him, were dispersed. [38] And now I say unto you, Refrain from these men, and let them alone: for if this counsel or this work be of men, it will come to nought: [39] But if it be of God, ye cannot overthrow it; lest haply ye be found even to fight against God.

CHAPTER 11

JESUS CHRIST DIED, AROSE AND ASCENDED.

Early in His ministry, the Jews demanded a sign from Him in view of the many great things He was doing. Jesus Christ then responded, *"Destroy this temple, and in three days I will raise it up"* (John 2:19). This was a prediction of His impending death and resurrection. He also predicted to His disciples at several occasions that He would be killed, buried, and on the third day raised, just like Prophet Jonah was three days and three nights in the belly of the fish.

Crucifixion and Death.

Prophet Isaiah prophesied the crucifixion of Jesus Christ as follows:

Isaiah 53:5 "But he was wounded for our transgressions, he was bruised for our iniquities: the chastisement of our peace was upon him; and with his stripes we are healed."

Jesus Christ was scourged, which resulted in His loss of much blood to the extent that He was disfigured beyond recognition as Isaiah prophesied:

Isaiah 52:14 " As many were astonied at thee; his visage was so marred more than any man, and his form more than the sons of men:"

He was then crucified on the Roman cross between two robbers on the eve of the great Passover – *"Then were there two thieves crucified with him, one on the right hand, and another on the left"* (Matthew 27:37). This was in fulfillment of the prophecy of Isaiah:

Isaiah 53:12 "Therefore will I divide him a portion with the great, and he shall divide the spoil with the strong; because he hath poured out his soul unto death: and he was numbered with the transgressors; and he bare the sin of many, and made intercession for the transgressors."

The Bible says that Jesus Christ died (gave up the ghost). All four Gospels recorded the death of the Lord Jesus Christ thus:

Matthew 27:50-51 "Jesus, when he had cried again with a loud voice, yielded up the ghost. 51 And, behold, the veil of the temple was rent in twain from the top to the bottom; and the earth did quake, and the rocks rent;"

Mark 15:39 "And when the centurion, which stood over against him, saw that he so cried out, and gave up the ghost, he said, Truly this man was the Son of God."

Luke 23:46 "And when Jesus had cried with a loud voice, he said, Father, into thy hands I commend my spirit: and having said thus, he gave up the ghost."

John 19:30 "When Jesus, therefore, had received the vinegar, he said, It is finished: and he bowed his head, and gave up the ghost."

This death was as voluntary as it was compelling. What does this mean? One of three instances of Jesus talking about His voluntarily laying down His life is as follows:

John 10:17 "Therefore doth my Father love me, because I lay down my life, that I might take it again."

At the same time, Jesus Christ had earlier told His followers that He was doing His Father's will all the time, just like Isaiah the prophet said that it was the pleasure of the Father for Jesus Christ to suffer and die for humanity:

Isaiah 53:10-11 "Yet it pleased the Lord to bruise him; he hath put him to grief: when thou shalt make his soul an offering for sin, he shall see his seed, he shall prolong his days, and the pleasure of the Lord shall prosper in his hand. 11 He shall see of the travail of his soul, and shall be satisfied: by his knowledge shall my righteous servant justify many; for he shall bear their iniquities."

Also when the "cup" came close, He prayed that the cup should pass; but if that was not the Father's will, let the will of the Father be done.

Matthew 26:38-39 "Then saith he unto them, My soul is exceeding sorrowful, even unto death: tarry ye here, and watch with me. 39 And he went a little farther, and fell on his face, and prayed, saying, O my Father, if it be possible, let this cup pass from me: nevertheless not as I will, but as thou wilt."

Luke 22:41-42 "And he was withdrawn from them about a stone's cast, and kneeled down, and prayed, 42 Saying, Father, if thou be willing, remove this cup from me: nevertheless not my will, but thine, be done."

But the emphasis here is on the fact that Jesus Christ died against the claims of some antagonists, religions and scholars that suggest various negative things. Some say He disappeared. The Docetists say that Jesus Christ was not really a flesh and blood man but only appeared to be one. In that case, the idea of dying was not applicable to Him. Some have said that Jesus was not even crucified in the first place. The Telegraph of

Friday, November 10 2017 said that a scholar had claimed that Jesus might not have died nailed to the cross for lack of evidence (to the scholar) that the Romans crucified prisoners 2,000 years earlier. But Jesus was not a prisoner! And one wonders whether the 'scholar' had studied extra-Biblical books and materials.

Burial of Jesus Christ.

And He was buried! The prophet had foretold His burial:

Isaiah 53:9 "And he made his grave with the wicked, and with the rich in his death; because he had done no violence, neither was any deceit in his mouth."

After Jesus died the Roman soldier pierced His side to ascertain that He had died, in fulfillment of the prophecies in the Psalms and Zechariah thus:

Psalm 22:16 "For dogs have compassed me: the assembly of the wicked have inclosed me: they pierced my hands and my feet."

Zechariah 12:10 "And I will pour upon the house of David, and upon the inhabitants of Jerusalem, the spirit of grace and of supplications: and they shall look upon me whom they have pierced, and they shall mourn for him, as one mourneth for his only son, and shall be in bitterness for him, as one that is in bitterness for his firstborn."

Fulfillment:

John 19:34-37 "But one of the soldiers with a spear pierced his side, and forthwith came there out blood and water. [35] And he that saw it bare record, and his record is true: and he knoweth that he saith true, that ye might believe. [36] For these things were done, that the scripture should be fulfilled, A bone of him shall not be broken. [37] And again another scripture saith, They shall look on him whom they pierced."

Then a rich man, Joseph of Arimathaea sought Governor Pilate's permission to take down and bury the body of Jesus Christ. With the help of another Jewish religious leader by the name Nicodemus[25], who earlier went to Jesus by night (John 3:1-2;

---

[25] Nicodemus in one occasion tried to defend Jesus Christ and His ministry. The reference is John 7:45-52 – "Then came the officers to the chief priests and Pharisees; and they said unto them, Why have ye not brought him? [46] The officers answered, Never man spake like this man. [47] Then answered them the Pharisees, Are ye also deceived? [48] Have any of the rulers or of the Pharisees believed on him? [49] But this people who knoweth not the law are cursed. [50] Nicodemus saith unto them, (he that came to Jesus by night, being one of them,) [51] Doth our law judge any man, before it hear him, and know what he doeth? [52] They answered and said unto him, Art thou also of Galilee? Search, and look: for out of Galilee ariseth no prophet."

7:50), Joseph of Arimathaea brought down the dead body of Jesus and buried it in his personal tomb in which nobody had previously been laid.

John 3:1-2 "There was a man of the Pharisees, named Nicodemus, a ruler of the Jews: [2] The same came to Jesus by night, and said unto him, Rabbi, we know that thou art a teacher come from God: for no man can do these miracles that thou doest, except God be with him.

John 7:50 "Nicodemus saith unto them, (he that came to Jesus by night, being one of them,)"

This burial of the body of Jesus Christ by Joseph and Nicodemus was a fulfillment of Isaiah's prophecy, which says;

Isaiah 53:9 "And he made his grave with the wicked, and with the rich in his death; because he had done no violence, neither was any deceit in his mouth."

The Resurrection of Jesus Christ And His Appearances.

The psalmist foretold that Jesus would not remain in the grave:

Psalm 16:10 "For thou wilt not leave my soul in hell; neither wilt thou suffer thine Holy One to see corruption."

In fulfillment of this, Jesus Christ arose on the first day of the week, being the third day of His death as He told the Jews He would. This is well presented by Luke thus:

Luke 24:4-7 "And it came to pass, as they were much perplexed thereabout, behold, two men stood by them in shining garments: [5] And as they were afraid, and bowed down their faces to the earth, they said unto them, Why seek ye the living among the dead? [6] He is not here, but is risen: remember how he spake unto you when he was yet in Galilee, [7] Saying, The Son of man must be delivered into the hands of sinful men, and be crucified, and the third day rise again."

Jesus Christ Made Physical Appearances.

In order to prove Himself and encourage His disciples, Jesus Christ made many physical, literal, personal appearances to His disciples at different times and at different locations. Details of these appearances are found in chapter 6.

He Physically Ascended into Heaven.

To ascend means to go up. It is noted that just like it was prophesied in the OT that He would ascend, Jesus Christ Himself announced several times that He would ascend into heaven – to His Father, from Whom He came. After commissioning His disciples for the global evangelism and discipling, He physically and literally ascended into heaven while His disciples were surprisingly watching and gazing into the sky even after He had gone out of their sight. He did not just suddenly vanish or disappear into thin air. The disciples watched Him ascend.

Jesus could not have been acting ascension into heaven. No man of his own volition decides to, and goes to heaven in his physical body. There were only two nearly similar instances of ascension into heaven in OT times – Enoch and Prophet Elijah.

Genesis 5:21-24 "And Enoch lived sixty and five years, and begat Methuselah: 22 And Enoch walked with God after he begat Methuselah three hundred years, and begat sons and daughters: 23 And all the days of Enoch were three hundred sixty and five years: 24 And Enoch walked with God: and he was not; for God took him.

2 Kings 2:1, 11-12 "And it came to pass, when the Lord would take up Elijah into heaven by a whirlwind, that Elijah went with Elisha from Gilgal." 11 "And it came to pass, as they still went on, and talked, that, behold, there appeared a chariot of fire, and horses of fire, and parted them both asunder; and Elijah went up by a whirlwind into heaven. 12 And Elisha saw it, and he cried, My father, my father, the chariot of Israel, and the horsemen thereof. And he saw him no more: and he took hold of his own clothes, and rent them in two pieces."

CHAPTER 12

JESUS CHRIST WAS DOING THE WILL OF GOD THE FATHER

The apostle Paul tells us that Jesus Christ was very humble. Paul says,

Philippians 2:5-8 "Let this mind be in you, which was also in Christ Jesus: 6 Who, being in the form of God, thought it not robbery to be equal with God: 7 But made himself of no reputation, and took upon him the form of a servant, and was made in the likeness of men: 8 And being found in fashion as a man, he humbled himself, and became obedient unto death, even the death of the cross."

The humility of Jesus Christ was characterized and evidenced by His doing the will of His Father all the time. The psalmist had earlier prophesied before the birth of Jesus Christ that Jesus would do the Father's will:

Psalm 40:7-10 "Then said I, Lo, I come: in the volume of the book it is written of me, 8 I delight to do thy will, O my God: yea, thy law is within my heart. 9 I have preached righteousness in the great congregation: lo, I have not refrained my lips, O Lord, thou knowest. 10 I have not hid thy righteousness within my heart; I have declared thy faithfulness and thy salvation: I have not concealed thy lovingkindness and thy truth from the great congregation."

Similarly, Prophet Isaiah foresaw and foretold that in view of the anointing of the Holy Spirit on Him, Jesus Christ would come to do the will of the Father as detailed in his prophecy as follows:

Isaiah 61:1-3 "The Spirit of the Lord God is upon me; because the Lord hath anointed me to preach good tidings unto the meek; he hath sent me to bind up the brokenhearted, to proclaim liberty to the captives, and the opening of the prison to them that are bound; 2 To proclaim the acceptable year of the Lord, and the day of vengeance of our God; to comfort all that mourn; 3 To appoint unto them that mourn in Zion, to give unto them beauty for ashes, the oil of joy for mourning, the garment of praise for the spirit of heaviness; that they might be called trees of righteousness, the planting of the Lord, that he might be glorified."

Jesus Christ Testified To Doing The Will Of The Father.

On various occasions, Jesus Christ testified to the fact that everything He did here on earth was in accordance with the will of the Father. He did nothing of His own accord as a humble and obedient Son. Commenting on Matthew 3:15, Ironside said that it is as if Jesus Christ said to John that He wished to submit to baptism as a pledge that He had come to fulfill every righteous demand of the throne of God on behalf of sinful men.[26] Relevant Bible references to this claim are as follows:

Matthew 3:15 "And Jesus answering said unto him, Suffer it to be so now: for thus it becometh us to fulfill all righteousness. Then he suffered him."

Matthew 7:21 "Not everyone that saith unto me, Lord, Lord, shall enter into the kingdom of heaven; but he that doeth the will of my Father which is in heaven."

Luke 2:49 "And he said unto them, How is it that ye sought me? wist ye not that I must be about my Father's business?

Luke 22:42 "Saying, Father, if thou be willing, remove this cup from me: nevertheless not my will, but thine, be done."

John 4:34 " Jesus saith unto them, My meat is to do the will of him that sent me, and to finish his work."

John 5:19 "Then answered Jesus and said unto them, Verily, verily, I say unto you, The Son can do nothing of himself, but what he seeth the Father do: for what things soever he doeth, these also doeth the Son likewise."

John 5:30-36 "I can of mine own self do nothing: as I hear, I judge: and my judgment is just; because I seek not mine own will, but the will of the Father which hath sent me. 31 If I bear witness of myself, my witness is not true. 32 There is another that beareth witness of me; and I know that the witness which he witnesseth of me is true. 33 Ye sent unto John, and he bare witness unto the truth. 34 But I receive not testimony from man: but these things I say, that ye might be saved. 35 He was a burning and a shining light: and ye were willing for a season to rejoice in his light. 36 But I have greater witness than that of John: for the works which the Father hath given me to finish, the same works that I do, bear witness of me, that the Father hath sent me."

John 6:37-38 "All that the Father giveth me shall come to me; and him that cometh to me I will in no wise cast out. 38 For I came down from heaven, not to do mine own will, but the will of him that sent me."

John 6:39-40 "And this is the Father's will which hath sent me, that of all which he hath given me I should lose nothing, but should raise it up again at the last day.
40 And this is the will of him that sent me, that every one which seeth the Son, and th on him, may have everlasting life: and I will raise him up at the last day."

---

[26] H. A. Ironside. *An Ironside Expository Commentary. Matthew.* (Grand Rapids: Kregel Publications, 1976), 22.

John 6:57 "As the living Father hath sent me, and I live by the Father: so he that eateth me, even he shall live by me."

John 8:29 "And he that sent me is with me: the Father hath not left me alone; for I do always those things that please him."

John 17:4 "I have glorified thee on the earth: I have finished the work which thou gavest me to do."

Not only that Jesus Christ did the will of His Father, but He also encouraged His disciples to seek to do the same, and pray so. You find some of this in the prayer template He gave them:

Matthew 6:9-10 "After this manner, therefore, pray ye: Our Father which art in heaven, Hallowed be thy name. 10 Thy kingdom come, Thy will be done in earth, as it is in heaven."

Matthew 12:48-50 "But he answered and said unto him that told him, Who is my mother? and who are my brethren? 49 And he stretched forth his hand toward his disciples, and said, Behold my mother and my brethren! 50 For whosoever shall do the will of my Father which is in heaven, the same is my brother, and sister, and mother."

Jesus Christ Was Rewarded.

Jesus Christ was obediently working out the will of the Father regarding His plan of redemption of mankind, rather than acting a man-made script; that is why Jesus Christ, before dismissing His Spirit, declared that it was finished.

John 19:30 "When Jesus therefore had received the vinegar, he said, It is finished: and he bowed his head, and gave up the ghost."

For being this obedient to the will of God the Father, God gave Jesus Christ a reward as the apostle Paul exposed in his letter to the Philippians:

Philippians 2:9-11 "Wherefore God also hath highly exalted him, and given him a name which is above every name: 10 That at the name of Jesus every knee should bow, of things in heaven, and things in earth, and things under the earth; 11 And that every tongue should confess that Jesus Christ is Lord, to the glory of God the Father."

CHAPTER 13

CONCLUSIONS AND RECOMMENDATIONS

Jesus Christ Was Supernatural.

Jesus Christ had an unusual virgin birth, the like of which never occurred before His, and will never occur again. National events, precisely a decreed census worked out to make possible His prophesied birth in Bethlehem. His virgin mother was Mary.

He performed many miracles that showed His authority over sickness and disease, death, demons and elements of nature. Jesus had power to multiply few resources to feed five thousand men in one instance, and four thousand men in another instance. He taught with great authority - not like the Scribes and Pharisees did. He had power to forgive sin on earth, an act the Pharisees deemed blasphemous because nobody has such power but God. Jesus Christ also did demonstrate the art of forgiving by asking the Father to forgive the people that were putting Him to death. He was also compassionate - a trait He displayed many times.

Jesus knew all things (**omniscient**) including the hearts of men. He knew who would betray Him ahead of the action; He knew that Lazarus was dead while He was far from Bethany, hometown of Lazarus. At the age of twelve He was able to engage teachers in the temple at Jerusalem, astonishingly asking them questions and answering theirs. His referencing during His teaching ministry was unequalled. Examples included His sign of Jonah, reference to the days of Noah and Sodom and Gomorrah; His reply to the question about divorce; the source of the baptism of John, paying taxes, the abomination of desolation by Prophet Daniel, etc.

Jesus Christ's humility surpassed that of any known human being, as He was obedient to His heavenly Father, and humble to the point of dying shamefully on the cross for sins He did not commit. He bore the Roman soldiers' bloody scourging, along with the piercing into His head of the crown of thorns with all the associated pains. He allowed Himself to be lifted alive on the cross, not dying on the ground from the (scourging) lashes that tore His skin and caused much bleeding. If He had died before being lifted,

201

it would not have been fulfilled His claim to draw all men unto Himself when lifted. He had said, *"And I, if I be lifted up from the earth, will draw all men unto me"* (John 12:32). While on earth He was present with the Father in heaven too.

The apostle John said, "Jesus did many other signs in the presence of the disciples, which are not written in this book" (John 20:30 ESV). If Jesus Christ was acting a script like a movie star, He would not have been able to perform the supernatural acts and the aspects that involved third parties, especially the birth, trials, crucifixion and death parts of the Jesus story. He would not have chosen to be born in a village like Bethlehem or in a manger. Neither would He have chosen nor accepted to be really crucified. He probably would have stopped at only the prophecies without preaching the beatitudes and the lessons He taught the Pharisees, Scribes and His disciples, which are not explicitly or implicitly in the prophecies.

RECOMMENDATIONS

It is clear that while walking the earth physically, Jesus Christ was not acting man-made movie script. Rather He was fulfilling prophecies that God revealed to the prophets of old. He did not come to earth to entertain the world. It is, therefore, wise to ask yourself what to do with what you know of Jesus Christ and His mission. What should you do with His teachings and promises? What should be your relationship with such a "Great Institution" and Supernatural Entity (Jesus Christ), notwithstanding that it is over two thousand years since He physically walked this earth. Should you continue on end to wonder what to do with Jesus Christ?

Jesus Christ contrasted His mission to earth with that of the devil as follows:

John 10:10 "The thief cometh not, but for to steal, and to kill, and to destroy: I am come that they might have life, and that they might have it more abundantly."

He came to give abundant life to ALL who believe in Him, who accept His finished work of salvation. No wonder He declared to that Jewish leader that went to Him by night, Nicodemus:

John 3:16-18 "For God so loved the world, that he gave his only begotten Son, that whosoever believeth in him should not perish, but have everlasting life. [17] For God sent not his Son into the world to condemn the world; but that the world through him might be saved. [18] He that believeth on him is not condemned: but he that believeth not is condemned already, because he hath not believed in the name of the only begotten Son of God."

In the last two passages above there is abundant life and there is everlasting life for WHOEVER believes in Jesus Christ. Abundant life is made available in this life and in eternity for them that believe in Him. Everlasting life starts from the moment you establish a relationship with the Christ and it continues to eternity. As per John 3:18 above, everyone is doomed who does not have the righteousness of Christ imputed on him or her. This imputation comes by believing in Him.

To establish a relationship with Jesus Christ, the first step is to accept that you are a sinner; ask God to forgive you of your sin, then invite Jesus Christ into your heart to become your personal Savior and Lord (Master). About Him the Bible says:

John 1:11-13 "He came unto his own, and his own received him not. [12] But as many as received him, to them gave he power to become the sons[27] of God, even to them that believe on his name: [13] Which were born, not of blood, nor of the will of the flesh, nor of the will of man, but of God."

The apostle Paul explains that you are saved by taking the steps below:

Romans 10:9-13 "That if thou shalt confess with thy mouth the Lord Jesus, and shalt believe in thine heart that God hath raised him from the dead, thou shalt be saved. [10] For with the heart man believeth unto righteousness; and with the mouth confession is made unto salvation. [11] For the scripture saith, Whosoever believeth on him shall not be ashamed. [12] For there is no difference between the Jew and the Greek: for the same Lord over all is rich unto all that call upon him. [13] For whosoever shall call upon the name of the Lord shall be saved."

The promise of Jesus Christ is that all who believe in Him shall come back to reign with Him in His millennial kingdom on earth. There are many passages in the Bible that support and describe what will be the portion of all of us that believe in Him – all who belong to Him. Some of these passages are stated below.

---

[27] Sometimes you hear people say we are all children of God; so what difference does it make? No! We are all creatures of God. Only those that believe in the only begotten Son of God are His children. That is the implication of John 1:12.

Matthew 5:5 "Blessed are the meek: for they shall inherit the earth."

Matthew 19:28 " And Jesus said unto them, Verily I say unto you, That ye which have followed me, in the regeneration when the Son of man shall sit in the throne of his glory, ye also shall sit upon twelve thrones, judging the twelve tribes of Israel."

Matthew 25:46 "And these shall go away into everlasting punishment: but the righteous into life eternal."

Luke 22:28-29 "Ye are they which have continued with me in my temptations. 29 And I appoint unto you a kingdom, as my Father hath appointed unto me;"

Romans 5:17 "For if by one man's offence death reigned by one; much more they which receive abundance of grace and of the gift of righteousness shall reign in life by one, Jesus Christ."

Romans 6:23 "For the wages of sin is death; but the gift of God is eternal life through Jesus Christ our Lord."

1 Corinthians 3:21-23 "Therefore let no man glory in men. For all things are your's; 22 Whether Paul, or Apollos, or Cephas, or the world, or life, or death, or things present, or things to come; all are yours; 23 And ye are Christ's; and Christ is God's."

1 Corinthians 6:2-3 "Do ye not know that the saints shall judge the world? and if the world shall be judged by you, are ye unworthy to judge the smallest matters? 3 Know ye not that we shall judge angels? how much more things that pertain to this life?"

1 Corinthians 15:21-25 "For since by man came death, by man came also the resurrection of the dead. 22 For as in Adam all die, even so in Christ shall all be made alive. 23 But every man in his own order: Christ the firstfruits; afterward they that are Christ's at his coming. 24 Then cometh the end, when he shall have delivered up the kingdom to God, even the Father; when he shall have put down all rule and all authority and power. 25 For he must reign, till he hath put all enemies under his feet."

Colossians 3:2-3 "Set your affection on things above, not on things on the earth. 3 For ye are dead, and your life is hid with Christ in God."

2 Timothy 2:11-13 " It is a faithful saying: For if we be dead with him, we shall also live with him: 12 If we suffer, we shall also reign with him: if we deny him, he also will deny us: 13 If we believe not, yet he abideth faithful: he cannot deny himself."

1 Thessalonians 4:13-18 "But I would not have you to be ignorant, brethren, concerning them which are asleep, that ye sorrow not, even as others which have no hope. ¹⁴ For if we believe that Jesus died and rose again, even so them also which sleep in Jesus will God bring with him. ¹⁵ For this we say unto you by the word of the Lord, that we which are alive and remain unto the coming of the Lord shall not prevent them which are asleep. ¹⁶ For the Lord himself shall descend from heaven with a shout, with the voice of the archangel, and with the trump of God: and the dead in Christ shall rise first: ¹⁷ Then we which are alive and remain shall be caught up together with them in the clouds, to meet the Lord in the air: and so shall we ever be with the Lord. ¹⁸ Wherefore comfort one another with these words."

1 Peter 4:13 "But rejoice, inasmuch as ye are partakers of Christ's sufferings; that, when his glory shall be revealed, ye may be glad also with exceeding joy."

Revelation 1:5-6 "And from Jesus Christ, who is the faithful witness, and the first begotten of the dead, and the prince of the kings of the earth. Unto him that loved us, and washed us from our sins in his own blood, ⁶ And hath made us kings and priests unto God and his Father; to him be glory and dominion for ever and ever. Amen."

Revelation 2:24-26 "But unto you I say, and unto the rest in Thyatira, as many as have not this doctrine, and which have not known the depths of Satan, as they speak; I will put upon you none other burden. ²⁵ But that which ye have already hold fast till I come. ²⁶ And he that overcometh, and keepeth my works unto the end, to him will I give power over the nations:"

Revelation 3:21 "To him that overcometh will I grant to sit with me in my throne, even as I also overcame, and am set down with my Father in his throne."

Revelation 5:9-10 "And they sung a new song, saying, Thou art worthy to take the book, and to open the seals thereof: for thou wast slain, and hast redeemed us to God by thy blood out of every kindred, and tongue, and people, and nation; ¹⁰ And hast made us unto our God kings and priests: and we shall reign on the earth."

Revelation 20:4-6 "And I saw thrones, and they sat upon them, and judgment was given unto them: and I saw the souls of them that were beheaded for the witness of Jesus, and for the word of God, and which had not worshipped the beast, neither his image, neither had received his mark upon their foreheads, or in their hands; and they lived and reigned with Christ a thousand years. ⁵ But the rest of the dead lived not again until the thousand years were finished. This is the first resurrection. ⁶ Blessed and holy is he that hath part in the first resurrection: on such the second death hath no power, but they shall be priests of God and of Christ, and shall reign with him a thousand years."

In addition to the above, when we place our faith in Christ we receive the gift of the Holy Spirit to enable us to live the Christian life and bear fruit.

Acts 2:38 "Then Peter said unto them, Repent, and be baptized every one of you in the name of Jesus Christ for the remission of sins, and ye shall receive the gift of the Holy Ghost."

Romans 8:9 "But ye are not in the flesh, but in the Spirit, if so be that the Spirit of God dwell in you. Now if any man have not the Spirit of Christ, he is none of his."

1 Corinthians 6:19 "What? know ye not that your body is the temple of the Holy Ghost which is in you, which ye have of God, and ye are not your own?"

Ephesians 1:12-14 "That we should be to the praise of his glory, who first trusted in Christ. 13 In whom ye also trusted, after that ye heard the word of truth, the gospel of your salvation: in whom also after that ye believed, ye were sealed with that holy Spirit of promise, 14 Which is the earnest of our inheritance until the redemption of the purchased possession, unto the praise of his glory.

Bear in mind that all the prophecies about Jesus Christ in the OT and NT have been fulfilled except the prophecies regarding His Second Coming. In effect, since the prophecies were fulfilled to the letter, it is only wise and reasonable to rest assured that the yet-to-be-fulfilled prophecies will definitely come to pass. The apostle Peter said that some scoffers had made jest of the prophecies of the Coming back of the Lord Jesus Christ:

2 Peter 3:1-13 "This second epistle, beloved, I now write unto you; in both which I stir up your pure minds by way of remembrance: 2 That ye may be mindful of the words which were spoken before by the holy prophets, and of the commandment of us the apostles of the Lord and Saviour: 3 Knowing this first, that there shall come in the last days scoffers, walking after their own lusts, 4 And saying, Where is the promise of his coming? for since the fathers fell asleep, all things continue as they were from the beginning of the creation.
5 For this they willingly are ignorant of, that by the word of God the heavens were of old, and the earth standing out of the water and in the water: 6 Whereby the world that then was, being overflowed with water, perished: 7 But the heavens and the earth, which are now, by the same word are kept in store, reserved unto fire against the day of judgment and perdition of ungodly men.
8 But, beloved, be not ignorant of this one thing, that one day is with the Lord as a thousand years, and a thousand years as one day. 9 The Lord is not slack concerning his promise, as some men count slackness; but is longsuffering to us-ward, not willing that any should perish, but that all should come to repentance.

[10] But the day of the Lord will come as a thief in the night; in the which the heavens shall pass away with a great noise, and the elements shall melt with fervent heat, the earth also and the works that are therein shall be burned up.
[11] Seeing then that all these things shall be dissolved, what manner of persons ought ye to be in all holy conversation and godliness, [12] Looking for and hasting unto the coming of the day of God, wherein the heavens being on fire shall be dissolved, and the elements shall melt with fervent heat? [13] Nevertheless we, according to his promise, look for new heavens and a new earth, wherein dwelleth righteousness."

The Bible says that "if any man be in Christ, he is a new creature: old things are passed away; behold, all things have become new" (1 Corinthians 5:17). As it is with an individual, so it is with society. Every society remains backward until it embraces Jesus Christ and Christianity. Christianity brings education and liberty for all, because where the Spirit of God is, there is liberty (2 Corinthians 3:17). Jesus Christ is the light of the world as He stated and added that anybody that follows Him shall not walk in darkness but shall have the light of life (John 8:12).

So, I recommend to you, brother/sister, to put your trust today (in fact, NOW) in the Lord Jesus Christ and become a son (including daughter) of God in Christ Jesus.

But if you are already a child of God, are you doing the work, which Jesus Christ assigned to His disciples – to be His witnesses from Jerusalem (including your family) to the uttermost parts of the world?[28] If not, prayerfully start today. There is a reward for your work for Christ as the apostles stated:

1 Corinthians 3:11-15 "For other foundation can no man lay than that is laid, which is Jesus Christ. [12] Now if any man build upon this foundation gold, silver, precious stones, wood, hay, stubble; [13] Every man's work shall be made manifest: for the day shall declare it, because it shall be revealed by fire; and the fire shall try every man's work of what sort it is. [14] If any man's work abide which he hath built thereupon, he shall receive a reward. [15] If any man's work shall be burned, he shall suffer loss: but he himself shall be saved; yet so as by fire. 2 Corinthians 5:9-10 "Wherefore we labour, that, whether present or absent, we may be accepted of him. [10] For we must all appear before the judgment seat of Christ; that every one may receive the things done in his body, according to that he hath done, whether it be good or bad."

---

[28] Acts 1:8 - But ye shall receive power, after that the Holy Ghost is come upon you: and ye shall be witnesses unto me both in Jerusalem, and in all Judaea, and in Samaria, and unto the uttermost part of the earth.

1 John 2:28 "And now, little children, abide in him; that, when he shall appear, we may have confidence, and not be ashamed before him at his coming.

Revelation 3:11-12 "Behold, I come quickly: hold that fast which thou hast, that no man take thy crown. [12] Him that overcometh will I make a pillar in the temple of my God, and he shall go no more out: and I will write upon him the name of my God, and the name of the city of my God, which is new Jerusalem, which cometh down out of heaven from my God: and I will write upon him my new name."

Revelation 22:12 "And, behold, I come quickly; and my reward is with me, to give every man according as his work shall be."

Jesus Christ is Lord!

Appendix 1
About The Author

The Author, Dr. Daniel Ukadike Nwaelene was born into a Christian family. He became saved at the age of eleven years. Over many years, alongside his secular jobs, he served in different capacities and ministries in two well-known member-churches of the Nigerian Baptist Convention. Some of the offices held include chorister, Associate Church Training Director, Church Secretary, Financial Secretary, Deacon, Chairman of Diaconate, Sunday school teacher, Minister for Education and Outreach, and pioneer Pastor of Royal Priesthood Baptist Church, Aseese near Lagos.

Currently this author is a minister (associate Pastor) in Community Baptist Church, Yonkers, New York, U. S. A.

Academically the author obtained a Bachelor's degree in Business Administration; Master of Business Administration (Management); Bachelor of Theology, Master and Doctor of Theology (Pastoral Theology). There were other diplomas that need not be listed.

His secular work saw him through Information Technology (IT) management for twelve years and five years of senior management (as General Manager, Corporate Services) in May & Baker Nigeria PLC, a pharmaceutical manufacturing corporation, all before retiring to private business prior to relocating to the United States.

The author is married to Patricia, and they are blessed with two sons and daughters that also know the Lord to His glory.

Appendix 2
About This Book

Acting Movie Script or Fulfilling Prophecies? is the second published work of this author, even though the writing began before that of the first one (*Jesus Christ: Savior, Judge and King of the World* or JSJK for short). It was in the process of researching and collating data for this book that the title and content of JSJK were revealed. All attention was then diverted to the new revelation. As the work on JSJK was concluding the outstanding parts of this book were made available (inspiration-wise).

At one of the author's quiet times, having been overwhelmed by the deeds, miracles and teachings of Jesus Christ the question was dropped on his mind, "Could Jesus Christ have been acting as a movie actor what He read in the Scriptures? Having believed in Him these many years, the author quickly tried to dismiss the question as coming from the devil. But the Spirit asked him, what if an unbeliever asked the same question to disprove Jesus Christ's Deity, what would be the answer? This led to going to the Scriptures, Yonkers Library, and the Internet to search for facts to prove that Jesus was not just acting man-made movie scripts but was fulfilling the old time prophecies concerning God's plan for redemption of lost mankind.

It is very likely that some other people may have been asking similar questions. Happily they have an answer in this book. *Acting Movie Script or Fulfilling Prophecies?* is a book for general consumption of everybody that can read the English language. It is targeted at all persons who desire to know. Through the prophet Hosea the Lord said, "My people are destroyed for lack of knowledge;" (Hosea 4:6).

All but a few of the Bible references are fully quoted from the Holy Bible (King James Version). So, reading through the book automatically creates an opportunity to read many portions of God's Word. Details of the works and teachings of Jesus Christ form a major part of the book. Many of the prophecies about Jesus Christ the Messiah and the fulfillment of such prophecies are also detailed.

When you read through with an open mind, the author believes you will be convinced that Jesus Christ was not an actor, but the Son of God, who came to save all believing mankind from eternal damnation in hellfire to heaven where we will spend eternity with God in His kingdom.

Bibliography

Bultema, Harry. *Commentary On Isaiah*. Grand Rapids: Kregel Publications, 1981.

Freeman, Hobart E. *An Introduction To The Old Testament Prophets*. Warsaw: Faith Ministries & Publications, 1983.

Hill, Andrew E & John H. Walton. *A Survey Of The Old Testament*. Grand Rapids: Zondervan, 2009.

Ironside, H. A. *An Ironside Expository Commentary. Matthew*. Grand Rapids: Kregel Publications, 1976.

Pentecost, J. Dwight. *The Words And Works Of Jesus Christ*. Grand Rapids: Zondervan Publishing House, 1984.

Ryrie, Charles C. *Basic Theology*. Wheaton: Victor Books, 1986.

Thiessen, Henry Clarence. *Introductory Lectures In Systematic Theology*. Grand Rapids: WM. B. Eerdmans Publishing Company, 1949.

Walvoord, John F. *Daniel: The Key To Prophetic Revelation*. Chicago: Moody Press, 1971.
Walvoord, John F. *Every Prophecy of the Bible*. USA: Chaiot Victor Publishing, 1999.

Walvoord, John F. Matthew: *Thy Kingdom Come*. Chicago: Moody Press, 1974.

Willmington, H. L. *Willmington's Guide To The Bible*. Wheaton: Tyndale House Publishers, INC., 1981.

Young, Edward J. *The Book of Isaiah Volume 1*. (Grand Rapids: William B. Eerdmans), 1965.

Young, Edward J. *The Book of Isaiah Volume 2*. Grand Rapids: William B. Eerdmans, 1969.

Young, Edward J. *The Book of Isaiah Volume 3*. Grand Rapids: William B. Eerdmans, 1972.

Disciple's Study Bible, New International Version. Korea: Holman Bible Publishers.

Life Application Study Bible NIV. Carol Stream: Tyndale House Publishers, Inc. and Grand Rapids: Zondervan, 1997.

Scofield, C. I. Ed. *The Scofield Study Bible,* 1945.

Crump, William D. *The Christmas Encyclopedia.* N. Carolina, London: McFarland & Co, Inc. Publishing, 2001.

Encyclopedia of Religion Second Edition Vol. 9. USA: Macmillan Reference, 2005.

Laymon, Charles M., ed. *The Interpreter's One-Volume Commentary on the Bible.* Nashville: Abingdon Press, 1971.

Wenham, G. J., J. A. Motyer, D. A. Carso, R. T. France, eds. *New Bible Commentary, 21st Century Edition.* Downers Gove; Leicester: Inter-Varsity Press, 1994).

The New Interpreter's Dictionary of the Bible, Me – R, Vol. 4. Nashville: Abingdon Press, 2009.

O'Collins, Gerald, S. J., Edward G. Farrugia, S. J.' *A Concise Dictionary of Theology.* New York/Mahwah, N.J.: Paulist Press, 2000.

Richardson, Alan and John Bowden, eds. *The Westminster Dictionary of Christian Theology.* Philadelphia: The Westminster Press, 1983.

Marshall, I. Howard, A. R. Millard, D. J. Wiseman, eds. *New Bible Dictionary, 3rd Edition.* Leicester: Inter-Varsity Press, 1996.

Gross, A. L., ed. *The Oxford Dictionary Of The Christian Church.* New York: Oxford University Press, 1997.

Vine, W. E. *Vine's Complete Expository Dictionary of Old and New Testament Words.* Nelson Publishers, 1996.

Whitaker, Richard E.. *The Eerdmans Analytical Concordance To The Revised Standard Version Of The Bible.* Grand Rapids: William B. Eerdmans Publishing, 1988.

Young, Robert. *Analytical Concordance To The Bible.* New York: Funk & Wagnalls – A Division of Reader's Digest Books, INC.

Wikipedia, the free encyclopedia.

Wikipedia: *Prophet.* http://www.thefreedictionary.com/prophet

Scripture Index

SUBJECT INDEX

Overcome	25,169
Parable	7,48,49,83,88,96,97,98,99,103,104,142,143,144,146,147,182,191
Pentecost	43,131,133,134,212
Pharisee	44,56,57,66,67,70,74,84,101,104,158,167,169,171,175,180,185
Pinewood	5
Pray	8,16,19,23,27,48,56,68,76,81,85,94,100,128,133,143,146,149,158
Preach	10,50,58,59,63,64,83,105,122,128,130,134,198
Precept	25,27
Priest	23,27,48,56,68,76,81,85,94,100,128,133,143,146
Priesthood	29,30,107,165,171,191,209
Priest-King	29,30
Prophecy	14,15,28,33,39,41,52,60,64,103,107,111,115,130,137,196,212
Prophesy	14,16,17,21,22,134,137
Prophet	19,23,27,48,56,68,76,81,85,94,100,128,133,143,146
Prophetic	14,29,38,43,191,212
Redemption	6,60,94,148,200,206,210
Religion	12,13,18,127,194,213,249
Remission	53,124,135,206
Repent	23,43,45,46,83,99,100,135,136,140,182,206
Repentance	24,45,132,150,192,206
Reproach	13,111
Resurrection	4,7,9,32,46,120,121,122,127,133,135,148,169,191,193,196,204
Reward	85,86,91,142,151,153,154,200,207,208
Righteousness	23,27,48,56,68,76,81,85,94,100,128,133,143
Sabbath	10,57,58,70,74,75,77,111,120,140,143,169,177,187,188
Sacrifice	26,29,30,45,107,189,191
Sadducee	44,176
Salvation	6,31,57,58,60,136,152,198,202,203,206
Sanctify	27,141,149
Satan	18,58,74,116,148,179,205
Saviour	36,149,150,165,166,170,192,206

Pacific Book Review

helping authors succeed!

Pacific Book Review

In our world, it is impossible not to come across a situation in which faith and belief does not come into direct conflict with the discovery of new sciences and advancements in technology. The divide between believers and non-believers has never been stronger, and as a result questions regarding the validity of a particular belief system or aspect of that belief system begin to arise. The fight against doubt is something all believers have to struggle through, and as Henri Poincare once said, "To doubt everything, or, to believe everything, are two equally convenient solutions; both dispense with the necessity of reflection."

In author Daniel Ukadike Nwaelene Thd's *Acting Movie Scripts or Fulfilling Prophecies?* the author hopes to answer the question many unbelievers have about Jesus Christ, which is whether or not he was truly the son of God or an incredibly talented actor bringing the prophecies of old to life to make himself into the son of God. The author uses biblical references and scripture to detail each prophecy that was given about the savior, and how Jesus proved himself through these scriptures why he fit into the prophecy naturally.

The author did a great job of crafting a well-researched and captivating read. The amount of time and effort the author put into compiling this information was evident in the amount of detail the author included in his research, and the wealth of information the book included helped to illustrate the author's message about Jesus and his actions which led to his inclusion as the son of God. The comparisons the author had of both the Old and New Testament accounts of what the Messiah would appear as and the actions he would take was in particular fascinating, as the Old and New Testaments have become a topic of debate even amongst the Christian faithful over the years, and seeing the author's research and study of these subjects was engaging to behold.

This is the perfect read for those who enjoy non-fiction reads, especially those that are Christian or believe in the Christian teachings of Jesus Christ. I particularly enjoyed the history and culture study that this book provided, and the ways in which the author was able to connect and tie everything from Jesus's appearance and attitude with the expectations that so many people had about the Messiah leading up to and during Jesus's teachings.

Thought-provoking, engaging, and mesmerizing, author Daniel Ukadike Nwaelene, Th.D's *Acting Movie Scripts or Fulfilling Prophecies?* is a must-read non-fiction book on religion and Christian faith overall. The structure and tone the author strikes brings a scholarly approach to the subject matter, while the faith aspect of the book brings a more personable touch to the reading experience. The terminology, history, and culture that ties into this subject made for a powerful reading experience.

www.ingramcontent.com/pod-product-compliance
Lightning Source LLC
Chambersburg PA
CBHW060801120626
46557CB00001B/57